Boxing, Masculinity and Identity

Boxing, with its extremes of violence and beauty, discipline and excess, has always been a source of inspiration for writers and filmmakers. Permeated by ideas of masculinity, power, 'race' and social class, boxing is an ideal site for the exploration of key contemporary themes in the social sciences.

Boxing, Masculinity and Identity: The 'I' of the Tiger explores the changing sociology of identity – especially gender identity and the meaning of masculinity – through the sport and art of boxing.

Drawing on ethnographic research as well as material from film, literature and journalism, the book takes in the broad cultural and social terrain of boxing. It considers the experience and understanding of:

- Masculinity and gendered identities.
- Physical embodiment: mind, body and the construction of identity.
- Spectacle and performance: links between public and personal social worlds.
- Boxing on film: the role of cultural representation and spectatorship.
- Methodologies: issues of authenticity and 'reality' in the social sciences.

Boxing, Masculinity and Identity will be of great interest to those following courses in sociology, sport, gender studies and cultural studies.

Kath Woodward is Senior Lecturer in Sociology at the Open University, UK, and a member of the Economic and Social Research Council's Centre for Research on Socio-Cultural Change (CRESC).

Boxing, Masculinity and Identity

The 'I' of the Tiger

Kath Woodward

Routledge
Taylor & Francis Group

LONDON AND NEW YORK

First published 2007
by Routledge
2 Park Square, Milton Park, Abingdon, Oxon OX14 4RN

Simultaneously published in the USA and Canada
by Routledge
270 Madison Ave, New York, NY 10016

Routledge is an imprint of the Taylor & Francis Group, an informa business

Typeset in Goudy by
Keystroke, 28 High Street, Tettenhall, Wolverhampton
Printed and bound in Great Britain by
MPG Books Ltd, Bodmin, Cornwall

British Library Cataloguing in Publication Data
A catalogue record for this book is available from the British Library

Library of Congress Cataloging in Publication Data
Woodward, Kath.
Boxing, masculinity and identity: the "I" of the tiger / Kath Woodward.
p. cm.
Includes bibliographical references and index.
1. Sports–Sociological aspects. 2. Boxing–Social aspects.
3. Gender identity. 4. Masculinity. I. Title.
GV706.5.W66 2006
796.83–dc22   2006016938

ISBN10: 0–415–36770–0 (hbk)
ISBN10: 0–415–36771–9 (pbk)
ISBN10: 0–203–02018–9 (ebk)

ISBN13: 978–0–415–36770–7 (hbk)
ISBN13: 978–0–415–36771–4 (pbk)
ISBN13: 987–0–203–02018–0 (ebk)

Contents

Figures

Dedication

For Steve, Richard, Tamsin, Jack and Sophie and my sister Sarah.

For HP who introduced me to boxing and for Col who loved sport.

For Sam who died while I was writing this book.

Acknowledgements

Copyright for all the images, Empics, Nottingham.

Thanks to Sylvia Lay-Flurrie and Margaret Marchant for all their help with the final typing and getting the book sent off and to Gill Gibson and Lewis Summers of Rotherham Library for their help chasing books and films.

I have benefited enormously from discussions with my colleagues in Open University research groups. I am grateful to Raia Prokhovnik and the Feminist Reading Group for the many stimulating discussions about developments in feminist work and to the psycho-social research group, Wendy Hollway, Peter Redman, Margie Wetherell and Joanne Whitehouse-Hart.

Thanks to Brendan Ingle and all the boxers who talked to me and let me watch them training at the gym in Sheffield.

Chapter 1

Introduction

There is a moment in Ron Howard's 2005 film of the life of the boxer James Braddock, *Cinderella Man*, which stars Russell Crowe as Braddock when

> Crowe walks into the ring for the final climactic fight, and the entire arena, packed with extras – thousands of them – falls silent. This total silence, in such a place and at such a time, is eerie, almost dream-like. And you realise that the dreams of every single person at that moment are riding on this man. That's the power of film and the performance and, ultimately the power of the game.
>
> (Horowitz, 2005: 3)

This is a moment of identification with a boxing hero. Boxing still has the power to draw in its audiences as well its participants, because the sport and its stories feed dreams and aspirations of success. This moment is about more than the 'thrill of the fight' as the *Rocky II* theme song, 'The Eye of the Tiger', goes. It is also about the 'will to survive'. The audience is bound up with the fortunes of Braddock: the white, working-class hero who is taking his chance in the ring, pursuing a path of honour in order to provide for his family. This statement points not only to the power of film, but also to the power of boxing and in particular boxing heroes, especially male heroes. Fantasy and reality are entwined in the construction of such heroic figures. The audience is implicated in the film's narrative structure framed around the justice of Braddock's plight and moral course which his actions represent. Whatever the economic and social constraints, this boxing hero seeks to shape his own identity. Those watching buy into this assumed agency and desperately want him to fulfil his dreams. This is a moment in which multiple aspects of identification are condensed. The draw of the fight and the projection of the audience's desires onto the central character combine the psychic investments that people make with the social and cultural meanings about identity that are produced by texts such as films. Of course, this moment is cinematic and not an actual fight. Real fights are not the sanitized drama of Hollywood. Boxing aficionados are keen to argue that boxing is 'real', it is not a drama (Oates, 1987), but it is a major argument of this book that fantasy and reality are inextricably combined. Public stories, symbolic representations, unconscious desires and anxieties and embodied experience and iterative practices are all constitutive of identity. The mechanisms in play at such moments as represented in *Cinderella Man* and more widely, for example in the more routine, everyday practices through which identities are reconstituted and the investments in such heroic (and not-so-heroic) figures of masculinity are what this book is about. Such boxing moments present a means of exploring the interrelationship between psychic and social dimensions of identity and, more specifically, of understanding the making and re-making of masculinities.

These processes of identification, whether of boxers themselves, the audience of such films and spectators of the sport itself and those who buy into its culture, are not straightforward. The film narrative of *Cinderella Man* and the real-life biography of its hero may be a simple story of good and evil and present an honourable route out of poverty and disadvantage, but the attraction of boxing and the pull of a heroism that depends on this version of masculinity are more puzzling. Boxing masculinities carry many of the features of traditional, hegemonic masculinity. It is a sport characterized by corporeal contact, courage, danger and in some cases violence, which might seem out of place in the contemporary world of change and fragmentation and the emergence of more ambiguous, less traditional gender identities. One might also expect to find resistance to the challenge of new masculinities and strong ties to more traditional, gendered identities in boxing. This raises questions about how different identities can cohabit in a terrain of transformation. What is the relationship between contradictory versions of masculinity and how do they coexist? Sport is often characterized by gender divisions and inequalities and hence polarized gender identities. There is a tension between the increased opportunities offered by sport and resistance to change, although sport remains a site of resistance, especially in terms of transforming masculinities (Messner, 2002). Such tensions are highlighted in boxing. Boxing is still something of an anomaly in a world of transforming gender relations and the emergence of greater social inclusion and equality in social relations based on gender, 'race', 'ethnicity', sexuality and dis/ability. If boxing is a bastion of traditional masculinities, how does this persist in a climate of change, for example when even feminists argue that we live in 'post-feminist times'? Or is there less radical transformation taking place in the wider world? How do these identifications operate for women? The attraction of boxing, not only to participants, but also to spectators, fans and all involved in its culture suggests that such versions of masculinity retain strong, if contradictory, claims.

I have chosen to focus upon men's boxing and masculinities because of their troublesome features. In many ways the continued success of such a sport is difficult to comprehend. Boxing is dangerous, but not only because of the risk of injury. Other sports are more hazardous in terms of the scale and number of injuries sustained, but boxing is exciting for its overt expression of aggression, because it carries the promise of risk. Boxing is the Dark Continent. It is frightening. I have followed boxing since my very first experience of the sport, very much at a distance, as a very young child, creeping into my parents' room in the middle of the night to listen to the radio with my father. He was listening to Rocky Marciano, the only undefeated heavyweight of the twentieth century, beating Jersey Joe Walcott in 1952; a key moment in the annals of boxing. I certainly picked up on the excitement, if not the visible violence. As a follower, although not a practitioner of boxing myself, I am only too aware of the troubling nature of a sport which is exciting because it carries the risk of injury and violence played out in public in front of the spectator. However, boxing survives in a changing climate of more fluid identities and greater gender equalities. Boxing masculinities do not fit so comfortably within a framework of flexibility and contingency in explaining how identities are taken up as other versions, such as those of 'new men'. Men's boxing still retains a high degree of cultural dominance and the genealogy of the sport is strongly configured around its associations with masculinity. Joyce Carol Oates expresses this powerfully as 'Boxing is for men and is about men, and is men' (1987: 72). Oates' comment is not only an empirical observation about the people who take part, but an expression of the powerfully gendered metaphors of the sport. This is not to say that women are not part of the sport and its history. Women's boxing has a long history and the sport has achieved considerable popularity, especially in the US in recent years, but, as I shall demonstrate, it is men's boxing especially that recreates legends of heroism and constructs the myths of masculinity in which practitioners and followers invest. Boxing is not just about men; it is about masculinity. However, this is not a masculinity reserved for men. Personal investments in public stories are more often related to heroic masculinities, but this does not of course limit their appeal to men. Boxing masculinities are configured within histories and mythologies of belonging which resonate with the desire to locate the self in relation to roots and the past, which extend beyond the specific gender identifications in boxing.

Expressions of the desire to belong and to stabilize identity are features of traditional masculinity that present another anomaly in theorizing identity. Increasingly, analyses of identification and of the self are informed by critiques that stress the hybridity and fluidity of identity, in opposition to fixity and certainty. Boxing is thus troubling in the contemporary world. Masculinities in this field do not exist in some separate cultural terrain but co-exist with other identifications and other versions of selfhood. Such masculinities can be construed as attempts at reconstructing the self through myths of origin invoking the roots of identity. Or they can be seen as responses to an unsettled and unsettling world of transformation and change, especially in relation to gender roles. Examples of attempts to secure the self and to establish some sense of belonging demonstrate some of the difficulties that emerge from framing identity in a sea of discursive uncertainty. Identification in a sport like boxing promises some security in knowing what masculinity means, but such attempts at setting boundaries of selfhood cannot be adequately explained as either false consciousness or misrecognition. If we think we can say who we are with some degree of surety, for example by tracing our identities back to some original source, we risk being accused of being deceived and in a state of false consciousness. This accusation could be based on the claim that the sense of security such identities afford has no substance, or because such identities are dependent upon and determined by social forces outside ourselves. Identities are reproduced and configured through discursive practices and regimes which are characterized by uncertainty. The resolutions adopted, for example in attempts to secure some sense of self in bounded masculinities, require more than a discursive explanation, which sees them as shaped and determined by cultural forms and practices. The powerful draw of such masculinities highlights the interrelationship between stability and uncertainty and demonstrates the need for a synthetic approach that combines different elements in the reconstruction of identities, the social and the psychic, the particular and the universal and agency and constraint.

The interpellation (Althusser, 1971) of public moments, such as those represented in films, are only part of the processes of assembling the self. Selves are reconstructed through the iterative practices and routines of everyday life. Public representations and spectatorship are, of course, only parts of boxing culture. Boxing involves the most rigorous training programmes in the gym. Thus the sport brings together the routine of the gym and the spectacle of public contests; it combines everyday embodied practice and public stories of celebrity, heroism and anti-heroism. Boxing combines the embodied practices and the daily physical grind of training with aspirations that are forged in particular economic and social circumstances and the aspirations which recruit boxers are firmly grounded in a material reality of social, economic and cultural disadvantage. Fantasy and reality are inextricably enmeshed. Boxing is *par excellence* an example of a space where the two meet; where celebrity and the routine, fantasy and corporeal, material and social reality and aspiration and desire become one. Thus boxing offers a route into exploring some of the mechanisms of identification that incorporate, routine practices, embodiment and psychic investment through personal and public representations.

In order to consider some of the regimes and apparatuses of identification through which masculinities are forged in boxing, this book combines analyses of the habitual and the routine, for example of everyday experience of training in the gym, with deconstruction of the spectacular, more public events, including media and literary coverage of the sport. This analysis brings together personal and public stories. This book explores the recruitment of people in the gym and in the ring and as spectators and followers who are implicated in boxing masculinities through the routine embodied practices of the sport and through its representation. Masculinities are made and remade through the body practices of routine and embodiment is a key concept in understanding the habitual. Identity formation can be understood through habit, *habitus* and bodily practices. Such a theoretical framework lends itself well to the corporeal engagement in the sport and the reproduction of embodied selfhood. However, whilst such approaches most effectively address the embodied self they are less successful in engaging with the fantasies and psychic investment which link personal and public stories and the interrelationship between the particular and the universal. The violent spectacle of boxing and its physical dangers for boxers suggest the appeal of unconscious aspects of identification. Traditional masculinities as enacted in boxing may offer the promise of secure boundaries to the self but they are based on extremely dangerous practices. What is even more troubling is the spectatorship of such a risky, if exciting sport which invokes unconscious fears and desires. Identity has to be embodied because 'we are our bodies' as Bourdieu has argued, but the investment made in boxing masculinities is not just about those who engage in the sport. It is about those who watch and those who buy into its culture and collude with its identifications. Boxing masculinities have to accommodate these tensions and ambivalences between heroic success and fear of failure. My argument demands a synthesis of embodiment and discursive meanings, as reproduced through public and personal narratives and spectacles, both in the ring and on film. These aspects of identification involve acknowledgement of unconscious desires and anxieties.

Boxing, Masculinity and Identity works through some of the identity puzzles that are thrown up by boxing in order to engage with contemporary debates about masculinity, including ambivalence and contradiction in the processes of making up the self. Boxing is used to acknowledge the power of representation and the 'thrill of the fight' as well as the more routine, embodied aspects of identification through which subjects are recruited into gendered identities, starting with processes of identification and boxing masculinities.

Chapter 2, 'Masculinity on the ropes? Boxing and gender identities' focuses upon masculinities as gendered identities. It addresses changes and continuities in relation to the transformations that have taken place in academic concerns with identity, subjectivity and the self and how identities might be seen to have been transformed, rethought and re-enacted. There has been both an increased interest in masculinity as the subject of academic enquiry and the suggestion that new masculinities have emerged in recent years. In sport, pro-feminist critiques have been developed (for example, McKay et al., 2000; Messner, 2002) drawing upon feminist theories and methodologies, which have put masculinities, as gendered identities, under the spotlight of research. Masculinities are still seen to be constructed in relation to femininity as well as within a deeply racialized context. The chapter then explores some of the specific dimensions of masculinities in relation to sport and specifically to boxing, as a place where one would expect hegemonic masculinity to be holding on and resisting the tide of ambiguity and contradiction and the advent of the 'new man'. Key moments in boxing history are identified. Focusing on gender, 'race' and 'ethnicity', my arguments are framed by political and moral discourses. Boxing history is marked by social exclusion and processes of 'othering' especially through racialization, ethnicization and gender differentiation and by notions of honour which are gendered through their associations with militarism. The persistence of gender binaries and the mechanisms through which they are constructed raise important questions about how and why women might 'do' masculinity in sport or whether there are alternative reconfigurations of gender identities. This discussion focuses on the tension within sport as a field with the potential for the transformation of selfhood and on oppositions and resistances and highlights the key dimensions of boxing masculinities in the history of the sport, which incorporate the articulation of class, 'race' and 'ethnicity' with gender.

Chapter 3, 'Outside in, inside out: routine masculinities', focuses on ways of knowing and addresses some of the big debates about the problem of methods in researching gender identities in boxing. This is illustrated by the specific difficulties which beset researchers, comparing 'insider' participant observation studies with 'outsider' non-participant observation. Boxing research really highlights these methodological issues and addresses the problems of investigating processes of identification. Most ethnographic research into boxing has been carried out by men, who have 'joined in' and who are not surprisingly very proud to include tales of their own sparring endeavours as well as, in some cases, their adventurous encounters with assorted perils within the account of the research (for example, Wacquant, 1995a, 1995b, 2004; Sugden, 1996; Beattie, 1997; de Garis, 2000). Few ethnographies of sport by male researchers acknowledge or make visible the researcher's gendered identity and maleness passes unquestioned (Wheaton, 2002). These debates are used to explore the question of ontological complicity (Merleau-Ponty, 1962) as is the issue of accessing authentic 'truth', which have much wider application outside sports research. The interrelationship between insiders and outsiders also contributes to an exploration of the networks and connections through which masculinities are reconstructed and reinstated. This chapter also considers some of the debates about the status of the texts that are deployed in different methodologies and the relationship between ethnography, interviews and analysis of other texts, including the 'public' stories of the press, the film and television media and literary sources. My aim is to highlight the necessity of combining the personal and the public and the inside and the outside, which includes the psychic and the social and to develop a methodology that synthesizes these dimensions using different texts as well as different dimensions of identity. My argument suggests that the personal stories yielded by ethnography and other qualitative methods have to be explored along with analyses of the public stories manifest in media representations of boxing as a sport which occupies a contentious place in public debates and there has to be some acknowledgement of situated knowledges and partial visions (Haraway, 1991). Much of the existing research in boxing has involved participant observation and ethnographies which have taken place in the 'situation' of the gym and has involved some embodied collusion in its routine training practices. Embodiment is the concern of the next chapter.

Chapter 4, 'Boxing bodies and embodied masculinities' focuses on the status of bodies in the processes of identification. Boxing is all about bodies; two bodies in the ring and the physical ordeal of training in the gym. Boxing images foreground bodies and the body is central to the issue of how and why people box. Chapter 4 looks at the problem of bodies in the making of the self and reviews some of the literature on theories of the body, before going on to develop a notion of embodiment that encompasses cultural and gender differentiation. This chapter focuses on bodies in processes of identification. Boxing, even more than other sports, might appear to be an activity where the body is central, but much of the discussion of the sport has assumed a mind/body split where the self is associated with the mind which seeks control over the body. This dichotomy is one key area of debate in this chapter along with the other ways in which the gendered body has been theorised in relation to social constructivist approaches, for example Foucauldian notions of the regulation and disciplining of the body, which are interesting in relation to the body regimes and regimens in a sport such as boxing. Merleau-Ponty's understanding of 'embodiment' is particularly useful in overcoming the problem of binaries and as contributing to Bourdieu's approach to embodiment encompassing the active construction of identities within sport within the context of investment in cultural capital and in particular physical capital, in the case of boxing. However, theories of the body need to address the diversity of bodies, their materiality and their differences. The enactments, through which meanings about gendered identities are produced and re-produced, are located within specific social and cultural spaces and in the context of the different and mostly unequal operation of power. These specificities and inequalities have to be incorporated into the analysis of embodiment and the status of the agentic body which plays its part in self definition where the material body and the concept of embodiment are crucial components of gendered identification. This chapter demonstrates first, that there is more to identity formation than routine bodily practices, even the iteratitive practices through which masculinities are forged and second, that the reiteration of body practices has to be explored in relation to the wider arena of culture in which stories of masculinities are told. The next chapter looks at what else is going on, especially in the more visible wider arena.

Chapter 5, 'Public stories, personal stories: heroes, celebrity and spectacle', shifts the emphasis onto the public arena in which subjects are recruited. This chapter links personal and public experiences through an exploration of the primacy of the visual and the visible and the public stories that are told about boxing and its masculinities. What is visible is also shadowed by what is invisible and this chapter also explores omissions as well as inclusions in public stories. It explores some of the ways in which boxing offers a site for research which is characterized by a combination of the routine, disciplined practice of its practitioners, the spectacle of performance and the legends and stories of celebrities and, especially, heroes which shape the understanding of those who participate, those who watch and the wider community. This chapter starts with the primacy of the visual and the visible within the framing device of the ring, which provides a synthesis of the public and personal spheres condensed within the image. It goes on to explore the interrelationships between the evidence of ethnographic research and the personal stories told in the gym and the media stories and mythology which permeate the sport at all levels. This includes some discussion of the contemporary phenomenon of celebrity and, which is more important, of the heroic narratives that constitute the genealogy of the sport and, in relation to spectacle, of some of the ways in which boxing illustrates the Bakhtinian notion of carnival with its spectacle and excess. This chapter engages explicitly with the 'attraction of repulsion' which characterizes boxing, its spectacles and the interpellation of subjects through spectatorship. Masculinities reconstituted and enacted in boxing are marked by the elisions and tensions between anxiety and aggression, attraction and fear and public and personal stories. The discussion of public and personal stories is informed by the experience of the tensions between discipline and control on the one hand and excess on the other, made manifest in the beautiful bodies and the damaged bodies which, as a very real possibility, haunt those who participate in the sport.

Chapter 6, 'When the going gets tough: going to the movies', revisits the phenomenon with which this Introduction began and takes up another dimension of the interrelationship between public and personal stories, especially in relation to fantasy and 'reality'. It explores some of the ways in which masculinities are made and remade through the representation of films, for example in the fight film genre and what could be called 'boxing films'. Cinema is used to develop a critique of masculinity as experienced, re-presented and re-produced through complex networks which combine symbolic systems in the public arena with the psychic investment of the spectator. The range covers the highly acclaimed *Raging Bull* as well as the Muhammad Ali films and the more populist *Rocky* series, as well as some earlier examples of what could be called the heyday of traditional boxing films in the 1940s and 1950s. Ali's heroic status, manifest at so many sites, is a strand through several chapters in the book. Again the ways in which heroic status is re-defined and questions about how far women can occupy heroic identity positions, through the performance of masculinity, through investment in its heroic tropes or in a reconfigured femininity is explored, citing, for example films that feature women boxers, like Clint Eastwood's *Million Dollar Baby*. This chapter draws upon textual analysis, audience research and psychoanalytic readings of the representation of violence in the cinematic context and links critical analysis of violence within boxing such as Kevin Mitchell's critique of the 'glamour of violence' to both the film narratives of boxing heroes such as Jake La Motta, Rocky Marciano and Muhammad Ali himself and their reception. It also engages with the problematic of the fictional, partly real Rocky Balboa of the *Rocky* series. The chapter also examines the ambivalences in these representations and the contradictions they reproduce, all of which contribute to the development of theories which offer explanations of the enactment, representation and experience of masculinity in the context of the management of anxiety through processes of identification.

Chapter 7, subtitled: 'I could have been a contender', the final chapter, brings together the different strands of the book, arguing for a synthetic, situated approach which combines the public and personal narratives and the routine

Transformations occur in complex ways. Boxing is a site at which there are strong expressions of the desire to stabilize and secure identities and a sense of belonging, but the processes of identification have to be examined in the context of social change and the dynamic interrelationship between the personal and the social. This entails first looking at some of the interrelationships and tensions in identity formation. This chapter starts with questions of identity and goes on to look at how masculinity in particular can be conceptualized before working through some of the pivotal points of identification in the genealogy of boxing in order to highlight some key aspects of processes of identification. My focus is largely on men's boxing as a sport which is used to explore contemporary debates about identity by focusing on masculinity in this context. I include discussion of the place of women in boxing in order to interrogate the relational aspects of gender identities. Masculinities are configured through the mechanisms through which femininities are also re-produced.

First, the chapter focuses on rethinking masculinity, especially within the field of sport and problematizes masculinities in boxing. Second, arising from the discussion of masculinity the chapter addresses some of the theories of identity which inform recent debates, located within the wider cultural field. The discussion of identity highlights the relevance of technologies of the self, the application of narrativization approaches and psycho-social understandings of identification. This discussion informs my approach to understanding identity in the rest of the book. Third, it focuses upon the genealogy of boxing as a field in which masculinities have been constituted, highlighting the dimension of the sport to demonstrate key components in the configuration of masculinities.

Gender identities: masculinities

Gender identities in boxing are marked by difference in very visible ways. The discussion has highlighted not only relational aspects of identity formation but a particular emphasis on dualisms. This appears the more so because this is an historical moment when there seems to be greater uncertainty about identity than at some points in the past. For example, Anthony Giddens' work on the crises of identity in late modern society (1991) foregrounds the insecurities of personal as well as collective identities and Zygmunt Bauman has written about the profound anxiety that typifies the decision making and life projects of women and men in western societies (2004). As Bauman has argued, the new social relationships of late capitalist society have given rise to the desire to return to a familiar and restricted world that creates barriers to the outsider (whoever the outsiders might be) (2004) and these anxieties can be seen to extend across a range of identifications. Indeed such insecurities might be a distinctive aspect of globalization and to encompass a wider field than western societies alone.

Gender identities have become the focus of concern about instability and uncertainty. Kobena Mercer's much quoted statement about the late twentieth century focus upon crises of identity also has some specific, gendered applications.

> Just now everybody wants to talk about identity . . . identity only becomes an issue when it is in crisis, when something assumed to be fixed, coherent and stable is displaced by the experience of doubt and uncertainty.
>
> (1990: 4)

Masculinity has also been a particular target of the interrogation of insecurity in establishing a sense of belonging and of setting some boundaries about selfhood (see for example, Segal, 1997a; Whitehead, 2002). Much of the recent discussion of masculinities has concentrated on loss of status for men, which has, for example, in debates about young people and educational achievement, or lack of it, focused upon young men's insecurities.

As Robert A. Nye notes in his review of recent literature on masculinity:

> Men are no longer the invisible, unmarked gender, the Archimedean point from which all norms, laws and rights flow; men are themselves the objects of the gaze of women, of other men and of a new critical scholarship that is deeply informed by the feminist insights . . . and scholarship of pioneers in the study of masculinity.
>
> (2005: 1938)

Masculinity has been interrogated at a variety of different sites and outcomes have been framed within a range of negative, pessimistic positions and those which present more optimistic, positive understandings of change and possibilities of greater democracy and wider participation, especially in terms of gender. Some approaches which have adopted feminist theoretical frameworks have suggested that masculinities are being transformed and 'new' masculinities are emerging. However, such claims are more likely to be in studies of paternity, which has also been a significant site of male backlash against feminist advances, or of sexuality. In his analysis of men, masculinities and gender equality in the global arena, Bob Connell suggests that the most positive and liberatory critiques have been located within the more marginalized masculinities and that sport occupies a more pessimistic space in terms of the potential for subversion of heterosexist, patriarchal orthodoxies, even though there is support for change among some men (2005). This is largely supported by Michael Messner in his wide-ranging study, *Taking the Field*, in which he argues that, although conditions have improved in some ways the gender inequities generated by sporting institutions and by the social apparatuses in which they are enmeshed remain securely entrenched (2002). Messner maps peer collaboration in the performance of violent masculinity, which is most frequent in the revenue-producing contact sports. Status is accorded to conformity with a particular code of heterosexual masculinity, a 'manhood formula' (Messner, 2002: 123) that he describes from US media coverage and which he describes as a script that is rehearsed and replayed by gendered performances. These performances incorporate pleasurable erotic bonds which are reinforced by the imperatives of sport and strengthened by the threat of failing to be complicit in such relationships (Messner, 2002). This kind of analysis is written within a critical framework which addresses continuities in order to demand change and to create its possibility. Whilst some work on masculinities points to existing transformations, for example in the subversion of racialized, heterosexist norms, most also provide very useful deconstructions of the operation of masculinity in order to highlight more progressive alternatives and to make explicit that which had been assumed and unstated and therefore unchallenged (Whitehead, 2002).

Some of the detailed work that has been conducted on masculinities has pointed to the complicity or collusion that takes place at particular sites of which sport is a good example. Connell's concept of hegemonic masculinity remains most useful for exploring some of the ways in which masculinities are constituted in historically specific contexts. Much of the engagement of recent work on masculinity has been in dialogue with Connell's conceptualization. Connell's use of the work of Antonio Gramsci (1971), especially his notion of hegemony, which had more frequently been applied to class formations yields particularly relevant applications to a study of gender identities with the benefit of retaining the importance of class. Hegemony does not simply signify dominance and class, or for my purposes gender in the construction of the social order. Hegemony is not directly the outcome of ideological factors which shape the identities that are adopted and into which people are recruited. Hegemony is never assured and guaranteed; it involves contestation in the cultural terrain too. As Stuart Hall has argued in the context of class,

> Hegemony implied that the dominance of certain formations was secured not by ideological compulsion, but by cultural leadership. It circumscribed all those processes by means of which a dominant class alliance or ruling bloc, which has effectively secured mastery of the primary economic processes in society, extends and expands its mastery over society in such a way that it can transform and re-fashion its ways of life, its mores and conceptualization, its very form and level of culture . . . hegemony is understood as accomplished . . . principally by means of winning the active consent of those classes and groups who were subordinated within it.
>
> (1985: 51)

Gender articulates with class in the configuration of masculinities in sport. Connell also points to the advantages of Gramsci's theory of hegemony in relation to gender using patriarchy as part of the cultural dynamic of contemporary social life. It is the emphasis upon the intersections of social and cultural life which make the concept so useful.

> Hegemonic masculinity can be defined as the configuration of gender prac-tice which embodies the currently accepted answer to the problem of the

legitimacy of patriarchy, which guarantees (or is taken to guarantee) the dominant position of men and the subordination of women.

(1995: 77)

This involves dynamic and contingent processes. As Connell suggests, 'When conditions for the defence of patriarchy change, the bases for the dominance of a particular patriarchy change' (Connell, 1995: 77). Not only is the dynamic of transformation built into Connell's analysis, the lack of prominence or even visibility of the institution of hegemonic masculinity is also noted. Following Gramsci, hegemony operates as a version of assumed, taken-for-granted knowledge which becomes 'common sense' (1971). However, common sense is fragmented, 'disjointed and episodic, one belongs simultaneously to a multiplicity of mass human groups' (Gramsci, 1971: 324). Common sense 'is a collective noun, like religion: there is not just one common sense, for that too is a product of history and part of the historical process' (Gramsci, 1971: 325–6).

As Connell claims, it is not the case that 'the most visible bearers of hegemonic masculinity are always the most powerful people. They may be exemplars, such as film actors, or even fantasy figures, such as film characters' (Connell, 1995: 51), or, I would add, sports stars. Another aspect of Connell's original work that is useful for my purposes is the *complicity* with the hegemonic project that can be demonstrated by those who are not rigorously and overtly engaging with the hegemonic project. Not all men are active participants in sport and certainly not in boxing, but many are complicit in the masculinity that is therein affirmed, for example through spectatorship, even from the comfort of their armchairs or in the pub or club. Connell suggests that the majority of men gain from 'the patriarchal dividend, the advantage men in general gain from the overall subordination of women' (Connell, 1995: 79). This would conform with Messner's 'manhood formula' with its collusion of beer drinking, bonding and violence on an interactional level (2002). Alcohol consumption is, of course, another potential source of exclusion from this formula, for men too. The interactions of sports cultures and networks of masculinity have resonance of earlier times, both in the occupation of public spaces that were denied to women and in the forms of association, such as The Fancy in the early nineteenth century. The Fancy, which gave its name to an illustrated journal published between 1821 and 1826, edited by Pierce Egan and detailing memoirs of famous publicists and accounts of sporting events, is used to describe the amusements of sporting men in the Regency period. The Fancy constituted a social network of men, whose lives were organised around sport. Prize fights provided the focus for the social lives of those men. Although Connell usefully points to the invisibility of some performances of masculinity and especially of complicity with hegemonic masculinity, boxing offers a space in which masculinities are very visible and invoke associations with physicality, risk-taking and even violence, that those who wish to buy into that masculinity but who are not participants in the sport have to accommodate in other ways. Interactions outside the sport offer one possibility, for example with other manly activities such as gambling and other not-so-legal 'entertainments', as does spectatorship, either of fights or of fight films, which offers a much more open field for collaboration. All of these are part of what have become the 'stratified deposits' of common sense (Gramsci, 1971) of boxing culture. There are strong associations between hegemonic masculinity and those who identify themselves or are identified as men. The resilience of traditional masculinities in sport is linked to the marking of gender differences and the ways in which bodies are inscribed through apparatuses of classification, which are powerfully embodied.

Identities, concepts and formulations

Recent academic work has shifted in its focus upon the concept of identity and in some instances has preferred the notion of identification, as a more dynamic idea which focuses on the processes through which identities are forged and maintained or transformed. I use both identity and identification. I wish to retain the concept of identity as a means of conceptualizing the interface between the personal and the social and the 'inside' and the 'outside'. 'Identity' permits acknowledgement of the intensity of the personal and psychic investment, made in a sport like boxing, for example, through the deep commitment of both routine bodily practices and the dangers of the sport, as experienced by practitioners and witnessed by spectators. The concept of identity extends beyond the notion of being subjected without the exercise of some agency. Much of the literature on boxing has emphasized structural, especially economic, social and cultural factors, which shape and indeed determine the identity of the boxer. However, the notion of subjection or even the more dynamic idea of subjectification, cannot adequately accommodate either the psychic investment that is made or the ways in which individuals might make choices in relation to the performance and expression of gender identity.

The concept of identity is also preferred for its history of association with identity politics which allows for both a politics of location (Hall, 1996) and some understanding of active engagement and transformation. Identity carries political connotations and offers the possibility, however fragile, of resistance and challenge to structural and discursive constraints. The identification processes that are implicated in making up the self, which are strongly gendered, ethnicized and racialized, are produced within discourse. However, identity always involves some negotiation between the self as agent in the discursive field in which the self is positioned. Even in a sport like boxing identification is not a simple story of inevitable positioning in an economically, racialized discursive field.

I use identity in this book in preference to subject, although there is overlap between the use of 'self' and identity, in order to highlight the engagement with and investment in identity positions and the possible failure as well as success of processes of identification. Identity and identification permit ambiguity and failure as well as agency and consequently resistance, which are difficult to accommodate in theories of subjectification which posit agency as arising only from the manner in which the self is assembled (Butler, 1990; Rose, 1996). Sport and perhaps boxing especially, however excluded and marginalized its participants, has also been a site of resistance to oppression and illustrates the politics of challenge and subversion too.

> On sport's level playing field, it is possible to challenge and overturn the dominant hierarchies of nation, race and class. The reversal may be limited and transient, but it is nonetheless real. It is, therefore, wrong to see black sporting achievement merely as an index of oppression; it is equally an index of creativity and resistance, collective and individual.
>
> (Marqusee, 1995: 5)

Boxing, like many other sports, is also a site of resistance; black boxers, like Caribbean cricketers, are not simply conforming to an expected regime of compliance. Sport is a route of resistance too (Carrington, 2002). This is certainly not to underplay the significance of social and economic factors which are clearly of enormous importance in the formation of gender identities in a sport like boxing. It is only to suggest that neither an emphasis on structural constraints nor an overly discursive explanation can fully account for the dynamic and situated identifications that are possible.

Embodiment is a key dimension of identity and one that carries particular meanings in the field of sport. Bodies are important components in the relational processes of differentiation through which identities are forged. For example, masculinity in boxing is particularly embodied and produced through understandings of the body, which is deployed to create differences, notably a most polarized difference between women and men. Difference is also marked by impairment. Physical damage is not accidental in the ring; it is the main purpose of the activity. This is reflected in boxing reports which list the damage inflicted; injuries are constitutive of the whole experience of the fight. In a typical example, from a super-middleweight fight between Joe Calzaghe and Jeff Lacy, the report includes not only the boxing competences but the physical harm suffered, recorded round by round.

> The American was gashed around both eyes, with his nose and mouth seeping blood by the time he was sent to the canvas in the final round. The last three rounds made uncomfortable watching as Lacy stumbled around.
>
> (Rawling, 2006)

Boxing identities are classified by the material body, its physical capabilities and its size as measured by weight categories. Body weight is measured with great precision. Male flyweights cannot be over 112 pounds, bantamweights not over 118 pounds and heavyweights have to be over 195 pounds (with no upper limit). Body weight is more than a means of organizing the practices of the sport; it carries meanings, with heavyweights having the highest status in the history of the sport.

As Oates claims, 'is there any athlete however celebrated in his own sport, who would not rather be heavyweight champion of the world?' (2002: 154). Bodies are lived and represented and the lived body has been the focus of a great deal of work in sport as Chapter 4 demonstrates. Bodies present problems for theorising identity. One relates to the question of agency and to the extent to which body and self are one or whether there is a mind/body split. How bodies are gendered and differentiated presents another dilemma in rethinking the body. For example how far is gender influenced or even determined by corporeality? This could be translated into a question about the interconnections between men and masculinity.

These are embodied identities that are intimately concerned with negotiating the relationship between personal investment and the biographies people bring to the identification process and the social forces which shape them. The interrelationship between the personal and the social which is intrinsic to identity formation involves material corporeality. Identification includes economic and social material circumstances and those that are specifically corporeal. Boxing bodies and those in other sports are implicated in the routine practices through which those bodies are regulated and disciplined. One powerful means of understanding these embodied identities is through the regimes which create, reinstate and inscribe them and through which selves are positioned and assembled.

Technologies of the self-regulating bodies

Sporting bodies are highly disciplined and regulated not only through the regimes of the gym and through training, but also through the bodies which regulate the sport. Increasingly these regulations derive from governmental sources, operating in more or less interventionist ways. Sport carries enormous potential for social transformation. Boxing has a long history as a route out of poverty, which has not only been seized upon by individuals but also recognized by government, for example through the provision of boys' clubs, gymnasia and the development of provision in schools. More recently sport has become a target of interventions which seek to promote social inclusion and new versions of citizenship (Wagg, 2004; Woodward, 2005). Sport has become implicated in the regimes of governmentality in liberal democracies. Some of the most productive work on identity, identification and the making of selves has been done in dialogue with Foucault's work, for example on governmentality in the case of Nikolas Rose. Such approaches have emphasized the processes through which subject positions are produced and reproduced using the idea of subjectification (Rose, 1996, 1999 [1989]). The body is targeted as the site of intervention, in a sporting version of the biopolitics which permits the state to invade the private space of the domestic and the corporeal in order to secure overall benefit (Donzelot, 1980). This was later construed in a more disembodied dimension of governmentality (Rose, 1999 [1989]).

In the context of boxing, the target group is disaffected and disadvantaged youth, predominantly young men. As recently as 2004, the then UK Home Secretary, David Blunkett, is reported as saying,

> The discipline of amateur-boxing training can give young people the chance to keep fit, learn sportsmanship and self-discipline and benefit from the support of a mentor in their boxing coach.
>
> (in Williams, 2004)

The reference to 'sportsmanship' is not incidental and draws upon differentiated traditions of boxing masculinities. In this configuration of the sporting corporeal ethic, not only is there the establishment of a causal link between the healthy body and the healthy mind, but there is also a rationale for this particular version of the state implanting body techniques upon individuals (Elias, 1983). The body is thus the target of state interventions through which identities are sought to be transformed. Bodies here are not disciplined through the prison or the asylum (Foucault, 1973, 1977a), but through similar, if much more diffuse, heterogeneous and subtle injunctions. The strategies operate to 'enjoin an internal relation between the pathological individual and his or her body in which bodily comportment would manifest and maintain a certain disciplined mastery exercised by the person over himself or herself' (Rose, 1996: 31). The techniques through which selves are recreated incorporate both routine bodily practices and a self-regulation which permits some agency. The arduous regimes of boxing are designed to enable its practitioners to regulate themselves. The rigours of the gym are highly disciplined by those who engage in them and not only imposed from outside.

Although the idea of techniques through which selves are constituted does challenge the notion of 'docile bodies' which are largely determined, Foucauldian approaches still present an excessively discursive, social constructionist view of the body and thus the self. If the body is conceived as inscribed by the regimes which regulate it and remains largely a cultural artefact or solely social construction, recognition of the materiality of the body is severely limited. Judith Butler endeavours to link the materiality of the body to the performativity of gender, through her emphasis on the regulatory practices through which 'sex' is materialized (1993). Performativity is not 'the act by which a subject brings into being what she/he names, but, rather, as that iterative power of discourse to produce the phenomena that it regulates and constrains' (Butler, 1993: 2). Butler's work has particular importance for the exploration of gendered identities within boxing because it provides a route into the problematic of the performance of masculinity and its relationship to gender categories. This addresses my earlier point about the association between those who are classified as men and the masculinities they enact and with which they identify. For Butler there are no fixed gender categories prior to regulatory processes. The matter of bodies, for Butler, is the effect of a dynamic of power. However, she is keen to reinstate the 'matter' of bodies, that is the physical condition, which includes anatomical sex. Bodies, at least the matter of bodies, will be dissociable from the regulatory norms that govern their materialization and the signification of those material effects (1993). Gender identities are created through iterative practices, but people speak as if they had a gender identity prior to those practices. Thus she links the way in which the 'speaking "I" is formed by virtue of having gone through such a process of "assuming" a sex with the question of *identification*' (Butler, 1993: 3, italics in original). This argument still suggests somewhat disembodied identities and very fluid theoretical categories of body, but very constraining categories of regulatory practices, which might be extremely difficult to resist. Butler's notion of performativity goes much further than the sociological idea of performance (Goffman, 1959) upon which she draws and has some relevant applications to a study of gender identities in boxing, especially in relation to women and the matter of how women can 'do' masculinity. Butler opens up new ways of thinking about gendered, embodied identities. Her approach is also particularly useful for addressing how women can 'do' masculinity and men can 'do' femininity and subversion might be a possibility, however challenging. Transformation of gender stereotypes and exclusions would come through different techniques and regimes. The body, though material, would not be the final arbiter of who can and who cannot perform masculinity.

There are other ways of reconfiguring gender identities, even within boxing and there are other ways of addressing the interrelationship between the personal and the social dimensions of identity.

Storied selves

One set of regulatory practices through which gendered identities are forged and reinstated in boxing is the mythology and public stories of the sport. Iterative practices do not only include the daily routine, the body practices of the gym and the preparation for and engagement in competitive sport. Gendered identifications are not confined to practitioners. Boxing identities are situated within particular narratives which have both a well-established tradition and enormous purchase at every level. These public and private stories are explored in much more detail in Chapter 4. Lyn Jamieson uses the term 'stories' to describe different accounts of social change (1998) and includes the stories of everyday life told by 'ordinary people' as well as the accounts, told in a more public forum, by academic researchers as well as by politicians, scientists, religious leaders and other public figures. She expresses a preference for the word 'story' because it retains a structure and a coherence without requiring a hierarchical distinction between different kinds of accounts, those of the 'experts' or those in power, and those of 'ordinary people', which in sport could include the insiders and practitioners and fans and those positioned outside this discursive field. Although the idea of 'stories' might be somewhat misleading, suggesting fabrication, it has considerable application in the field of sport, because of the synchrony in the accounts that constitute meanings and which combine public and personal stories, those of celebrity and those of routine practice. Stories are told in the gym, in the media and through more formal narratives, for example in film and literature, as a means of making sense of how we are positioned and position ourselves within this field. Stories circulate in the public arena, but are recreated through the desires and dreams of those who invest in them. As Henrietta Moore suggests 'narrative is a strategy for placing us within a historically constituted world. . . . If narrative makes the world intelligible, it also makes ourselves intelligible' (1994: 119). Even though the practice of boxing might be taken for granted as a part of the *habitus*, stories are what provide coherence. It is not so important whether our stories can be verified or disproved, because it is how these narratives are constructed that people make sense of themselves. Such stories provide a means of exploring how the psychic operates within the social and how personal and public stories combine. This is what is relevant to the exploration of identity and, in this instance, of identities which are configured around a dynamic belonging.

The production of identities through narratives is a dynamic process.

> We achieve our personal identities and self-concept through the use of narrative configuration, and make our existence into a whole by understanding it as an expression of a single unfolding and developing story. We are in the middle of our stories and cannot be sure how they will end; we are constantly having to revise the plot as new events are added to our lives. Self then, is not a static thing or a substance, but a configuring of personal events into an historical unity which includes not only what one has been but also anticipations of what one will be.
>
> (Polkinghorne, 1988: 150)

The stories may change and adapt to circumstances; there is fluidity in these narratives of identity, yet there remains the desire for unity and for a sense of belonging in situating the self, and of being situated, in making sense of experience by putting together the often disjointed and fragmented pieces of everyday life, as well as the narratives of celebrity and the crises and traumas as well as the more banal aspects of routine, into some kind of structure. The narrativization of the self (Ricoeur, 1991) and the ways in which identities are recreated and transformed through both the private and public stories that are told provide another route into comprehending the pivotal moments through which identification takes place (Woodward, 2002).

Embodied selves are implicated in these stories, through the routine practices of sport as well as through the visibility of boxing bodies: beautiful and broken bodies. Identity is thus constructed and investments are made in identity positions through locating the self in these narratives, many of which are heroic legends which offer both recruitment possibilities and exclusions. These are not simple narratives, however, and like the processes of identification are beset by contradiction and ambivalence.

Such narratives, for example in the biographical accounts of the lives of boxing heroes and celebrities, usually trace the central character's life back to home and origins, however depressing. Identity stories, however they are told, often engage with authenticity and a search for roots. This is particularly appealing in boxing narratives, with the sport's apparent risks and dangers. Investment in a traditional masculinity such as is enacted and experienced in a sport like boxing can be explained through the desire to achieve some stability in a rapidly changing world; not that boxing can operate outside of those changes. This desire for stability resonates with the need to belong, which has more transformative potential and is less retrospective. Much of the debate about identity has been set within a consideration of myths of origin and attempts to trace roots. As Stuart Hall has argued, developing the work of the anthropologist James Clifford, identity can more usefully be understood as making sense of where you come from through the routes you have travelled, rather than seeking out some original source and one's roots (Hall, 1990). Routes provide us with the narrative of the journey that has been made, with pivotal points along the way and contribute to a more dynamic sense of what is involved in the taking up of identity positions and relate more closely to the conceptualization of identity as configured through narrativization.

Narratives are structured around pivotal moments which create possibilities for identification. For example, in a Foucauldian sense, stories put subject positions 'into discourse' (Foucault, 1978) and make identities available. Such stories are part of the social dimensions of identity since they are part of the cultural currency of the time. However, this raises questions about why some stories work and how and why some of these available identities are taken up. How does the psychic operate within the social? What are the processes whereby people buy into the subjectivities constructed in the narrative? Identification involves the psychic investment and more troubling unconscious desires and disruptions that are also implicated, for example, in a sport like boxing which appears so brutal and primordial.

Psycho-social selves: dealing with the real

Understanding identity as necessarily involving some psychic as well as social dimensions invokes notions of the unconscious. Whilst a major emphasis of this book is upon discursive explanations of identity formation, I also wish to argue that theories of how selves are constituted have to address not only the personal, but the psychic dimensions of these processes. As Butler argues, it is necessary for Foucauldian discourse theory to accommodate psychic dimensions (1993). Arguments which develop Lacanian critiques and prioritize symbolic systems and representations still have considerable purchase in analyses of public stories, such as films. Althusser's concept of interpellation offers one means of understanding the psychic–social relationship (1971). The process of recognizing oneself as named through an identification which operates at the level of the unconscious has enormous power. Whatever the limits of this Althusserian concept (Hirst, 1979; Barrett, 1991), especially in its inherent assumption that there must be a subject prior to the identification process of interpellation by which the subject is 'hailed', it clearly has application in this context not only as a 'summoning into place' of the subject (Hall, 1996) but as a means of capturing particularly well the intensity of the moment of identification and the investment in identity that is so powerfully expressed in boxing. The moment of identification with the boxing hero as in the example of the film *Cinderella Man* cited in the Introduction, is a moment of being 'hailed'. Those who watch are interpellated, feeling themselves 'named' by the hero: 'yes, that's me!' It is more than an association: we are recruited into this subject position in the narrative. Interpellation may be a moment of misrecognition (Heath, 1981) but it nevertheless incorporates the relationship between the discursive, social 'outside' and the investing, psychic 'inside'. The notion of moments of being hailed into an identity position also suggests the possibility of such moments constituting the narratives through which particular identities are constructed and reconstructed. However, just as interpellation 'works' when the subject is recruited, there are also occasions when subjects do not recognise their names. This raises questions about who is and who is not interpellated by particular versions of masculinity, including if and how women might be summoned into this position.

The recognition of unconscious desires and their expression resonates powerfully with the identification mechanisms implicated in sport. Sport can be seen as an outlet for the feelings and emotions that 'civilized' societies constrain and regulate. Sport provides a regularized outlet for the expression of routinely repressed instincts, such as aggression (Elias and Dunning, 1986). Elias admits that sport also generates and increases emotional tension and this argument has been used to explain the phenomenon of football hooliganism that is the violence that has sometimes ensued after football matches (Dunning *et al.*, 1988; Dunning and Rojek, 1992). Boxing, too, is generative of strong emotions both inside and outside the ring, especially outside the ring, although the whole *raison d'être* of boxing is to contain and discipline its protagonists. The conflict and aggression of the sport becomes a focus for the projection of the fears and anxieties of spectators as well as of those who are involved in boxing in the ring. This process of projection is more complex than either a simple channelling of aggressive feelings or a collective identification generated by the structure of the competition. Boxing invokes excess and disrupts the narrative of the civilizing process in more troubling ways. Psychoanalytic theories also encompass excess and that which it is difficult, if not impossible, to explain rationally. The Lacanian 'Real', for example as developed by Slavoj Žižek (1989) offers another means of engaging with some of these more troublesome aspects of identification and the relationship between the psychic 'inside' and the social exterior. This is not a discursive real of what can be represented, for example in the practices, performances, public representations, stories and culture of the sport, but represent a gap within the subject; the Real cannot be symbolized.

Whilst psychoanalytic theories have been deployed to support the argument that identities are fragmented and fluid, they are also subject to the criticism that psychoanalytic approaches are based upon universal and essentialist claims (Woodward, 1997a). Boxing masculinities highlight the tension between the fixity and fluidity of identity. Initially one might expect not only some degree of certainty but also some element of fixity in the masculinity that is produced in this context. It is because boxing makes such polarities so explicit that it provides a particularly useful site for the exploration of the negotiation and accommodation of such differences and relationships in the identification process. Some of this discussion has been translated into other debates about what can be known and said and what cannot be symbolized, and between the socially constructed and the 'real'. It is very hard to escape from Oates' claim that boxing is *real*, especially in the pain and suffering that it involves. The material body and the economic, social and cultural structures which shape experiences and set the parameters of the self are crucial elements in the reconstruction of gender identities. These structures are nonetheless made meaningful by the ways in which they refract the unstated and even un-symbolizable eruptions of unconscious desires and address some of the contradictory processes that are implicated in identification with boxing masculinities.

The drama as well as the routine of boxing is manifest in its genealogy. Boxing offers its own key moments in shaping identities and opportunities for identification. The sport is characterized by and features many of the most important dimensions of identity where the social and personal come together, which are often framed by ethical tensions. Notably boxing is coded as honourable through its associations with the disciplines of militarism and heroic endeavours and in another strand as offering an honourable route out of poverty. On the other hand, boxing as 'dark trade' has a history of association with low life and entertainment. It is these associations which inform identity formation and particularly resonate with masculinities. What are the pivotal points in the boxing story, particularly those in the public domain?

Boxing: histories and meanings

This section focuses upon the articulation of class, racialization and ethnicization as key aspects of the reconstruction of gender identities in boxing within discourses of morality and politics. Matters of who it is possible to become through identifications with boxing masculinities have to be traced through the routes that these boxing masculinities have travelled. Although the versions of masculinity that are made available through the sport may say more about who those who take them up want to *become*, it is also necessary to understand where they come from. However contradictory, it is these boxing stories which make up the 'common sense' of more contemporary masculinities. What is important about the history of boxing masculinities?

All sport occupies a cultural terrain in which political, social and economic matters are implicated and these are most dramatically and powerfully represented in boxing along with its distinctive features of excitement, danger and transgression which make boxing such a stimulating subject for cultural commentators. In his list of the ten greatest moments in US sport, the sports writer and award winning author Thomas Hauser cites two boxing examples: Joe Louis's defeat of Max Schmeling in 1938 and Joe Frazier's defeat of Muhammad Ali in 1971. Hauser's second greatest moment in US sport, the Joe Louis–Max Schmeling fight, is set in the context of the great depression of the 1930s, just before the outbreak of the Second World War. Hauser describes the fight as speaking 'to issues of democracy and totalitarianism. It was viewed as a test of decency and freedom versus Nazi philosophy. For the first time many white Americans openly rooted for a black man against a white opponent' (2005b: 6). The politics of race is apparent in Hauser's fifth great moment on the list: with Ali and Frazier symbolizing the divide in politics. He quotes the television commentator, Bryant Gumbel, who describes Ali as 'the symbol of black pride, parading black feelings about black heritage, speaking out against racial injustice. And the other guy just went along . . . how you stood on Ali became a political and generational litmus test' (quoted in Hauser, 2005a: 7).

Racialization and the politics of race

'Race' has figured greatly in the configuration of masculinities in boxing. Boxing in the US has at times been more emphatically marked by 'race' and racialization, as well as the ethnicization that has characterized boxing in Britain at particular points. Boxing has retained its strong associations with the urban poor and with particular ethnic groups, such as the Irish and groups of black people, whose status in US society might be measured by their participation in boxing (Michner, 1976). As Sugden points out, fighting a way out of the ghetto is an oversimplification, but it still has considerable purchase in the twenty-first century both in the experience of individuals and in the public stories that are told about boxing. Sugden argues that in the US, as in Britain,

> By the middle of the nineteenth century, on both sides of the Atlantic, and increasingly in other parts of the world, urban poverty, racial and ethnic discrimination and relative deprivation had been established as the common denominators of prize fighting and subsequent professional boxing.
>
> (1996: 24)

Success at the sport and especially in the ring came to be used to symbolize not only individual prowess but also racial superiority. Whilst black boxers might have been most drawn to the sport for economic and social reasons, US society still sought to maintain white supremacy, for example by rejecting contests between black and white opponents, especially if it was more likely that the black boxer would win. Jack Johnson holds a special place as a champion heavyweight who was badly treated by the white establishment. Not only was his boxing prowess an anathema to white racists, he was vilified as a womanizer and sexualized as a danger to white women. Johnson fled to Europe but eventually returned to fight and was defeated by a white Texan, Jess Willard, to the satisfaction of many white fans:

> Whatever the circumstances most white Americans rejoiced in the return of the heavyweight crown to their race. Willard became an instant hero, one who brought renewed confidence to the physical and moral strength of white America.
>
> (Sammons, 1988: 44)

Intervention and regulation of boxing has not always served only to protect its protagonists. Boxing was legalized in the US after the demise of Jack Johnson, but a prohibition against fights between black and white boxers was also established, which was not abolished until the black boxer Joe Louis beat the white American James Braddock in 1937. This was another pivotal moment in boxing history, representing Joe Louis's come-back after his defeat by Max Schmeling, Hitler's champion. Again boxing had been implicated in the configuration of politics through a re-articulation of athleticism and racialized corporeal ideals, in this instance promoting fascism and the rise of the Third Reich.

> Schmeling set out to win the heavyweight championship of the world as Hitler goose-stepped through Europe. Each would use the other to achieve his goals, and each would come perilously close to succeeding.
>
> (Sammons, 1988: 107)

In 1938 Joe Louis beat Schmeling in New York City and the US celebrated the triumph of good over evil (Sammons, 1988) and Louis went on to dominate the heavyweight category and achieved heroic status because of this and also through his support for the US war effort throughout the period of the Second World War.

Race and racist policies have been formalized in boxing, for example through the prohibition of contests between black and white contenders. However, as I have suggested boxing has also provided a route not only out of poverty but also of political resistance. Muhammad Ali's story, however heroic in retrospect, has not been a straightforward one and there has been a vast number of works devoted to his biography (notably Mailer, 1975; Hauser, 1991; Remnick 1998; Early, 1999; Marqusee, 2000; Lemert, 2003). Ali's story incorporates so many of the tensions, contradictions and key elements that characterize boxing and its identifications. Ali, like Joe Louis, was an African-American who sought boxing as the route to success, in Ali's case by following the amateur then professional path, after winning a gold medal at the 1960 Olympics. Ali's victory against the odds and in six rounds, over 'bad guy' Sonny Liston in 1964 was a pivotal moment. It raised questions about the status of the black heavyweight champion. Liston, the 'bad guy', with all his illegal entanglements, had beaten Floyd Patterson the 'good guy', but how was Ali, formerly Cassius Clay, a name he rejected as a slave name after his fight with Liston in 1964, to be seen? Clay had been backed by the lawful businessmen of Louisville, whereas Liston retained his connections with the mob and the criminal underworld (Lemert, 2003). Clay's defeat of Liston created a new version of heroic black masculinity. Not only did Clay proclaim, 'I am the greatest', after this fight (Hauser, 1991: 78), he also stated, 'I talk to God every day . . . the real God' (in Lemert, 2003: 73), which heralded his adoption of the name Muhammad Ali and his membership of the Nation of Islam. In this binary configuration of 'good' and 'bad' black masculinity Ali was both a celebrity performer and a political activist. He was involved in the Nation of Islam and a strong supporter of civil rights and refused the draft to fight in Vietnam in 1967. Ali was also a spectacular performer and perhaps a celebrity before the cult of celebrity really took hold in the west (Scambler, 2005). Charles Lemert, drawing on different sources, quotes Ali after his victory in 1964:

> I am the greatest! . . . I don't have a mark on my face . . . I upset Sonny Liston . . . I just turned twenty-two years old . . . I must be the greatest . . . I showed the world . . . tell the world . . . I talk to God every day . . . the real God . . . I'm the king of the world . . . I shook up the world . . . I am the prettiest thing that ever lived.
>
> (2003: 73)

Ali shook the fight world in Miami in 1964, but he also had enormous impact upon the wider world, although his path to heroic status, when he was ultimately accepted more generally as a US hero, was a rocky one, especially because of his explicit political activism and assertion of Black civil rights, which led to the loss of his title as well as the threat of imprisonment. Racialized and racist politics had occupied the ring through the prohibition against black and white contests, but Ali represented a very active resistance. Even in the most constraining of contexts, there are opportunities for resistance and for the reconfiguration of identity. Collective resistance condensed in the agency of the boxing hero can be transformative.

It is not only in the ring that the politics of race has been played out. Until Don King's arrival, the promotion of the sport had been dominated by white men. As Ali has himself pointed out there might be two black men slogging it out in the ring but the profits would largely accrue to white promoters and investors (Ali and Durham, 1975). Sammons points to the massive profits gained through television deals (1988) and with satellite and cable broadcasting such revenues have accounted for a large amount of boxing revenue. Exploitation, especially of the journeymen who do not make it to the big time persists (Sammons, 1990). Even at the top, especially for women, for example, for boxers like Laila Ali and Jacqui Frazier, the million dollar purse is a new phenomenon and in general there are limited rewards and racialization and gender articulate in different ways, temporally and spatially.

The story of boxing is not a simple one and there are complexities and contradictions in the working through of the tensions between boxers and promoters, in relation to race and inequality, even between women and men and especially between the 'good guys' and the 'bad guys', for example as embodied in the Mike Tyson story. Boxers can be praised and vilified, seen as representative of their communities and people and rewarded and exploited. Tyson is a prime example of the ambivalence of boxing and its black heroic figures.

> Tyson has had two distinct, if somewhat contradictory uses for the racialized history of professional boxing. His identification and expropriation of the great white fighters made him a mainstream figure, depoliticizing his masculinity by making him someone who identified with whites, and so someone with whom whites could, on some level, identify . . . But, as Don King knew . . . [i]dentifying with black fighters of the past – or more precisely, with the street life that produced them – promised to re-politicize Tyson's masculinity and stave off charges of racial inauthenticity. The 'Public Enemy' myth . . . was Tyson's most convincing role, if only because it fit so neatly into the roles scripted for young and physically powerful black men in the American mind.
> (Early, 2002: 203)

Public stories are not all of success and acclaim, nor distinctly of heroism and honour; honour too can be reconfigured. Boxing is contentious in diverse ways: for its manifestations of exclusion and segregation by 'race', 'ethnicity', class and gender. These structural aspects of differentiation operate within gendered discourses of honour with strong associations with masculinity wrought particularly through militarism. Honour is inflected in particular ways in the genealogy of boxing, which resonate with contemporary identifications with masculinity in the sport.

Honour, war and masculinity

Men's boxing, in particular, has long been associated with the notion of honour which is deeply embedded in military codes and practices. The history of boxing includes various forms of pugilism ranging from classical times which included the beautiful bodies of Ancient Greek athleticism and the no-holds-barred combat of *pankration* to bare knuckle fighting in fairground booths, prize fighting and the massive commercial enterprise that boxing became in the last century. This suggests a complex and multi-layered genealogy with contradictory messages, but heroism coded within discourses of honour and militarism persist into the twenty-first century as is demonstrated by its description as the 'noble art'.

Many boxing histories include the associations of boxing and honour in the classical world and foreground the centrality of pugilism in construction of courageous and honourable masculinity. Boxing in the classical world also served as entertainment, which illustrates the reiteration of the ambivalence between aristocratic articulations of honour and the gross mass spectacles of the arena, which nonetheless provided a route to free citizenship for gladiators who excelled. Gladiatorial combat usually involved weapons and animals and was not limited to the one-on-one corporeal combat more strictly classified as boxing. The Roman poet Virgil, writing in the first century BCE, who drew upon Ancient Greek notions of heroism describes Aeneas's challenge in the Aeneid, Book V, 'Now let anyone who has a valorous heart and a quick resource come forward, ready to box with fists gloved in hide' (Virgil, 1956, v: 130).

He then goes on to describe the fight between Entellus and Dares that would be quite comprehensible in the contemporary world.

> Each at once took position, alert, on tip-toe with eagerness, undismayed, and with arms raised in the air. Holding their heads high and well out of the reach of blows, they began to spar in interplay of fist with fist, warming to the fight.
> (Virgil, 1956, v: 132)

Jackson Knight's translation of Virgil, although lacking some of the hyperbole of contemporary journalism, combines honour with aggression:

> The heroic Entellus, as active and as fearless as ever in spite of his fall, returned to the fight all the fiercer, with a new force kindled by rage. His shame together with his confidence in his own valour, set his strength on fire . . . There was no pause, no respite. The heroic Entellus battered Dares and sent him spinning.
> (Virgil, 1956, v: 133)

Whilst expression of conflict in the language of heroic endeavour is culturally and historically specific, the equation of defence of one's body and attack on that of another, the immersion of discourses of honour in body practices and pugilism has a very strong hold and informs more recent retelling of boxing legends and the gender identities that are forged therein. Hand-on-hand combat has continued up to the present, although there have been variations along the way, not the least by the Romans, who are probably most famous for their gladiatorial competitions which provided mass entertainment and diversion. Honourable endeavour, whether articulated by aristocratic fighting or the investment in physical capital by the dispossessed as a means of gaining freedom is a strand in boxing history which retains strong resonance from its earliest times.

Boxing's encoding of honour also carries strongly classed dimensions. Although the sport has been associated with the poor and marginalized, it has links with more elevated class status, for example with self-defence, including fist fighting, and notably, duelling skills, being part of the young gentleman's repertoire in the eighteenth century. Fist fighting often had less disastrous outcomes than duelling and therefore was preferable as a means of satisfying honour in cases of injured pride in such disputes (Gorn, 1986). Boxing continues to draw upon such discourses of honour and self-respect, especially in relation to masculinity and the need to establish boundaries to the self and maintain esteem within a tradition that elides physical and moral strength. Pugilism combines institutionalized approval of corporeal combat as a legitimate and morally acceptable means of solving disputes with personal justification and affirmation of identity, or more specifically, masculinity. There is no such space for the affirmation of femininity. The association of men with warfare is one contributory factor to this exclusion. Masculinity and honour along with the association of boxing with military training reinforce particularly gendered strands within the genealogy of the sport.

Boxing history has parallels with military history with its warrior legends, which has provided only a marginal role for women. Configurations of this version of masculinity have frequently been based upon gendered polarizations. Gorn suggests that by the turn of the twentieth century, pugilism, for example as practised in the gymnasium movement, was linked more closely to a particular version of masculinity, set in direct opposition to the threat of an ever-encroaching and debilitating femininity,

> Alive in every nerve, the boxer was in complete control of his body, negating by example the pervasive fears of over-civilization, nervous breakdowns and neurasthenia. The ring countered effeminizing tendencies, preparing men for a life of strife.
>
> (1986: 202)

This version of masculinity, embedded in militaristic codes of honour had to be reasserted, for example after women had entered areas of economic life during the First World War. Nearly a century ago, women were seen to have begun to occupy other previously denied locations. However, as G. Stanley Hall wrote just after the war,

> War is, in a sense, the acme of what some now call the manly protest. In peace women have invaded nearly all the occupations of man, but in war male virtues come to the fore, for woman cannot go 'over the top'.
>
> (1920: 102)

Whilst there are continuities and resonances of earlier articulations of the sport, boxing also carries different temporal and spatial nuances and inflections. For example, there are some differences in the history of the sport in the US and in Britain. However, the Roman legacy of associations between sport and the techniques of war and militarism have remained strong. These links have been expressed in the expectation that young men should fulfil their patriotic duty and fight for their country. Refusal has been interpreted as cowardice rather than acting on principle. However, masculinity can be framed within a subversion of regimes of truth that consolidate honour with particular practices. For example, Joe Louis enlisted in the army, conforming to that integration of pugilism and the military, but Muhammad Ali refused and suffered as a result, being stripped of his world championship, although he did successfully appeal against his prison sentence. Ali drew upon his skill and success as a boxer to express political opposition. Before the 'Rumble in the Jungle' in Zaire in 1974, Ali is reported as telling a reporter,

> Nobody is ready to know what I am up to. People in America just find it hard to take a fighter seriously. They don't know that I'm using boxing for the sake of getting over certain points you couldn't get over without it. Being a fighter enables me to attain certain ends. I'm not doing this for the glory of fighting, but to change a whole lot of things.
>
> (Mailer, 1975: 79)

In this contest, whilst Foreman could be seen to accept boxing as the 'vindication of the American dream' (Sugden, 1996: 191), Ali used boxing as a platform for political activism which rejected that dream as a betrayal of the interests of black people and turned 'his back on America, Christianity and the white race' (Marqusee, 2000: 10). Ali's career followed a circuitous path, but his rehabilitation in the 1970s took place at a time of political corruption in the US when Ali 'stood tall as a man who stood by and literally fought for his principles' (Sugden, 1996: 46). Ali was able to deploy his public success to reconfigure a version of honourable masculinity. Moral and political tensions have been negotiated in different ways at different times. Boxing history has been marked by different understandings of the public spectacle as well as its trajectories of honour. Boxing has always served as an entertaining spectacle through classical times and, for example with its later resurgence as public spectacles in the eighteenth century, in boxing booths and at fairs.

High life, low life, discipline and regulation

As John Sugden argues in his book *Boxing and Society*, boxing is reminiscent of those sports that characterized pre-industrial cultures, along with animal based sports such as bear baiting and cockfighting (1996). Boxing is in many ways different from the individual and team sports of the twentieth and twenty-first centuries, with its elemental one-on-one, body-on-body contact. However, whatever the extent of the regulation of contemporary boxing it remains strongly shaped by its associations with the unregulated practices of earlier times, including the eighteenth century practices of fairground entertainments and boxing booths. Contemporary gendered technologies of selfhood draw upon the associations of women's fighting, for example in fairgrounds with low life and with immorality rather than any honourable endeavour.

Women's prize fighting was also an important element in entertainments in the eighteenth and nineteenth centuries (Hargreaves, 1996). However, women's fighting has not been situated quite so firmly within the same discourses of honour, for example as a means of settling disputes, as has men's. Women have tended to be associated with the lowlife of boxing, with both boxing and wrestling being 'characterized as disreputable and dangerous, and self-contained in working-class venues' (Hargreaves, 1994: 183). This association with low life is sexualized, drawing on traditional repertoires of the Madonna and the whore, whereby gender and sexuality elide in popular categorizations of women's behaviour.

Masculinities were also constituted through class alliances. For example popular fighters like James Figg, Britain's first national champion in 1719 (Gorn, 1986) also offered to train young gentlemen in the 'noble art'. Figg made money from his fairground bouts and then advertised his services to young gentlemen who might benefit from acquiring some of the arts of self defence (Brailsford, 1988). The 'noble art' learned as self-defence was less likely to include performance in the ring however, although there was something of an alliance between the aristocracy and the migrant agricultural and urban poor. Combat was undertaken by the poor and dispossessed agricultural workers of the itinerant and some of the minority groups such as diaspora Jews and immigrant Irish people, who nonetheless were offered a route out of poverty and a chance to gain some recognition through the sport (Gorn, 1986); then as now. The culture of boxing, rather like blood sports in the contemporary world, brought together the poor and marginalized and the aristocratic and well-off. Sugden points out that not only were there very few rules in operation in the ring in the early nineteenth century, these were dangerous times in the public spaces of the city. He suggests that,

> In 1719 there were few rules associated with pugilism. In addition to punching, kicking was tolerated and wrestling holds and throws were permitted, as was the practice of gouging – inserting fingers and thumbs into the opponent's eye sockets. By the end of the century the sport had been taken over by a fraternity whose passions revolved around blood, gore and a wager. While strength, nimbleness of foot and power and speed of punch were attributes in a fighter . . . being game and having 'bottom' (being lion-hearted, resolute and, above all, long-suffering) were considered to be even more important. The more prize fighting developed as a public spectacle and a gambling forum the more organised the sport became.
>
> (Sugden, 1996: 15)

This presents another strand in the narrative along with a reworking of heroism to incorporate both daring and unrestrained aggression and long-suffering endurance. Sugden suggests that gambling played an increasingly important role integrated into the organization of the sport (1996). Gambling and other nefarious activities on the periphery of legality constitute some of the collusions of masculinity within sport and operate to reinstate a 'manhood formula' (Messner, 2002). The networks through which these masculinities and their alliances are forged draw in others, including commentators and journalists. They remain part of the networks of masculinity in which any transformations or reformulations might be accommodated. There are other elements in these alliances. The eighteenth century also saw the advent of sports journalism Pierce Egan, who has been considered as one of the first sports journalists and who wrote most graphically and entertainingly about the sub-culture of boxing (Reid, 1971) and all its associated activities in his famous collection, *Boxiana*, published in 1812. Egan might have been a forerunner of the sports journalists and writers, some of whom are discussed in Chapter 4, who, without necessarily taking part themselves as pugilists, seek to be part of the boxing scene and to buy into its culture and its gender identities.

Although pugilism in Britain experienced great popularity in the early nineteenth century, social and economic changes led to new alliances and reconfigured discourses of morality which contributed to its transformation and to the demise of prize fighting. Prize fighting was first outlawed in 1750 and, as gambling became illegal and the sport lost its aristocratic support, it seemed doomed. It had lived for too long 'outside the pale of respectability for there to be now any hope of gradual amendment' (Brailsford, 1988: 157). As Sugden notes, bare knuckle fighting was forced underground in Britain by the 1830s, although it did receive something of a revival in the US at this time (1996).

Looking back on the earlier period when James Figg achieved fame, it already represented some nostalgia for a less regulated period than the later nineteenth century was to become. It was certainly a period of enormous interest in boxing as an exceedingly violent sport in which there were frequent fatalities in the ring, although this was a violence which reflected that of the world outside the ring (Gorn, 1986; Elias and Dunning, 1986).

Boxing was one of the first sports to be organized around a set of principles, governing practice, but in effect doing little to reduce the brutality inflicted in the ring (Sugden, 1996). Broughton's rules were introduced in 1843 and governed the practice of prize fighting until the Marquis of Queensberry's rules, with the imposition of the use of gloves, a limited number of three-minute rounds, weight equilibrium and the standardization of refereeing in the late nineteenth century. Again, the extent to which these rules, which remain in place today with few amendments, reduced violence and damage in the ring is strongly disputed (Gorn, 1986; Sugden, 1996). However, Queensberry's rules did contribute to the transformation of boxing, especially to the development of the amateur sport so that professional boxing could grow almost as a legitimized branch of amateur boxing. Amateur boxing has provided the training ground for those who want to turn professional and provides a useful, well-regulated route into earning a living by boxing. The distinction between amateur and professional boxing presents another technology of regulation. Of course the status of the amateur–professional relationship has different meanings in different parts of the world. In the UK and

US amateur boxing represents a pathway to professional competition, for example via local gyms or, more recently, through participation in the Olympic Games. Professional boxing largely carries higher status in the UK and the US and in the gym the rules governing amateur bouts are seen as repressive and constraining of the greater aggression expressed in the professional sport (Woodward, 1997b). However, in Cuba, for example, there is much stronger congruence between amateur status and the honour of representing the country and there are heavy proscriptions against turning professional.

Debates about the regulation of boxing represented in the historical shift from bare-knuckle fighting to professional and amateur boxing, demonstrate the ambivalent status of the sport and its occupation of a moral 'low ground', especially as positioned by those who lay claim to the moral high ground. These tensions, apparent in the nineteenth century in what Sugden calls the 'campaign against the popular recreations of the pre-industrial, urban labour pool, of which the crusade against prize fighting was part' (1996: 27) re-emerge in different manifestations at different historical moments, but I cite the instance here as illustrative of the moral framework in which debates about boxing, whether men's or women's, are so often set. Prize fighting in the late eighteenth and early nineteenth century was characterized by more informal than formal regulations, for example through its association with The Fancy, which was slang parlance for the collective name for prize fighters and their devotees and associates. Such networks through which masculinities are secured persist into the present as part of the collusions of hegemonic masculinity (Connell, 1995) and are constitutive of the 'manhood formula' (Messner, 2002). Although boxing is now strictly rule-governed there is a resonance of its earlier forms of association and the closure around its groupings; the practices of The Fancy, however, do seem more suited to the timescales and routines of pre-industrial life. Such networks provide support for hegemonic masculinity and for subversions of the regulatory regimes of boxing. Contemporary boxing gyms are often the focus for information about quasi legal or illegal activities including dog-fighting and bare-knuckle fighting (Beattie, 1997; Mitchell, 2003). These practices are all constitutive of the regimes of masculinity that are enacted and experienced in boxing. What has come to be taken for granted as the 'common sense' of boxing masculinities might be challenged and reconstructed.

Questions remain about how these apparatuses relate to experience and to what extent they shape the masculinities that are embedded in the culture of boxing or how far they might be capable of transformation and renegotiation.

Is boxing for men?

Joyce Carol Oates has written extensively and influentially on the subject of boxing; most emphatically, men's boxing. Whilst the dominance of men's boxing may be unstated and assumed in much of what is written about the sport, in Oates's work it is centre stage. Because her statements are so explicit, I think it is worth citing some of them in order to get a picture of what cultural meanings she draws upon in making her claims that 'boxing is for men'. In her book *On Boxing*, Oates invokes the language of boxing and its associations with machismo, as expressed in the names of boxers, such as, 'Hector Macho Man Commacho', former World Boxing Organization (WBO) Lightweight Champion. Placing a traditional, macho masculinity above factors shaped by class and socio-economic position she writes,

> It was once said by Jose Torres that the machismo of boxing is a condition of poverty. But it is not surely a condition uniquely of poverty? Or even of adolescence? I think of it as the obverse of the feminine-in-man that has its ambiguous attractions for all men however 'civilized'. It is a remnant of another earlier era when the physical being was primary and the warriors' masculinity its highest expression.
>
> (1987: 76–7)

> Boxing is a purely masculine activity and it inhabits a purely masculine world – which is not to suggest that most men are defined by it; clearly most men are not. And although there are female boxers – a fact that seems to surprise, alarm, amuse – women's role in the sport has been extremely marginal . . . Men fighting men to determine worth (i.e. masculinity) excludes women as completely as the female experience of childbirth excludes men . . . A celebration of the lost religion of masculinity, all the more trenchant for being lost . . .
>
> (Oates, 1987: 71–3)

This clearly establishes the female/male binary with its separate spheres sanctioned by biology and the notion that men project their fears of femininity and of fragmentation onto the fight scenario. Oates also sites the gladiatorial combat that not only informs boxing with its one-on-one conflict in the ring, but also has resonance in most other sports. Even Test cricket can be represented by the individual bowler set in direct opposition to the batsman, surrounded by a close field and focusing on the square, as if it were a contest between two men, as in the 2005 Ashes series between England and Australia. Much of the commentary at key moments in this series deployed not only the lexis of war but also pugilistic and bellicose discourses of one-to-one combat. Bowlers take on titles reminiscent of boxers, 'The Assassin', 'The Destroyer' and batsmen hold their bats, as Michael Vaughan the English captain did on 12 August 2005, after scoring a captain's century, as if it were a gladiatorial sword (*Guardian*, Friday, 12 August, www.guardian.co.uk), and 'putting the Aussies to the sword' (*Daily Telegraph*, 12 August 2005, www.telegraph.co.uk). Masculinity in these terms is strictly hierarchical – two men cannot occupy the same space at the same time (Oates, 1987: 73).

Whilst this may seem like hyperbole it does underpin much of the reporting of sport, where competition is framed within the discourse of a dualistic combat; resonant of that between two warriors; a kind of 'clash of the Titans'. This is a space which is not only limited to two men at a time, it is one which it is difficult for women to occupy at all, certainly without attempting to perform the same masculinity that men are enacting, which is one from which women have largely been excluded historically.

Oates identifies boxing as male, and even a celebration of machismo, through an essentialist discourse in which boxing is construed as a masculine activity with childbirth as a female concern. Whilst these polarities may be a bit extreme she is giving voice to some of the dualisms that inform the practice of gender identities and the investments people make, which demonstrates the pull of a particular language of belonging. Boxing carries heroic status through its genealogies of war and warriors, which childbirth clearly does not. Also in Oates's albeit literary and thus somewhat embellished account boxing is not only hierarchical and competitive and although it is spectacle, 'it is *not drama*. It's real' (1987). This 'reality' suggests the materiality of the body and the pain experienced in training and in the ring and focuses upon an essentialized understanding of the body based on what Butler calls 'anatomical sex' (1993). However, it is possible to conceptualize identity as encompassing the material body in an embodied self which is reconstituted, not only through embodiment but also through the imaginary and which embraces the dramatic moments of identification. The main binary picked out by Oates is that between women and men; a dualism underpinned by that of nature and culture with nature in a strongly dominant role, which in one sense subverts the more usual equation of men with culture and women with nature.

Men's boxing carries different meanings from women's boxing in all sorts of ways, for the participants, the spectators, the media and probably most significantly the promoters, although there is an increasing number of women, for example in the US, who are engaging in competitive boxing (Women's Boxing Archive Network, 2005b). Whilst women do participate in the sport in increasing numbers, it is more difficult for women to situate themselves within the genealogy of boxing and especially within its heroic narratives. Women also work out at boxing gyms and enjoy feeling in control of their own bodies, which periodically receives media coverage, perhaps because it is seen as unusual (Randall, 2004) although the increased popularity of the sport is also extensively covered by the Women's Boxing Archive Network (WBAN, 2005b) as well as by academic study including ethnographies, or at least observations, if not participant observations (Lafferty and McKay, 2005).

Whilst theories of identity, especially the theorising of gender identities become ever more concerned with intersectionality and the interrelationships between different dimensions of identity, boxing is ever more constructed around resistance to the rhetoric of transgression and interconnections and remains entrenched in binary logic. This was expressed in the destruction of the 'myth of

Tyson' by Lennox Lewis in their heayyweight world championship fight in Memphis in June 2002, post facto, being coded the triumph of 'good' over 'evil' and as a 'morality tale' (Engel, 2002: 2), although it was also a 'compelling spectacle . . . two strong men, sweat glistening urged on deafeningly by the crowd' (Engel, 2002: 2). Boxing embodies and makes real these binaries and this dualistic thinking pervades the rhetoric of boxing in the press and in the gym; strong/weak, big/small, success/failure, pro/amateur, brave/cowardly all have to be negotiated by those who participate in its practices. However, the question is whether this is indicative of meanings being produced in opposition to secure hegemonic masculinity or expressive of more complex aspects of identification and the desire to stabilize the self and to establish a sense of location and of belonging achieved through an accommodated settlement.

The involvement with this particular sporting activity has particular reso-nance for presenting oneself as 'tough' and as a 'real man' in the tradition of a particular form of physical, dominant and dominating masculinity (Oates, 1987). Masculinity is inextricably enmeshed with race and class and location (Early, 1994), but these articulate with masculinity in the production of gendered identities in relation to the sport. As Loic Wacquant observes, 'That boxing is a working-class occupation is reflected not only in the physical nature of the activ-ity but also in the social recruitment of its practitioners and in their continuing dependence on blue-collar or unskilled service jobs to support their career in the ring' (1995b: 502). This follows Pierre Bourdieu's claim that 'the body is the most indisputable materialization of class taste' (1986: 190), which is explored in more detail in Chapter 3. According to Bourdieu different social classes operate with different tastes and lifestyles and have different and unequal access to cultural capital (1986). Bourdieu has argued that working-class bodily types constitute a form of physical capital that has a lower exchange value than that which has been developed by the ruling classes (1978). Working-class people have more limited access to the means of converting physical capital into cultural capital and their physical capital is predominantly devalued. Thus boxing could be seen as a largely male, working-class engagement in converting physical capital which is also practised by those who are socially excluded through racialization and ethnicization.

Boxing illustrates well the centrality of masculinity in sport and is rich in illustrating the multiple points at which attempts are made to secure the domi-nance of masculinity. Boxing offers a focus on the mechanisms of embodiment and the regulatory practices, representations and narratives through which selves are interpellated. The creation of regimes of truth operates through the 'common sense' assumptions of boxing and its invocation of particular narratives as well as its powerful attraction as a way of making up the self in the face of structural constraints such as economic disadvantage, social exclusion and racism. These versions of masculinity are situated. They are constituted in specific contexts, spatially and temporally which lends support to their particularity.

Conclusion

Processes of identification bring together the diverse and different components of identity providing a space in which regulatory, disciplinary practices, narratives which circulate in the wider field as well as within the sport, embodiment and unconscious forces, combine to inform an understanding of how identities are remade. Selves are reconstructed through personal investment in the stories that are told, as well as through embodied practices.

Masculinities are reconstituted through diverse mechanisms. An exploration of the genealogy of the sport demonstrates the primacy of particular dimensions of identity which indicate the interrelationship between the personal and the social in the constitution of the self. Whilst there are clearly specificities in the processes through which selves are reconfigured within boxing, identification cannot be situated outside the wider social and cultural terrain and boxing offers a good example of the personal social interface at a time of change and uncertainty. However, this returns to one of the big questions which inspire this book, which is linked to the draw of boxing. How do boxing masculinities work? How are identities reconfigured through the genealogies through which 'common-sense' assumptions about masculinities are made? Why do people want to engage in the sport and buy into its culture? Why do people watch boxing? Why is this a version of masculinity that has appeal and how does it work – or not work? Who else is implicated in these identification processes and who is complicit in the configuration of masculinities at this site?

The body, or more specifically bodies, since bodies, like selves are differentiated and diverse, are central to boxing, as they are to any discussion of identity, but the primacy of 'the body' in boxing has great impact and can be troubling, especially in relation to risk and danger, in practice and spectatorship. The formalized practices of classification based on corporeality also foreground the importance of the material body. Gender identities are embodied. This is a masculinity that displays the contingent dimensions of anatomical corporeal sex, gender identity, racialized identity and performance, but presents problems for rethinking identity. Does a focus upon the material body necessarily underpin essentialized understandings of identity which cannot accommodate agency? What is the relationship between the material body and inscribed social and cultural practices? In order to address these questions in the rest of the book I have set up some of my major concerns here.

The making of selfhood within boxing is often based on a binary logic, especially in relation to gender. Such an identity, or set of identities, might involve strong investment in and identification with traditional masculinity, as distinguished from femininity which is construed as its psychic and material opposite. Although the sport seems characterized by dualisms, these are problematic too and even boxing myths and legends include contradictory heroes. Media stories invite oppositional thinking in terms of good and evil, success and failure, but it is apparent that a more complex set of narratives and identifications is emerging.

The moral discourses which frame many boxing stories can be translated as expressive of the desires and aspirations of identification and a need to belong, which involves at least a moment of recognition. Even if boxing may not ever ultimately deliver, it might and there is a sense in which identity is about being as well as becoming, to turn around Stuart Hall's statement about identity being more about becoming than being (1990). Identities are incomplete and the expression of the desire to belong and to stabilize identity through the practices of particular masculinities is testimony to that incompleteness.

Developments of Foucauldian theory have been immensely useful especially in shifting the focus onto the processes through which subjects are constituted. However, they do still present problems in relation to the success of the reproduction of identities. The notion of governmentality might suggest that subjection is a successful process through which subjects live out self-governing subjection as inscribed in the apparatuses of governance. Gender identities are fragmented and subjects are not simply reproduced. The processes of making up the self include transgression and resistance and disruption. Although the processes of identification are iterative, they are also transforming and I want to argue that not only are there discontinuities and resistances, but that also the subject is implicated in the process, which would suggest that subjects actively take up or invest in identity positions. I suggest that one way of accommodating this is to deploy the notion of belonging, which is not confined to the search for fixity and the security of a bounded identity. Roots and belonging have been linked to closure and a misrecognized stability, but the desire to belong can be dynamic and active. Belonging can also involve mobility, transformation and contingency as well as fixity and stability, especially when understood in the context of the narrative structures with which those recruited into such identity positions situated themselves. Thus, it is not possible to disentangle the practice of the sport and its more public representations, which include embodied practice and fantasies and aspirations. Identities are forged through both.

Identities, especially masculinities lived and experienced in and through boxing, are forged through networks and associations. These may operate in changing rooms, in social spaces where people associate before and after the gym or the sporting event at which they have been spectators, as well as through more informal channels of television, film, the internet and other spaces in which it is possible to collude with particular versions of masculinity or even to resist them. This book also addresses some of these public spaces in which people might be interpellated and which are also constitutive of masculinities. Identifications take place within a wider social context than the specific field of sport and even binaries of good and evil are reconstructed within transforming and transformed cultural regimes. Boxing stories are retold within changing contexts. Boxing stories are also told by sociologists and a variety of 'experts' and in the next chapter, I discuss some of the problems of researching the sport which clearly have resonance for the process of investigation much more widely.

total 'surrender' to the experiences of the field, and especially the fact that I regularly put the gloves on with them, earned me the esteem of my club-mates, as attested in the term of address 'brother *Louie*'.

(Wacquant, 2004: 10–11)

These extracts illustrate different 'ways of knowing' about boxing. They are all examples of knowledge produced in some way 'from the inside'. They also pose questions about how it might be even possible to attempt to answer any of the questions that might be raised about so compelling and extraordinary a sport, especially in contemporary societies. What is so seductive about this version of masculinity that invites such identifications and collusions? These quotations cover the local space of the gym as well as competitive fights on the global arena and link the immediacy of contemporary experience to the historical narratives of boxing. Boxing research has to incorporate all these aspects: the public stage and the genealogy of the sport and its routine everyday practices. Getting 'inside' the routine and the local can present more problems for the researcher than investigating public boxing stories. However, getting 'inside' involves more than practising the sport. Immersion can take different forms. For example Oates is a fan but not a boxer herself and as a woman has a different form of outsider status, although she could, of course, be 'doing masculinity'. Similarly 'routine' includes rigorous daily practice in the gym and the routine practices of the fan, going to fights and following the sport. What does immersion in the field mean for research into gender identities and how do these considerations impact upon routine masculinities?

The first of these quotations is a more literary account of the Ali–Foreman 'Rumble in the Jungle' in Zaire in 1974 and is taken from Norman Mailer's famous book *The Fight*. Mailer is both a writer of fiction and a boxing fan and in this text draws upon his considerable literary skills to convey the excitement and the immediacy of the contest. Much of the knowledge that is produced about boxing derives from literary or at least journalistic sources; sometimes the two elide. Joyce Carol Oates, whose work is also quoted here is in a similar category to Mailer, a fan and a writer and is distinguished by her gender as well as the strength of her writing. Mailer achieved significance as a boxing writer through his association with a particular event and with Ali, who carries considerable status in the annals of heavyweight boxing as well as in popular culture, whereas Oates is cited by so many academic writers especially because of the power of expression and the range of her critique. John Sugden and Loic Wacquant are both sociologists who cite Oates in their work. These sociologists are, however, differently placed; their engagement is with the routine practice of the field and, especially in Sugden's case, with the wider social, economic and cultural context of the sport. Both write of the appeal of pugilism and of buying into its culture. In Sugden's case there is some avowed surprise, given that he would not classify himself as a fan. He too cannot resist the 'thrill of the fight', however seedy the surroundings, thus demonstrating the totality of boxing culture and not just the draw of its most

Chapter 3

Outside in, inside out
Routine masculinities

Introduction: knowing boxing masculinities

The bell! Through a long unheard sigh of collective release, Ali charged across the ring . . . They collided without meeting, their bodies still five feet apart. Each veered backward like similar magnetic poles repelling one another forward, they circled, they feinted, they moved in an electric ring, and Ali threw the first punch, a tentative left. It came up short. Then he drove a lightning-strong right straight as a pole into a stunned center of Foreman's head, the unmistakable thwomp of a high-powered punch. A cry went up. Whatever else happened Foreman had been hit. No opponent had hit George this hard in years and no sparring partner had dared to.

(Mailer, 1975: 177–8)

When the boxing fan shouts 'Kill him! Kill him!' he is betraying no peculiar individual pathology or quirk but asserting his common humanity and his kinship, however distant, with thousands upon thousands of spectators who crowded into the Roman amphitheatres to see gladiators fight to the death. That such contests for mass amusement endured not for a few years or even decades but for centuries should arrest our attention.

(Oates, 1987: 42)

I am not a fight fan, but I have had this dormant passion roused in me in dirty back-streets in Belfast, in decaying sports palaces in Havana and ringside Madison Square Garden. I have also noticed how it spreads in a concentric wave from those closest to the action to those at the back of the theatre, accompanied by a collective baying for the despatch of the weakening victim.

(Sugden, 1996: 177)

Being the only white member of the club . . . could have constituted a serious obstacle [but] the egalitarian ethos and pronounced 'color-blindness' of pugilistic culture are such that everyone is fully accepted into it so long as he submits to the common discipline and 'pays his dues' in the ring . . . my spectacular moments. *Boxing and Society* incorporates ethnographic studies of gyms in three different countries and a critical analysis of the sport that engages with the reasons why people participate in it as well as the pull of boxing as a spectator sport. Wacquant acknowledges more explicitly in this extract a socio-logical understanding of the need for total immersion in the field for his project of understanding the embodied practices of boxing and his own participation. The extract which is from Wacquant's notebooks of an apprentice boxer (the subtitle of his book, *Body and Soul*) is also particularly interesting in its illustration of the way in which participating in, or colluding with, hegemonic masculinity might override differences of class and 'race'. He notes the egalitarian ethos of the gym which welcomes all-comers who are willing to put on the gloves, although he might also have commented on the incredible generosity of his friends at the gym in accepting a white academic as an honorary black person. There may even be some irony in their acceptance of him as a very privileged white man, albeit, as he says, as a Frenchman, giving some outsider status in terms of ethnicity, which passes without reflection. The extract is included to raise questions about reflexivity in the research process. Wacquant's focus upon embodiment offers interesting material with which to address the outsider insider relationship and how it is configured.

All of these quotations demonstrate immersion, which has been recognized as a key strategy of the qualitative researcher (Hammersley and Atkinson, 2003) in some way and each of these writers is 'inside' to a greater or lesser extent. Boxing raises some big issues about the processes through which knowledge is produced and especially about the relationship between the researcher and the subject of the research, about how the logic of the 'inside' and the 'outside' is constituted. Boxing invites such dualisms and privileges notions of inclusion and exclusion as one of the defence mechanisms in play in a sport that is so often under attack in the public terrain. Oates suggests that boxing represents an extreme version of male–female polarization, with women's experience of childbirth at the other end (1987). The actual experience of childbirth is currently limited to those whose bodies are not only categorized as female but also possess ovaries and a uterus and thus represents a particularly corporeal constraint, whereas the constraints in boxing are cultural and historical, although one might say no less forceful in their imposition of closed boundaries. However, as both Oates and Sugden posit, in the above quotations, social constructions and cultural histories are insufficient to explain the continuing attraction of boxing, especially its spectatorship. This is what is really difficult to access and to get 'inside'. There is also some slippage in the meanings of 'inside' and 'outside'. For example in a sport that is as subject to criticism as boxing, 'insiders' are those who are empathetic and support the sport rather than seeking to ban it.

Boxing presents a special and distinctive field of inquiry even within the study of sport. Boxing has a contradictory presence in contemporary culture and supporters are aware of the censure it provokes. However, boxing still invites participation and the desire to buy into just a little bit of the hyperbole which the sport attracts among commentators and researchers. Those who study other sports are much less likely to boast of their involvement. In cricket there are few stories of facing West Indian fast bowlers at their prime or of scoring a century off Shane Warne. There may be apocryphal tales of meeting a celebrity, indeed whole books have been written by academics about sports stars (Cashmore, 2004a, 2004b), including Muhammad Ali and Mike Tyson. Boxing demands some complicity in its masculinities and claims to authenticity, not only among journalists but also among academics. What constitutes authenticity, can be construed in different ways; through actual participation in the body practices of the sport, through being a 'true' fan or through being part of a sporting culture, as in the manner of what Sugden calls modern fandom (1996), which may be characterized by following a sport, even following the most successful or celebrity player, rather than having strong identification with a sports hero or team that has a long history of affiliation and personal and group investment (1996). Hence contemporary sports research includes both ethnographies of the sport itself including its body practices and extensive studies of fandom and spectatorship and especially the media coverage of sport. My questions relate to rethinking the relationship between insider and outsider status in all these situations, but which are highlighted by ethnography and the related issues of objectivity and subjectivity in the application of some acceptable criteria for carrying out research and in the pursuit of generally acceptable findings.

Some of these methodological questions as well as their concomitant epistemological issues have been most effectively addressed within feminist debates, although, not surprisingly, not in the context of boxing. Feminism in sport is largely associated with a focus on women in sport and with an agenda for change (Scraton and Flintoff, 2002). Eliot Cashmore, in what is avowedly a textbook on sports studies, includes a discussion of feminism in his chapter on 'Sports emasculated' and describes women's increased participation in sport as 'de-gendering' (2005: 152). Whilst putting women who do sport into the discursive regime of sport is one very important aspect of the feminist project, as is providing explanations for women's exclusion and inclusion and their current experience, the major feminist contribution upon which I want to focus in this chapter is how feminist methodologies and epistemologies might inform a critical analysis of sport. Feminist work has focused upon gender difference, albeit from very different perspectives, but what is most useful for my purposes is its concern with the centrality of gender difference and the need to deconstruct difference and to put gender into analyses of the situation. The major concern of this book is with gendered identities in boxing, especially how masculinities are lived, experienced and represented and in this chapter I am emphasizing how such knowledge is produced and especially how it might be investigated. Those who conduct the investigations and generate knowledge are also complicit in the processes through which knowledge is reproduced. Whilst individual research projects do, of course, outline their methodological approaches, I wish here to address the more general issues that are raised and which derive from a consideration and review of boxing research. This is also designed to progress the arguments of those whose research into sport draws upon feminist perspectives, such as those of McKay, Messner and Sabo, and are described as 'pro-feminist' (2000). Such work includes engaging with masculinities and with making men visible as men, rather than assuming men as the homogenous, non-gendered norm of humanity, moving beyond the female/male binary and putting women into the discursive regime of sport. I would like to bring more to the debate and to include situated perspectives and reflective processes, including those implicating the researcher and the field, which are concepts that may not derive directly from sports research but definitely have a place there.

Although I have followed boxing through my life I come to it as a research subject from work which has focused on an area largely seen as at the other end of the gendered spectrum, motherhood. Not only work carried out by women, but research within an avowedly feminist framework in this field, has been subjected to criticisms of excessive 'ontological complicity' and on occasion of essentialism. An example of this is the criticism levelled at French feminist work on embodied gender difference such as the earlier work of Luce Irigaray, who has argued that the notion of gender cannot embrace the specificity of women's embodiment (1991). She demands the recognition of embodied gender difference and presents a powerful critique of the lack of recognition of women's bodies and women's lives in western culture. This is one aspect of the criticism that has been made of feminist work in relation to its epistemology. The other stresses methodology, for example where the starting point of research is women's experience (Stanley and Wise, 1993; Smith, 1997). In particular feminist standpoint epistemology, a hotly contested conceptualization, has been criticized, for example, by Wacquant, as holding 'that women's subjugation puts them in a privileged position to produce true knowledge' (1993: 497). There are several issues here. One relates to the status of the dichotomy of objectivity and subjectivity upon which this dilemma is based and the privileging of one aspect of this dualism. The second concerns the related methods through which knowledge is produced and especially the production of the insider and outsider status of the researcher and whose voices count. This is what triggers my interest in the tensions implicated in the situation of the researcher. Some questions emerge from my experience. Do you have to have 'been there'? Is being 'inside' about embodiment as understood by Merleau-Ponty and Bourdieu? How might the development of Chicago School ethnography involving the participation of men in boxing research be privileged? Does ethnography have to be embodied through the same mechanisms as those of the research site? In some instances the 'insider status' of the ethnographic participant observation might be subject to dismissal as too prone to an excess of sympathy, empathy, subjectivism or even reductionism, for example when applied to the work women do in relation to women's lives. On the other hand an 'outsider' might be subjected to the criticism which might be made of research into women's lives which is conducted without an acknowledgement of the situation and which claims 'objectivity' determined by 'insider' status. There are, of course problems in this classification of the relationship as one organised around an 'inside' and an 'outside' since research processes can never be wholly one or the other.

The majority of ethnographies conducted in boxing have been carried out by men (Wacquant, 1995a and b; Beattie, 1997; de Garis, 2000) and the great boxing books, especially the biographies of Muhammad Ali (such as Hauser, 1991), histories of the sport and expositions of its social significance (for example, Sammons, 1988; Early, 1994; Gorn, 1986) have male authors. Sugden's work illustrates immersion into the culture of boxing which includes useful reflections on the process as cited in the quotation at the start of this chapter (1996). There has, of course been work done on gyms where women box (for example, Mennesson, 2000) but women researchers are more likely to conduct research by observation and interview, rather than emphasizing participation (for example, Lafferty in Lafferty and McKay, 2005). Few ethnographies of sport by male researchers acknowledge or make visible the researcher's gendered identity and maleness passes unquestioned (Wheaton, 2002). This complicity does not only apply to ethnographic accounts and it extends into other areas of sports research where there is participation in and collusion with the gendered sporting culture even if there is not physical involvement by the researcher in the actual sporting practices (Messner, 2002). Ethnography is one particularly pertinent approach to research. These debates are used to explore the question of 'ontological complicity' (Merleau-Ponty, 1962) as is the production of authentic 'truth' or an inside world, sometimes couched in terms of the objective/subjective dualism, which have much wider application outside sports research. In order to interrogate the collusions of masculinity consideration of immersion has to address the status of different texts and the relationship between ethnography, interviews, historical accounts and analysis of other texts, including the public stories that might include the press, the film and television media and literary sources.

Producing knowledge: methodologies

An important example of ethnographic research into boxing carried out by men who have 'joined in', is that of Loic Wacquant. Wacquant describes his experience of conducting an ethnography of boxing in the Woodlawn gym in Chicago as being that of an 'observant participator', rather than the more familiar participant observer (2004: 6). This approach permits the most engaging, detailed coverage not only of the ultimate experience of competitive fighting but also the routine of 'being in the gym, talking and laughing . . . and just *living* and *breathing* there, among them soaking up the atmosphere of the gym like a human sponge . . . [feeling] so much pleasure simply participating that observation becomes secondary'(2004: 4n). Wacquant goes on to say that his involvement in the gym, to the extent that he felt reluctant to return to his academic life and take up a post at Harvard, provoked Pierre Bourdieu to comment that Wacquant might be letting himself be 'seduced by his object'. Wacquant's story of seduction is one

However, access to research sites, like boxing gyms is difficult for women and problems are exacerbated by the gendered culture of the sport. There are strategies to gain entry and others to ensure continued acceptance. Given the sexualized positioning of women within boxing, for example where female partners of male boxers would be seen as distracting the fighter and reducing both his energy and concentration, there are wider implications. This is translated into the presence of any woman in the gym. Consequently one tactic is to be the maternal figure, an extension of a family figure, like the mothers who deliver small boys to youth sessions, or the family members of the trainer, who is thus not threatening and largely asexual (Woodward, 2004). The other is as the gender neutral outsider, which can be possible as an academic, although there might be some scepticism and being associated with other agencies such as the news or television media for initial contact can be very useful (Woodward, 1997b). Such 'outsider' character- istics as class provided access to some of the gym's more famous members since they thought I must be from a TV company or a national newspaper. 'Outsider' status has to be negotiated and acknowledged explicitly and this has worked in other situations where I have been involved in work in an all male environment such as professional football (Woodward, 2005). Distancing had to be embraced as my distinction as researcher was as outsider in terms of gender, class, biography and locality.

Personal involvement in the body practices of the sport is a key means of gaining access and one of ethnography's major strengths. However, participation is not everything, nor does it necessarily access a more authentic 'truth' than observation and interviewing. As Belinda Wheaton (2002) has pointed out, few ethnographies of sport by male researchers acknowledge or make visible the researcher's gendered identity; maleness passes unquestioned. Wheaton draws upon her own experience as an 'insider' in her ethnography of windsurfing and she reflects upon her insider status, arguing for the critical distance that is also a vital part of ethnography. Although there have been assertions in favour of the superiority of the status of the 'outsider' and a privileging of 'objectivity' in the continuum that has been constructed from complete participant to complete observer (Hammersley and Atkinson, 1995), this separation of the inside and outside is problematic. As Wheaton argues, the dualism of 'inside' and 'outside' has limitations but the recognition of differently situated positions does highlight the necessity for reflection about the researcher's own situation. The accounts of male 'insiders' in sport, especially in the case of sports like boxing, are interesting for their insights into the collusions of masculinity because of the personal investment made in these gender identities at the research site. 'Qualitative research has its own brand of machismo with its image of the male sociologist bringing back news from the fringes of society, the lower depths, the mean streets' (Morgan, 1992: 87).

However, throughout the research process there may be collusion in a particular version of masculinity which goes unnoticed and unrecorded when the researcher and the protagonists at the research site are engaged in the same,

competitive, embodied project. The embodiment of boxing and the implication
of the body in the activities and practices of the agents may make it difficult to
disentangle the diversity of the dimensions of masculinity. Active engagement
affords greater insights into the corporeality of the sport and, in the case of boxing,
more effectively addresses the question of how it is possible to keep going in what
can be so violent and painful an endeavour. This is demonstrated particularly
well in Wacquant's work (2004 especially). However, the more active the 'joining
in', the less room there is for a distancing from the research site and for reflection
upon and acknowledgement of the researcher's situated relationship with what
is being researched. Feminist approaches that acknowledge the position of the
researcher have the advantage of being explicit and direct in instating 'situatedness'. A focus upon the situation in which the mechanisms of the 'inside'–'outside'
binary is configured is more useful than the dualism that is the outcome of this
logic.

Public spaces: personal spaces

One of the questions which informs this chapter, along with how boxing
knowledges are produced, is what it is about boxing which so invites participation,
for example among the men who study boxing and who seem to want to buy into
its culture so whole-heartedly. Identification involves particular techniques and
use of language and these ways of performing masculinity are not restricted to
men. However, there is more to it because of the status of boxing as a sporting site
which is especially characterized by traditional or even hegemonic masculinity.
Following Bob Connell's earlier work (1983) which suggested that the demands
of every sport involve a specific balance between force and skill, it could be that
a greater weighting on force is decisive and the more likely that physically dominating hegemonic masculinity can be publicly celebrated. Wacquant describes his
own entry into the field as 'brute and even brutal' and sets his own investment in
this masculinity as a challenge: 'Would I be capable of *learning this toughest and
most demanding of sports . . . ?*' (2004: x, italics in original).

Hegemonic masculinity is based upon the exclusion and marginalization of any
versions of selfhood in which frailty, weakness or lack of courage are implicated.
This is translated into other dimensions of 'otherness' such as the inability to
compete and to be 'a contender' which render the subject incapable of securing
the boundaries of hegemonic masculinity. To position oneself within the
boundaries of this masculinity is a strategy for eschewing any associations with
weakness or the 'othered' selves that are excluded and for resolving the anxieties
of failure articulated in 'not being a contender'.

The practice in the gym cannot be entirely removed from the wider cultural
terrain or from the public stories that inform it. There are necessary links between
public and private space, even when the apparent site of investigation is the more
local, private space of the gym. Any reflection upon the implications of complicity
in gendered identities has to incorporate the interrelationship between what can,

for the sake of simplicity be called personal and public worlds, especially given the ever-increasing public presence of sport through its stars and celebrities and media coverage. Public and personal worlds are inseparable; not only does the public, social world operate within personal psychic realms, but the psychic is manifest in the social world of public stories, for example of heroism and toughness that dominate the public world of boxing. Much of the research that is carried out into sport as a field of study seeks to address this interrelationship through interrogations of the practice of sport.

Empirical research: knowing the field

One of the most influential approaches to the study of boxing derives from the work of Pierre Bourdieu, which has inspired a grounded empirical approach. In boxing, this has been taken up most enthusiastically by Wacquant who worked extensively with Bourdieu (for example, Bourdieu and Wacquant, 1992) and especially in Wacquant's development of Bourdieu's conceptualizations of embodiment, which are discussed in Chapter 4 in more detail. Bourdieu was one of the first sociologists to take sport seriously as a field of inquiry (1978) and his use of the concept of cultural capital has wide-ranging application. Bourdieu uses the concept of field in a specific way. It is especially useful for a study of sport because sport constitutes a field, as deployed by Bourdieu, who defines a field in his later work as follows:

> In analytic terms a field may be defined as a network, or a configuration, of objective relations between positions. These positions are objectively defined, in their existence and in the determinations they impose upon their occupants, agents or institutions, by their present and potential situation (*situs*) in the structure of the distribution of species of power (capital) whose possession commands access to the specific profits that are at stake in the field, as well as by their objective relation to other positions (dominations, subordination, homology, etc.).
>
> (Bourdieu and Wacquant, 1992: 97)

Bourdieu's studies of the way in which people's *habitus* signalled their place in the social system of class and taste hierarchies through practical repetition contributes towards an understanding of how gender identities are made and re-made in the field of sport. *Habitus* is the acquired patterns of thought, practice and taste which constitutes the link between social structures and social action (Bourdieu, 1977) and includes conscious, reflective practices and to some extent those that are unconscious. The *habitus* may be unconscious even when it directly influences the activity being undertaken as, for example, in sport. The boxer does not consciously focus on techniques that are part of this *habitus*. In fact it is more likely that the boxer only consciously focuses upon technique when something has gone wrong. However, this conceptualization of the unconscious is less the inner space of psychoanalytic theory than the unreflective practice of the *habitus* as is discussed in more detail in Chapter 4.

There are three issues in relation to developments of Bourdieu's work that are important to a study of boxing and impact upon methodological questions, notably the tension and interrelationship between 'inside' and 'outside' research, which I want to explore in this chapter. The first is the stress Bourdieu places upon the body and embodiment which has been understood to require immersion in the embodied social world. The second is the relationship between public and personal worlds, in sport manifest especially through the relationship between celebrity, spectatorship and routine practice and, lastly, the high priority Bourdieu affords sport as an indicator of class taste.

Bourdieu argued that sport played a particularly important role

> Sport is, with dance, one of the sites in which is posed with maximum acuity the problem of the relations between theory and practice . . . The teaching of a bodily practice [involves] a set of theoretical questions of the greatest importance, inasmuch as the social sciences endeavour to theorize conducts that are produced, for the vast majority of them, beneath the level of consciousness.
>
> (1990a [1987]: 166)

In order to access the embodied world of sport with its bodily practices that operate below the level of consciousness, it is imperative that the researcher becomes immersed in these practices. Following Marcel Mauss's argument that 'Before instrumental techniques there is the ensemble of the body' (1973 [1935]: 75). If, 'we are our bodies', then the researcher too learns through the body and to engage in bodily practices must require total immersion in these practices. Bourdieu suggests that in order to understand the practices, and explore the depths of the social world with its 'relation of presence to the world, being possessed by it, in which neither the agent nor the object is posited as such' (2000a: 141), one must join in. As practised by sociologists like Wacquant, this is an embodied engagement with Chicago school ethnography which goes further than traditional anthropologists' total integration into the research site. As Wacquant argues

> It is imperative that the sociologist submit himself [*sic*] to the fire of action *in situ*; that to the greatest extent possible he put his own organism, sensibility and incarnate intelligence at the epicentre of the array of material and symbolic forces that he intends to dissect.
>
> (2004: viii)

Whilst there are enormous strengths in this approach, it also raises many questions. How far is personal embodied participation privileged so that, for example, only women who have undergone childbirth could offer understanding of the depths of the experience? The vast majority of such research is based on interviews and observations and whilst women might encourage others to speak through an initial sharing of experience, the researcher's own experience rarely forms the central focus of the argument (for example, Akrich and Pasveer, 2004).

This also raises questions about the extent to which participation in the field can only be effected through routine body practices. How does the process of generalisation and the translation of one's own experience into a relationship with that of others take place and how can the experience be theorized? Related to this question about this overwhelming enthusiasm for the primacy and exclusivity of embodied engagement is a more traditional challenge in terms of its excessive subjectivism. Even if the objective subjective binary is rejected, as I suggest in the discussion of this tension below, there have to be some criteria and some means of generalizing from the data. Developments of theories of embodiment have made enormous contributions to the understanding of the relationship between agency and the body and the self (Wacquant, 1995a, b and c, 2004; Crossley, 2001, 2004, 2005), some of which is considered in more detail in Chapter 4. However, one of the problems of total immersion is the apparent mis-recognition of the wider field. For example, I would suggest that Wacquant's use of the male pronoun is neither chance nor an old-fashioned use of 'he' as some generic neutral pronoun where 'he' subsumes 'she'. It has to be 'he' in this *habitus*. Complete immersion may obscure the operation of inequalities, which are so crucial to Bourdieu's theories of inequality and the part played by culture in their reinstatement and persistence. Gender inequalities are particularly obscured and unstated or may lead to unsettling of the *habitus*. Gender presents a moment when habit may break down or habits may clash and disruption has serious implications for theories of the self (Burkitt, 2002). At points when the *habitus* breaks down the 'self is forced to reflexively monitor itself and the context in which it is acting in order to meaningfully reconstruct with others both self and situation' (Burkitt, 2002: 220).

The gendered immersion in a *habitus* in boxing research is taken for granted and largely unacknowledged, except insofar as there may be some reference women's spatial exclusion from the gym. A woman conducting such research would not be free to deny the gendered embodiment of its practices, nor not to reflect upon it. For example, as a woman conducting research at a gym, my approach was all observation. There was a complete separation between the researcher and the subject and I also had to negotiate my gender identity as an 'outsider'. There are other strategies for collusion. For example Oates is complicit as a fan, but in the gym there are fewer opportunities. In this instance gender offers an additional dimension to the relationship between researcher and the people being researched. The researcher has a spectatorial position, so that the research is not constructed around accessing any kind of 'authentic voice' of those who engage in boxing, but rather to explore the intersection between their stories and those which occupy the public arena in order to reach some understanding of how masculinities are constructed and experienced at this site (Woodward, 1997b,

2004). The researcher as outsider avoids the privileging of 'insider knowledge' and unrecognised collusion with the gendered identities being enacted at this site but this has to be countered by the more limited access to the understandings of those who box. However, by addressing both the stories that are told in the public arena and spectatorship as well as everyday body practices and regimens, there are different nodes at which the researcher can be an insider. There are not only different stories that are told, there are different identities into which recruitment is made possible. Private stories might concur or they might counter the public stories and especially the heroic legends which dominate them.

This raises the second issue which I would like to consider here. Gendered identities are enacted in the gym and in the sport in its wider representations and gender is part of the wider field. Insider status in as gendered a sport as boxing may marginalize the impact of this broader terrain. Immersion is not only in the bodily reflexive practices of the gym, it is also in the *habitus* of the sport which is at least in part constituted by its heroes and celebrities. As Wacquant observes the gym walls are decorated with posters of great moments (2004) and narratives of heroic masculinities are routinely exchanged in the gym (Woodward, 2004), but I would like to suggest that these are what make up the sport along with its routine practices and they are what interpellates boxers into the embodied masculinity that is also routinely practised. The one is no more real that the other, however drab and obsessive the routine of the gym with the 'endless and thankless preparation, inseparably physical and moral, that preludes the all too brief appearance in the limelight, the minute and mundane rites of daily life in the gym' (Wacquant, 2004: 6). Wacquant suggests that the researcher must 'not step into the ring by proxy with the extra-ordinary figure of the "champ" but "hit the bags" alongside anonymous boxers in their habitual setting of the gym' (Wacquant, 2004: 6). This argument makes a distinction between public and private spheres and between the fantasy of success and heroism and the reality of routine which fails to take account of the identificatory processes through which masculinities are made in boxing. On the scale that stretches between participation and observation there are problems that have to be addressed in espousing the 'observant participator' (Wacquant, 2004: 6) position. Whilst boxing in the gym might 'make sense' through engaging with its practices it is a partial understanding which does not take account of the psychic investment made by the boxers or the dreams and aspirations that inform the heroic masculinity into which they may seek to invest and which cannot be disassociated from the public stories that are told about the sport. This is not to make a case for the 'outsider'-only position dismissed as the 'gaze from afar' (Wacquant, 2004: 6) but to suggest the need for both reflection on the complicity or distancing of the researcher and the incorporation of the wider field of social and cultural dispositions into an understanding of body practices.

Bourdieu's work has contributed greatly to the understanding of social inequalities through cultural practices, especially in relation to class and this relates to the third issue I would like to raise here in relation to his work, which has methodological implications. The approach advocated in *Distinction* is informed by a model of the relationship between the universe of economic and social conditions and the universe of lifestyles' (1986: xi). This offers an extensive empirical cataloguing of the importance of cultural practices in shaping inequalities and differences that are linked to other operations of power, notably economic, using the conceptual category of capital, which includes economic, social and cultural capital, of which one aspect which has particular relevance to class distinctions in sport is physical capital, when what a person has to invest is their body. Although Bourdieu described this project as a sort of 'ethnography of France' (1986: xi) it depends heavily on grounded empirical research based on questionnaires and interviews rather than immersion in the field.

Whilst some of the detail of *Distinction* may be out of date and limited to the French context, the conceptual framework of the study is enormously useful and has clear applications to class-based sporting activities, which could be extended to encompass matters of gender and 'race'. Wrestling rather than boxing is the focus in this study but there are clear parallels and some of the findings on elite sport demonstrate very well the distinctive patterns of taste that shape and reproduce class differences. For example, in the case of 'smart clubs', for sports like golf and tennis, sailing or riding.

> There are more hidden entry requirements, such as family tradition and early training, or the obligatory manner (of dress and behaviour), and socializing techniques, which keep these sports closed to the working classes and which maintain them (along with parlour games like chess and especially bridge) among the surest indicators of bourgeois pedigree.
>
> (1986: 217)

Such sports co-exist along with what Bourdieu calls 'new sports' such as skiing, hang gliding or archery, 'whose common feature is that they all demand a high investment of cultural capital in the activity itself, in preparing, maintaining and using the equipment.' (Bourdieu, 1986: 220)

A sport like boxing demands physical capital and is associated with a different set of investments and generates the input of physical capital by black and minority white ethnic and working-class men.

Bourdieu's conceptual framework has relevant application to a study of sport especially boxing given its emphasis on class-based distinction. Wacquant's work is testimony to its enormous relevance to detailed empirical ethnographic work, drawing on Bourdieu's anthropological legacy and his development of theories of embodiment which lend themselves well to this kind of study. Whilst the approach and the concept of cultural capital has relevance to women's experience too (Hargreaves, 1994; Mennesson, 2000) and Bourdieu did write about masculinity (2001) overall his strategies underplay the importance of gender and masculinity is largely elided with a taken-for-granted patriarchy which is reproduced rather than challenged in Bourdieu's schemata. However, sports cultures transform and are transformed through human agency which draws upon different kinds of capital in the creation of new class-based, gendered and racialized *habituses* and Bourdieu's theory of practice continues to provide some useful approaches to investigating change and even the possibility of resistance as well as continuities. However, there is still a need to question the immersion of the researcher in the process. Wacquant has argued, following both Durkheim and Bourdieu that the hallmark of practice is that it has:

> 'a logic that unfolds directly in bodily gymnastics' without the intervention of discursive consciousness and reflective explication, that is by excluding the contemplative and de-temporalizing posture of the theoretical gaze, then few practices may be said to be more 'practical' than boxing.
> (2004: 48–9. The internal quotation is Durkheim, *Education and Sociology*, New York: Free Press, 1956 [1922] : 78)

The practice of research does require subjection to the theoretical gaze, especially when a particular methodology is privileged as accessing authenticity and even truth based on some kind of epistemological superiority; whether it is accorded to a more subjective or objective positioning.

Inside, outside: objective, subjective

The very notion of privileging insider status sets up the binary upon which it is based, which early studies of Chicago school ethnography sought to disrupt. However, taking the 'insider' role is part of a tradition in sports and cultural studies. Sugden acknowledges a debt to the Centre for Cultural Studies at Birmingham University in developing Chicago School ethnography to accommodate the socio-structural and power-related elements which frame sub-cultural experience and which are somewhat neglected in earlier ethnographies, including Whyte's *Street Corner Society* (1954) the seminal Chicago School ethnography. The dichotomized rubric of insider and outsider is inaccurate in many ways, being too concerned with differences between researchers and their subjects and less with commonality (Wheaton, 2002). The insider and outsider status of the researcher is closely connected to other debates about the process of producing knowledge through the research process, for example the interrelationship between objectivity and subjectivity. This is articulated in complex ways. The immersion of what Wacquant calls the 'observing participant' (2004: 6) may invoke, on the one hand, a perspective that is taken from the subjective position of the researcher and may therefore lack distance and objectivity, or on the other hand, may provide deeper insights which enrich the findings and create a more accurate picture of the field. Ethnography privileges the insider and processes of immersion, but these practices are very specifically gendered, in ways that are not always acknowledged. One way of exploring some of these processes is through reviewing the traditional dualism between objectivity and subjectivity and looking at how problems have been addressed by feminist approaches that have taken the matter of claims of bias and of the need to address situatedness very seriously and thus offer some strategies for critical thinking and possible resolutions to problems that have been identified.

Debates about objectivity have often been framed in the context of tensions between the validity of social science methodologies in relation to those of the natural sciences and more recently this is another dichotomy that has been extensively challenged. The social sciences and those who conduct qualitative research have often had to defend their position against attacks about the size of the sample upon which generalizations are based as well as the possibility of bias and the excesses of subjective involvement.

The objectivity that was associated with positivism has received limited support in recent years. For example Steven Ward suggests that realist epistemology has become unfashionable (1997). Ward was attacking, it must be said somewhat unfairly, a diverse range of approaches, including feminist, postmodernist and culturally relativist positions, but he does demonstrate some of the extremes in which objectivity and subjectivity can be expressed and may have some point to make about the excesses of subjective, experiential narratives which are unrelated to the field as well as rejecting any claim to truth and authenticity other than what truths they produce themselves. Ward's expression of the need to seek out universal truths is an extreme version of the objectivist position and illustrates another dimension of universalism.

However, as Caroline Ramazanoglu and Janet Holland point out in the context of feminist methodologies, those who challenge the primacy of objectivity in the objective/subjective dichotomy are in a contradictory position. The researcher who eschews the dominance of the model which asserts the possibility of objective truth still has to make a valid claim to the observations made and explanations offered about the nature of the social world being investigated (2005). For feminist researchers their project is to produce knowledge of what gender relations are, as a basis for emancipatory action that is in some way more 'true' than pre-existing, partial, patriarchal or male-centred knowledge. 'They still have the problem confronted by all social researchers of making their knowledge believable' (Ramazanoglu and Holland, 2002: 47).

Objectivity may be asserted through outside status. The researcher as outsider avoids the privileging of 'insider knowledge' but this may also have to be countered by the more limited access to the understandings of those who box. De Garis (2000) describes revelations and intimate exchanges in the showers which are not, of course, accessible to a woman in this context. Research into a sport like boxing may be especially susceptible to the reverse of the assertion of greater objectivity through outsider status as insider participation may be deemed an essential component of immersion in the field through which knowledge may be secured (Wacquant, 2004). However, immersion without acknowledgement of the researcher's situatedness, in this instance in particular in relation to gender, class and 'ethnicity' may obscure the claimed objectivity of any findings. My point here is to indicate the relevance of the gender specific experience of the researcher especially and to illustrate both positive and negative, gendered dimensions of ontological complicity which are linked to the debate about the relationship between objective and subjective experience of doing research and producing knowledge. Power and knowledge are always implicated in the process of doing research.

Reflection and situatedness

If Bourdieu's approach has been criticized for its emphasis on the reproduction of existing knowledge and social relations (Burkitt, 2002), what alternatives are there which might challenge existing 'truths', or at least the current dominant regime? As Donna Haraway has argued, in the context of feminist research, especially in relation to the methods of the social and the natural sciences, the pursuit of truth is slippery (1991). Feminists might want to challenge existing regimes of truth and assert another; thus they are split between 'truth' and objectivity on the one hand and relativism on the other. If one wants to resist and challenge existing knowledge systems, what escape routes are there? In a field of competing knowledges which one has greater claims to acceptance and to validity? Haraway develops the concept of the greased pole to illustrate the tension between realism and relativism and the problem of laying claim to objective truth. The aim of climbing the pole is to achieve authentic knowledge, to achieve 'enforceable, reliable accounts of things' (Haraway, 1991: 188). However this aim is set against a refusal to let go of the relativist claim that all knowledge is socially constructed and there is no reliable truth. Haraway suggest that it is not possible to hold onto the dualism of truth and relativism and that there must be an alternative. Her solution to the problem of the greased pole is to suggest that privileged knowledge should be abandoned in favour of partial visions and what she calls 'socially situated knowledge' (1991: 188). Partial knowledge includes embodied, knowledge that is produced from multiple perspectives. Haraway holds onto the possibility that some knowledge and some partial visions may be more reliable than others, thus retaining the requirement that knowledge be subjected to critical evaluation. This approach has been criticized, for example by Ramazanoglu and Holland (2005), as failing to specify the criteria by which some knowledge is to judged more valid than others. However what is useful about it for my purposes is the necessity that is asserted of situating the researcher who seeks knowledge and the recognition that knowledge is both partial and situated.

Sugden's *Boxing and Society* includes a range of tales of adventure and his own involvement in risky and threatening activities, but he also goes some way towards acknowledging his own position and reflecting upon his relationship with the field. He argues that for the researcher, 'it is only through total immersion that she or he can become sufficiently conversant with the formal and informal rules governing the webbing of the human interactions under investigation so that its innermost secrets can be revealed' (1996: 201). Sugden acknowledges the demands and dangers of his chosen strategy and admits that some of what he did was the direct result of his 'outsider' rather than his 'insider' status and that he experienced fear as a result. This is an important stage in the process of engaging with situatedness. As Sugden says in his conclusion 'We need to develop empathy with our subjects without getting emotionally tied to them . . . A few of my simple rules might help: be upfront about the research role . . . we are interested in naturally emergent (or concealed) social truths, not good stories' (1996: 211).

Sugden acknowledges that he is not an honorary member of the gym even if his situatedness does not extend to cognition of the complicity in masculinity that implicates him is the field. Masculinity in sport in reinstated and enacted around the networks that are configured around the 'insider'–'outsider' relationship. Sugden does recognize the need to acknowledge situatedness, although, as I argue in this book telling 'good stories' also provides raw material for the sociologist and is part of the research process and could be valued too.

A synthetic approach to the attraction of boxing

'Good stories' take different forms and, in boxing, also relate to the big moments of major contests. Mailer's account of the 'Rumble in the Jungle' in 1974 from which an extract is quoted at the start of this chapter, is such a boxing moment,

Figure 3.1 'Rumble in the Jungle' (Photo: © Empics)

condensing temporal and spatial particularities. Such a moment configures the particularity of the protagonists and the universal stories of the sport and its appeal, especially as articulated by narratives of heavyweight fighters. The heroic narratives of the public arena, even if these public stories are romanticized, glamorized or even, in some cases, demonized, inform masculinities which circulate the culture of boxing.

There are different strategies that can be adopted for incorporating different discursive fields into the analysis, which include an historical approach (for example, Sammons, 1988) and those of comparative studies (for example, Sugden, 1996) all of which are directed at addressing some of the issues raised in the quotations with which this chapter opened. One of these issues relates to the draw of boxing. In spite of the sport's obvious violence and aggression in competitive fighting, boxing remains a powerfully attractive spectacle in the twenty-first century. In order to explore the enormous attraction of boxing much of the literature focuses upon biographies or key moments, which, in boxing, are the big fights, such as the Ali–Foreman 'Rumble in the Jungle' in Zaire in 1974. Big moments such as this are worthy of study, in that they condense the meanings of the sport. The existentialist philosopher Jean Paul Sartre's analysis of boxing was far removed from the empirical work advocated by Bourdieu and represents the methods of the outside observer, but offers an alternative methodology that does seek to address the phenomenon of boxing by linking its different manifestations, temporality and spatiality. He presented a synthetic approach to boxing by suggesting that a particular fight has temporal specificity, but that this moment reproduces the individual boxer's life, so that we can only understand one fight by understanding not only the totality of the boxer's life but the totality of boxing. Boxing appears to be about individuals and 'from the very outset we note that the deep truth of every individual fight is competition for titles' (1991: 18). The whole of the sport, with its rules, promoters, hierarchies and spectators and indeed the wider social phenomenon of violence, is present at each fight.

> The two men very much (seemingly) at their ease, who climb into the ring amid the applause in their brightly coloured robes . . . contain within them the opponents they have already defeated and, via this mediation, the entire universe of boxing. In another way, you can say that the hierarchy supports them: that they are its illuminated peaks.
>
> (1991: 19)

Although the individual boxer may have been drawn into fighting through economic necessity, Sartre suggests that the violence that has its roots in scarcity and poverty is mediated in the ring through the sport, its rules, the adjudication and prizes. It becomes a spectacle with its own social values, notably that violence and the exercise of physical force represent strength and right, which draws on boxing genealogies of honour. The violence of the fight is not imaginary though; it is the embodiment of violence. Sartre argues that the incarnation of violence in a fight is a totalization as an expression of violence that has its origins elsewhere (outside the fight). Thus the fight is the incarnation of all violence and is 'real' and not imaginary or imagined in the sense that it is fantastical or unreal.

> the spectator of that putrified brawl is an actor, because it is really taking place in front of him. He encourages the boxers or finds fault with them, he shouts, he thinks he is making the event as it takes place. His violence is wholly present and he tries to communicate it to the combatants in order to hasten the course of the fight . . . It would not be violence without favouring, without preferring, without opting to be partisan.
>
> (1991: 25–6)

This approach has been deployed to bring together the particular and the universal in the condensation of a significant moment that a particular fight provides. Sartre's development of the understanding of the dialectical processes whereby meanings are produced which brings together the boxer and the social world provides a synthetic approach which can be used to analyse a temporally specific event, such as the 'Rumble in the Jungle', which permits a focus on the praxis of individual fighters (Culbertson, 2002). Culbertson suggests that there has to be a consideration of regressive and progressive aspects. For example, the regressive analysis addresses existential structures such as the details of Ali's early childhood. The 'progressive analysis identifies evidence of a fundamental project, or an original choice of the manner in which Ali lives his facticity or historialises his times' (Culbertson, 2002: 95). This method provides more than an 'add-on' summation of individual biography and the social and historical context in which the boxer performs his art. Synthesis must include the individual and, not only the time but the comprehension of that time by the individual boxer.

> Praxis would include Ali's political action, the way he deals with the media and his preparation, tactics and actions during the fight. The practico-inert would include the venue, 'pugilistic folklore', gym life, Ali's fame and any role that was perceived for him as representative of his race. His religion, or the Nation of Islam; there would also be the fact that Ali had been stripped of his title and endured a period during which he could not fight, the fact that Ali was no longer World Champion, and the violence and possibility of death that exists in boxing. The role of spectators, the media and Ali and Foreman themselves as mediating thirds would have to be analysed. In addition, issues of racial, class and religious identity and the role of big business, governing bodies and the media.
>
> (Culbertson, 2002: 95)

Material attributed largely to the regressive method, which might occupy some of the conventional sociological terrain has to be combined with the progressive phase of an understanding of the individual's perception of their times. Gender has to be incorporated into this synthetic approach as both particular, in how boxers perform gender, and universal, as a social structure, which makes versions of masculinity possible. This approach has the advantage of integrating the personal and social dimensions of identity and of acknowledging their inseparability, as well as providing a route into accessing the social world that is boxing that might bring together the social and cultural context and the individual practitioners in a more comprehensive analysis.

Conclusion

Although I have used some oppositions to frame the debate in this chapter, I have also demonstrated the limitations of making such distinctions. It is these very binaries which constitute the polarized logic of separation. However, revealing some of the mechanisms through which dualisms are forged does not diminish their impact. Objectivity and subjectivity cannot be disentangled, but this does not discount the necessity of providing some kind of criteria by which research findings might be made general and evaluated. What has been revealed to be more problematic is the suggestion that the research process through its empirical location might provide a spatial separation of personal and public worlds and between routine everyday practices and the dreams that are fed by more public representations, including celebrity. These dichotomies can be misleading and I have argued for a greater recognition of the interrelationships between discursive opposites, both conceptually and spatially. However, if dualisms, such as those of the 'insider' and the 'outsider' and the subjective and the objective are obscured and not expressed, complicity is denied and marginalized. Routine masculinities are built upon the configuration of an 'insider' world that is embedded in cultural collusion as well as body practices.

Being primarily an 'observing participant' and being immersed in a research site has the enormous advantage of the immediacy of 'being there' and in addressing the routine performance of masculinity. For example in boxing this facilitates a grasp of the embodied practices that make it possible, indeed essential to keep going even though one is experiencing extreme pain and distress, like the 'wall' in distance running, or transition in childbirth. However, there is a space between immersion in the field and the role of the researcher which requires some acknowledgement of the situatedness of the researcher in the process. Research into boxing which has deployed Bourdieu's approaches has been particularly productive in exploring embodiment and the routines and rituals of everyday life. Feminist critiques, although rarely applied to boxing, have a great deal to offer when addressing strategies for resolving some of the methodological problems that have emerged out of the tensions between the inside and the outside and between different forms of claims to validity which underpin the objective–subjective dualism. Oates is a good example of a woman who writes about boxing from in one sense an insider position, although not as practitioner, but as a very committed fan. She does not write from a feminist perspective, but despite her 'insider' status, she is quite explicit about her gendered situation. This illustrates how women are marked in sports writing and, whatever their level of expertise, cannot adopt a gender neutral stance nor even be silent. Women can only go so far in 'doing masculinity'. This may be because the masculinity that is in play in boxing is predicated upon risk-taking, danger, adventure, the practice of physical force and exclusivity, all of which constitute the making of traditional masculinities. The question is how far these masculinities are tied into the particularities of the bodies with which they are associated; that is men's bodies. Material bodies constitute important elements in understanding processes of identification. The suggestion that all knowledge is situated provides a route into reflection upon the position of the researcher as well as the subjects of the research. Reflection upon the gender identity and positioning of the male researcher as well as the more frequent occurrence of this practice among feminists might both cast light on the masculinities that are co-produced and demonstrate the partiality of the knowledge emerging from the research process. This is not to devalue the research, but to situate the knowledge so produced.

It is binary thinking which produces a devaluing of fantasy over reality and of the corporeal present over the desire to become that is so distinguishing a feature of identification processes. As Stuart Hall has argued 'cultural identity is a matter of "becoming" as well as "being". It belongs to the future as well as the past' (1990: 223). The future and the past can be more accessible through narratives and fantasies than through the embodied present. One of the ways of accessing the relationship between public and private worlds is to combine the routine body practices with the configuration of identities which is repeated in the public arena. This includes current celebrity as well as past legends which can be achieved through a more synthetic, Sartrean methodology. However, whilst I am arguing for recognition of the public stories that are told, they do not make manifest the whole picture and, as the evidence of different ethnographies indicates, boxing and consequently the masculinities that are experienced and created through the sport have different meanings in different places and at different times.

Some of the explanations of the violence associated with boxing appeal to its history and to the elemental, primordial aspects of one-on-one aggression, such as is suggested in the quotation from Oates at the start of this chapter. However, the empirical evidence does demonstrate a note of caution in making universal claims and indicates the need to acknowledge spatial and temporal particularities and to recognize the distinctiveness of the different sites at which boxing masculinities are enacted as well as the diversity of those engaged in the sport. Local experience has to be subject to evaluation through the theoretical frameworks of the social sciences too. It is also necessary to maintain a critical awareness of difference, which is possible through methodologies that grapple with the minutiae of everyday routines through ethnography, comparative studies and those historical works that cover a longer trajectory. The contribution of feminist and pro-feminist debates about how knowledge is produced and the implications of the methods that are adopted points to the necessary inclusion, whatever methods are adopted, of a situated perspective and of incorporating an analysis of power and its relationship to knowledge into the approach.

As has been shown in the discussion in this chapter, one of the big attractions – and enigmas – of boxing is its corporeality. One of the problems thrown up by boxing is the relationship between men and masculinity as expressed in the gendered differentiation of bodies. Much of the research discussed in this chapter which is representative of work done on boxing deals with boxing bodies. Chapter 4 is all about bodies; about why the body is central to boxing and what boxing bodies can tell us about different ways of thinking through the body and theories of embodiment.

Boxing bodies and embodied masculinities

Introduction

Boxing, even more than other sports presents an activity in which the body is central. Boxing is all about bodies, whether in the production of the supremely fit body in the gym or in the one-on-one corporeal combat of the ring. The two bodies in the ring and their interaction provide the spectacle which draws the audience. The vast majority of a boxer's time is spent doing floor work, working on the pads, bags, jab bags and shadow boxing all of which form the demanding regimen through which the whole schema of boxing is achieved, experienced and inscribed on the boxer's body. The classificatory system of the sport is based on body weight with the heaviest bodies being accorded the highest status. Boxers are labelled by their bodies from heavyweight down to flyweight and fighting out of one's weight category is likely to yield a disastrous outcome.

Keeping or reaching their weight is a crucial concern for boxers. Not only is preparation for a fight a demanding and rigorous body-centred regime, but maintaining the correct weight for the contest may require fasting or an excess of last-minute exercise that can put enormous strain on the body. Boxing presents a wonderful opportunity for both the exploration of what Wacquant calls 'direct embodiment' (2004: 60) and the social and cultural spaces in which these bodily regimes are enacted and experienced. Boxers are their bodies, but what does this mean in terms of understanding gendered identity and the ways in which people might make sense of who they are through the body which they inhabit and which is who they are? What is the status of bodies in the processes of identification?

The interrelationship between the wider social and cultural context and the specificities of the corporeality of boxing has been assumed and taken for granted in many accounts. Problematizing the status of the body in relation to gendered identities in sport is a relatively recent field of inquiry especially in relation to masculinity. Not only has 'the body', or, more accurately, have 'bodies' become the focus of intellectual critical inquiry but, as was demonstrated in Chapter 2, so has masculinity. Men's bodies are no longer un-marked in terms of their gender or assumed to be 'natural', as the norm by which all other bodies are judged.

Some of the processes through which meanings about masculinity relate to embodiment have also been interrogated. Sport is one of the sites at which such investigations have taken place, which is not surprising given the interrelationship between male physicality and masculinity as a cultural identity. This chapter addresses some of the debates which have arisen, especially those relating to the idea that the mind and body are separate along with associated issues about the degree to which people are able to exercise agency and especially debates about embodied agency. The interrelationship between agency and structural constraints, including those presented by the material body is significantly played out in sport and boxing offers a most useful field for further interrogation of these issues.

In the late twentieth-century assumptions about the norms of the male body and its aestheticization were deconstructed and challenged. Men's bodies have become more explicitly the subject of the female gaze and the gaze of other men. Not only have men's bodies been incorporated into critiques of 'the body' but also the particularities and differences of those bodies have become the subject of a theoretical gaze. Theories of embodiment have begun to explore how men embody prevailing codes of masculinity according to variations of class, 'race', sexuality and able-bodiedness. How are these variations played out through individuality and difference and how are they evaluated? Sport and boxing in particular has played a major part in some of the ways in which questions about embodiment have been addressed in recent thinking, although some of the most creative thinking, in other respects, about these issues has, nonetheless, marginalized the importance of gender in addressing these debates. This chapter uses boxing as the trigger to explore and critique some of these ideas.

Beautiful bodies: broken bodies

Not only is boxing a sport distinctively marked by corporeality it also manifests some of the most extreme versions of embodiment through the beautiful body and the broken, damaged body. In boxing it is difficult to read the body as a text and a site of inscription. The boxer's body demands acknowledgement of physical materiality. The beautiful body incorporates not only physical fitness, muscle, skill and good looks, but also a whole set of physical experiences through which this version of masculinity is forged. Muhammad Ali at his peak must be one of the best examples of this beautiful body, but the ill health which has dogged his later years, albeit which he denies to have arisen from his boxing experience, presents another dimension of embodiment. Similarly Mike Tyson in his prime appeared both invincible and physically perfect whatever his emotional shortcomings (O'Connor, 2002). Ill health is one aspect of impairment, damage in the ring or even, although less dramatically, in the gym is another. Beautiful boxing bodies might be said to comply with an ideal that equates physical beauty with health, success and strength, both moral and corporeal, but they are always subverted by the threat of damage and the broken body.

It is the tension and the interrelationship between beautiful and damaged bodies and the excesses of violence that haunt boxers in the practice of their art. Damage ranges from the more personal experiences of minor injuries to public accounts of death in the global media, such as that of Bradley Stone and brain damage as in the case of Michael Watson. The year 2005 saw the first death of a woman in the ring when Becky Zerlentes died at the age of 34, after being knocked out in an amateur bout in Washington (Walters, 2005a). As the artist Sandor Szenassy, whose work includes boxers as subjects and whose patron was the boxing promoter, Frank Warren, is quoted as saying, 'People think we live in a civilised society. Boxing hurts our sensibilities, it reminds us that we don't' (*Independent on Sunday*, 16 July 1995). Boxing hurts our sensibilities because of its physical materiality and public display of hurt bodies, which is so integral to the masculinities from which the sport recruits.

Boxing abounds with stories which challenge civilized sensibilities. Oliver McCall suffered what was described as a nervous breakdown in the ring at his WBC heavyweight fight against Lennox Lewis in Las Vegas in 1997. 'At the end of the fourth round, when McCall threw just two punches, he was crying . . . and [it] needed just 55 seconds of the fifth to see that the man's problems were deep-rooted and mental' (Mossop, 1997: S7). McCall's body refused to respond from round four. This is conceptualized as 'mental failure' but what was evident is that McCall could not fight. This example illustrates the passive rather than the active synthesis of mind and body which is visible in the broken body in the ring in an unusual scenario. McCall became an object of pity and not of desire in what was perceived to be a loss of control of his body.

A more familiar incidence of the broken body is the damaged, injured body. The very famous case of the collision between Nigel Benn and Gerald McClellan in February 1995 has been described as Benn's greatest and his worst night (Mitchell, 2003, 2005b). It was certainly McClellan's worst night; a night from which he never recovered.

McClellan remained in an induced coma for eleven days after the fight while doctors eased the blood clot on his brain. McClellan no longer knows about boxing titles or records and can no longer see (Mitchell, 2003). Much of the debate has been framed within a moral dilemma about whether the film of the actual fight should be shown, for example on television after the event, but it also raises issues about the materiality of broken body in boxing which so often constitutes a broken self.

The beautiful body draws upon an aesthetic that has a long history, especially in bringing together notions of physical beauty, fitness and rectitude. Through much of the twentieth century men's bodies remained understood as 'natural', their constitution being a biological preserve linked to hormonal balance, but separate and distinct from the rationality of the mind, which, in the mind/body dichotomy, was accorded much higher status and largely coded male. The polarization of beautiful and damaged bodies is embedded in the genealogy of boxing and in its configuration of masculinities. Another version of the male

Figure 4.1 Broken body: Gerald McClellan in Benn versus McClellan, 1995
(Photo: © Empics)

body was the aestheticized body in relation to classical ideals following the eighteenth century revivals of the ideals of Greek sculptures, which include the figure of the boxer. The two best known statues are the bronze statue of the *Terme Boxer* and the *Belvedere Torso*. The *Terme Boxer*, a seated figure in a contemplative pose is cited as masterpiece of Hellenistic athletic professionalism. 'His head is realistic with cropped hair, low forehead, broken nose, cauliflower ears, numerous facial scars and a mouth suggesting broken teeth' (Smith, 1991: 54).

The marble *Belvedere Torso*, on the other hand is accorded nobility and grandeur from the realm of myth (Smith, 1991). The point is made that the latter is a classical heroic figure whereas the *Terme Boxer*, 'despite all his training and physique remains firmly earthbound' (Smith, 1991: 55). My point is that boxing is both fantasy and myth and the material, 'earthbound' body is the route into finding out how they interrelate. It is through the material boxing body and its practices that heroic status is achieved, rather than body and myth occupying separate spaces. Heroism is embodied and created through the agentic body and the beautiful body is elevated to heroic status, the more so in contrast with the damaged, impaired body which haunts all boxers.

The standards by which the beautiful male body was judged have been dominated by a classical aesthetic. There are comparable contemporary heroic bodies, one of the most notable of which, in more recent times, is Muhammad Ali, whose greatness might have been augmented by his dramatic physical decline. The beautiful body and the damaged body combine in the biography of a great boxing hero. This is a male hero nonetheless, because male bodies have been seen to exercise greater power, especially in terms of physical strength. However, as I suggest in Chapter 5 in the discussion of heroes and legends, Ali's daughter Laila Ali could be seen as sharing some of this status in a heroic woman's body. Women risk being relegated rather than elevated to the corporeal. As women, they are seen as subject to the whims, vagaries and cycles of the body, rather than achieving the control and mastery (*sic*) associated with the mind and with masculinity. When masculinity is embedded in corporeality as in a sport like boxing, what is emphasized is the control and discipline of the body rather than any unregulated excess of physicality. 'Mind over matter' might indeed be the guiding principle. However boxing has an ambivalent relationship to the unequal values attributed to the mind/body dualism, especially given the socio-economic and racialized aspects of the sport.

The body may be central to the 'noble art', but much of the discussion of the sport has assumed a mind/body split where the self is associated with the mind which seeks control over the body and there is still some residue, especially in the practices of the material body, of the notion that the mind can exercise control and dominance over the body. Resolutions to this problem, which has been perceived as dating back to Descartes' division of mind and body, have not always engaged with the gendering of the body or with other aspects of difference and diversity. Nor has discussion of embodiment always engaged with the subject/

object binary where subject refers to the active body and object to a body that is acted upon as a passive body and the body is construed as a passive object to be controlled, or not, by the mind. Aimee Liu's statement that 'I will be master of my own body' (in Bordo, 1993: 150), although arising in a very different context, has enormous resonance in sport. The Cartesian dualism and attempts to resolve it are key areas of debate in this chapter along with the other ways in which the gendered body has been theorised in relation to social constructivist approaches, for example Foucauldian notions of techniques of the self, the 'docile body' (1977a [1975]: 138) and the regulation and disciplining of the body, which are particularly interesting in relation to the body in a sport such as boxing. Foucault argued that the body is an inscribed surface, imprinted by history (Foucault, 1977b), through which power operates, but 'docile bodies', although saturated with disciplinary techniques (Foucault, 1977b) are not without resistance. Boxing bodies are highly regulated and self-disciplined through a set of routine practices and mechanisms so that the body becomes the inscribed surface of events combining the body practices and the traditions to which they belong. Boxing bodies are disciplined and regulated through techniques of the self (Foucault, 1988). However, boxing bodies bleed, sweat and are injured and, as I argue in this chapter, there are problems with what can be seen as such disembodied accounts (Segal, 1987, 1997a).

Bodies, if not boxing bodies, have been central to feminist critiques and these are deployed to demonstrate some of the limitations of undifferentiated theories which retain assumptions of the homogeneity of bodies. The relationship between the configuration of femininity as well as masculinity and the specific interaction between the two is crucial to any exploration of embodiment however extreme a social constructionist position that is adopted may be. The intersections of masculinity and femininity are crucial to a grasp of a re-valuing of gender in relation to identity.

Embodied identities

At one level, the relationship between the body and identity might appear relatively simple. 'One body, one self' (Fraser and Greco, 2005: 12). The body seems to present the boundaries of the self, with the body of each person demarcating each self and the limits of the self which takes on different identity positions. The body marks out space. Iris Marion Young, following the ideas of Merleau-Ponty, which are explored in more detail in relation to boxing below, claims that 'the body is the original subject that constitutes space; there would be no space without the body' (Young, 1990: 152). The body presents the unique location for the development of the self and for notions of continuity. The body becomes a focus for the self and, as Ian Burkitt suggests, individuals pursue wholeness in order to pre-empt the conflicts of fragmentation and alienation that characterize contemporary identifications. 'In resisting forms of domination and dividing practices, the body becomes a point of focus because it is located in relational networks, that individuals can integrate the various aspects of themselves into a whole person and can demand to be treated as such' (1999: 145).

The embodied masculinities that are forged in boxing can be seen as pre-emptive masculinities, where the centrality of the body and its practices provide a means of securing the self.

The body bears the scars and stigmata of the journeys travelled along the routes through which identities are made and re-made. However, as Mariam Fraser and Monica Greco argue, the relationship between body and identity occupies a contested terrain (2005). The uniqueness of the self has a very specific history. Its genealogy dates from historical moments when the notion of an autonomous individual, sometimes construed as the sovereign subject, was developed through the Cartesian distinction between mind and body of western culture. This distinction underpins the expression 'mind over matter' in everyday language. This most famous Cartesian dualism has not only held enormous sway in shaping common sense understandings of the self and of identity, but also has informed academic discourse. The claim that the mind can control the body as if they were separate entities might suggest that the mind can restrain the excesses of the body and operate within a rational and moral framework which is outside the scope of the body. As Steven Rose has pointed out, the mind/body dualism and the marginalization and devaluation of the body arose from the association of the body with 'biology', in an understanding which posits biology as the opposite of the social as well as the rational (1998). It is this body which eats, breathes, bleeds, feels pain and dies; these are the attributes of the body, which may seem so routine that they are not central to social investigation or so 'biological' that they are outside the terrain of the social and belong in the medical and biological sciences. Fighting and inflicting pain on others as well as receiving blows might occupy a more problematic place in this list of necessary bodily functions. There is, however, a need to engage with the physical dimensions of the body and with what Butler calls the 'anatomical body' (1993), but to which she attributes no agency or materiality beyond what is dynamically and discursively produced. This is not only because of the importance of the body in shaping experience, but also of the diversity of bodies and the embodiment of difference across class, 'race', 'ethnicity', disability, generation and gender, to name but a few aspects of these differences. The body has also to be seen as presenting constraint and limitations. The body breaks down and is damaged and impaired and, as is clearly apparent in relation to the boxing body, is constantly subject to the very material threat of severe damage as well as of routine stress and pain in training. Recognition of this is core to training. Avoidance of being hurt, being able to get out of the way and act defensively are key to the training regimen. Strategies include moving out of the way and pre-emptive strikes. In order to avoid injury oneself one ensures that one delivers the first blows. The body practices through which such defences operate are implicated in the defence of the self and the strategies that are adopted aim to secure the boundaries of the embodied self and to pre-empt damage.

Mind/body is not the only dualism, although it has been very important in recent work on the body which has taken this binary as its main area of dispute. It has also been expressed in different ways. The biological 'nature' of the body has been articulated in different ways at different historical times, but the nature/ culture divide gives expression to the traditional distinction. The relationship between nature and culture has been described as a binary opposition that at particular moments has been very unevenly weighted. More recently the nature/ culture dualism has been expressed in terms of the relative weighting accorded to genetic as opposed to social factors. Tensions have been expressed between the influence of people's genetic inheritance and the societies in which they live, in shaping who we are. Again the opposition is challenged by arguments which point to the ways in which knowledge about genes is also socially constructed, nature is also subject to social and cultural interpretation. In sport there has been an ever-increasing range of strategies deploying new technologies and scientific practices that constitute technoscientific interventions on and into the body in the pursuit of ever greater excellence in performance. Technoscience can be deployed to detect damage. For example, professional boxers undergo regular brain scans which visualize, but, of course do not prevent such impairment. Athletes, whilst having to negotiate the legal constraints of pharmaceutical interventions, combine the natural and the social in the process of becoming cyborgs (Haraway, 2000 [1985]). Donna Haraway's work, although not focused on sport, highlights the transformations of identity that are possible through the merging of boundaries between humans and technology. She has not simply deconstructed the divisions between the organic and inorganic, but has problematized the category of being human. Technological advances blur the boundaries of the closed human body and open up all sorts of liberatory possibilities (1992).

The body as the boundary of the self might appear to offer some certainty about 'who we are' where the body might seem to offer a source of security, which presents some fixity in locating people's sense of identity and in demarcating one embodied self from another. One aspect of engaging in sport is the apparent security that might be afforded by being able to exercise control through the body and the feeling of being at one with oneself that accrues from physical exercise. Boxing, especially in training, offers not only a sense of well-being that comes with being physically fit and 'feeling good' but also a sense of being able to defend oneself and of being 'in control' and of 'belonging to oneself' (Woodward, 1997b, 2004), which can also be coded as establishing the boundaries of a secured masculinity. Competitive sport offers more avenues for utilizing the body in order to belong, for example to the locality, such as the club or the nation at the highest levels as well as providing a means of achieving personal acclaim. As Pierre Bourdieu argues the body is the only tangible manifestation of the person (1986), although this focus might also seem to underplay the importance of the emotions, especially as explanatory factors in the identificatory processes involved in establishing a sense of belonging.

Women and men and gendered bodies

Not only do bodies eat, sleep, breathe and feel pain, they are also classified by gender based on bodily characteristics. Until recently in sport, gender was categorized according to decisions made at birth. Interventions that later transform or modify the external sexual characteristics of the body have presented problems for the regulating bodies of sport; or maybe the rigid classificatory systems of the sport's regulating bodies have presented problems for bodies that do not fit neatly into the female/male binary. In boxing this is troubling within the strongly contested terrain of disputation about women fighting men. Weight categories are not sufficient to keep women and men apart. For example the controversy over Ann Wolfe in 2005, having successfully defeated her female opposition then seeking male opponents, has invited strong arguments on both sides which open up questions about the categories around which boxing is organised. Much of the opposition that women experience in sport when wanting to compete on a level playing field with men is based on quasi biological arguments about the size and strength of women's bodies. For example in golf, women play a shorter yardage which is explained in terms of women's hitting power. In boxing, as a contact sport, these arguments are more problematic since other factors intrude upon the evaluation of weight and body strength. Debates about women fighting with men in the ring are linked to the performance of masculinity and femininity. Women boxers may be seen to be performing masculinity when they fight each other but the matter of how women are implicated in the embodied performance of masculinity is brought into stark relief when they actually fight with men. This presents a problem for the categories of 'sex' and 'gender', which feminists have addressed in different ways.

Sex and gender, as shaped by the physical, largely observable characteristics of the body are seen as key sources of identity. A distinction has been made between 'sex' and 'gender'. Some second wave feminists, notably Ann Oakley (1972) usefully argued that sex and gender were frequently elided to women's disadvantage, whereby cultural expectations of what was appropriate or possible for women was attributed to some biological law. The notion that women should be relegated to second class citizenship, or even no citizenship, because of anatomical difference from men, in particular the possession of a uterus, has a long history. Women have been excluded from activities ranging from sport (Hargreaves, 1994) to membership of the professions and posts in the military, because of their 'sex', which was claimed to be generative of dire outcomes such as Aristotle's 'wandering womb' or the psychic phenomenon of hysteria. Women still run shorter distances, play off different tees in golf and encounter a vast range of regulatory apparatuses and mechanisms based on assumptions about the primacy of biology and the body. Even when they are permitted to participate, women may adopt less assertive and competitive bodily practices. In effect they may 'throw like a girl' (Young, 1990). Women's role in societies, unlike men's, was seen to be determined by their biological sex, although the notion of fixed, binary differences between women and men are used to privilege men's status in competitive sport, either through physical attributes like speed, weight and strength or, more likely, more exciting, skilful performances which are much more loosely linked to corporeality. It is immediately apparent that there are difficulties in separating out some of these attributes which reside in the bodies of women or men, although in the past feminists sought to make a distinction between the biological characteristics of the body, the anatomical body and gender as a cultural construct. More recently the idea of an oppositional distinction between sex and gender has been challenged, most powerfully by postmodernist feminists such as Judith Butler (1990, 1993) and the term 'gender' is largely preferred. As Butler argues, sex too is a cultural construct. Donna Haraway also points out that the sex gender dualism cannot accommodate differentiation and this will not be possible unless we ensure that 'the binary universalizing opposition that spawned the concept of the sex/gender system . . . implodes into articulated, differentiated, accountable, located and sequential theories of embodiment, where nature is no longer imagined and enacted as a resource to culture and sex to gender' (1991: 148).

The meaning of 'sex' is strongly mediated by cultural understandings that make it impossible to differentiate between sex and gender. The use of gender permits an acknowledgement of this powerful cultural and social mediation (Price and Shildrick, 1999), although the sex gender binary 'does not pretend to explain class, race, or nationality, or anything else' (Moi, 1999: 35).

However, an analysis of a sport like boxing raises some interesting questions about the sex/gender dichotomy in relation to other discourses. It is not chance that Joyce Carol Oates reiterates her analogy between men and boxing and women and childbirth (1997, 2002). However, there is some slippage here between the bodily experience and the cultural assumptions that are made about it. Whilst childbirth and prizefighting are both largely painful experiences which involve extremes of physical distress and as Loic Wacquant argues of boxing, they are situations where 'the body takes over', they are very different. Whilst there might be technological or human interventions in childbirth to alleviate pain, there is no going back; the body takes over entirely. Agency only operates through going with the body, whereas in the ring a boxer can make decisions and can even opt out. One interesting analogy does, however, relate to agency. Labouring women are more likely to perceive themselves as in control when they do go with the body, rather than attempting to resist its demands (Akrich and Pasveer, 2004). However, childbirth involves at least two bodies, the one contained within the other and dependent upon it, so one would not want to extend the analogy too far. Each is an embodied activity which generates a range of associations which would appear to derive from the embodied experience, for example, the aggression linked to pugilism and the nurturing that is claimed to go with childbirth. Boxing is also so clearly organized on the basis of the body, for example in weight categories, the contact of the sport and its bellicose culture and language, all of which are associated with men and masculinity. Boxing is even called 'the

manly art', not only in historical accounts such as Elliot Gorn's 1986, *The Manly Art: Bare knuckle prize-fighting in America*, but these are the words frequently used to refer to the sport in ethnographic research (Wacquant, 2004). Women might participate in the 'noble art' but the 'manly art' highlights the exclusionary ethos of the sport and suggests that women who do box are joining in as pseudo men; 'doing masculinity', but as pretend men. Of course these are two very different areas of experience, but each is constitutive of gendered identity and there are useful parallels that can be drawn in relation to the role of the body in securing and making identity and the central role played by the body in shaping and regulating the identity positions that are available.

The claims which feminists have made about the devaluing of women and women's bodies through a reduction to their biology can be similarly applied to boxing, which mostly carries more cultural status than childbirth, but still manifests the same essentialist associations. The only difference is that if what is in operation here is hegemonic masculinity then the reductionism of the associations between body and identity still work in favour of masculinity in the gender binary if not in the mind/body dualism.

The contemporary focus on the body in the social sciences and humanities has been strongly influenced by feminist critics who have challenged the notion of a 'disembodied', somehow gender neutral (for which read white, middle class, male) person by stressing that the person, and thus the self, is necessarily embodied. The traditional universalizing of the self has been argued in conjunction with a denial of the body that is that self, in favour of a fallacious notion of an abstract, rational self which has largely been associated with a masculine person. Moira Gatens argues that, whilst the male subject is

> constructed as self-contained and as an owner of his person and his capacities, one who relates to other men as free competitors, with whom he shares politico-economic rights . . . [t]he female subject is constructed as prone to disorder and passion, as economically and politically dependent on men . . . justified by reference to women's nature.
>
> (Gatens, 1991: 5)

The 'thinking body' has been gendered but there is still a need for both the lived experience of the embodied self and a practical engagement with the world which includes action and intention. Ian Burkitt posits the 'thinking body' in which thinking is an embodied activity located within particular social and material contexts. All knowledge is thus 'generated in a community of speaking subjects and is an aspect of communication within relationships and interdependencies' (1999: 70). This notion of embodiment which is more inclusive of gender, also opens up the possibilities of diversity.

However, the gender divide operates powerfully in the routines and lived experiences of sport. Whilst the presence of women in men's boxing gyms is largely, although not universally, seen as disruptive, the men who box have also

been construed as threatening. Boxing is not an activity that signifies cultural capital of some magnitude. As Loic Wacquant says of the men at the gym which he, like Gerald Early, describes as 'proletariat', they attend 'to commune in the plebeian cult of virility that is the Manly Art' (2004: 14). The language may be somewhat overblown but the sentiments are not. It is clearly apparent that not all male bodies are assumed to be gender neutral nor do they represent a homogenous group set in superior opposition to the gendered bodies of women.

Feminists' renewed emphasis on embodiment reinstates gender differentiation. As Rosi Braidotti has argued, this focus on embodiment and the inclusion of corporeality in addressing matters of identity and subjectivity is developed 'by emphasizing the embodied and therefore sexually differentiated structure of the speaking subject' (1994: 3). This focus permits the inclusion of different embodied experiences. The emphasis upon experience and the meanings that people give to their own experience which is associated with phenomenological approaches to embodiment also makes it possible to incorporate an account of agency, so that people are not perceived to be the victims of their bodies but also implicated in attributing meanings to them. As Brian Turner suggests, this might transform our understanding not just of 'the body' but of actually

> living one's body . . . because of the concept of embodiment, we can break out of the dualism of the Cartesian legacy, phenomenologically appreciating the intimate and necessary relationship between my sense of myself, my awareness of the integrity of my body and the experience of illness as not simply an attack on my instrumental body but as a radical intrusion into my embodied selfhood.
>
> (Turner, 1992: 167)

How does this resolve the question of what is happening when women engage in an activity like boxing that does not conform to expected embodied gendered practices, as is sharply indicated by the controversy arising from women and men fighting together? Sex differences that reside in the body are usually what is invoked as the reason for excluding women from a sport or insisting upon specific regulations for women and for men. As Judith Butler argues, 'Sexual difference . . . is never simply a function of material differences which are not in some way marked by discursive practices . . . The category "sex" is, from the start normative; it is what Foucault called a "regulatory ideal"' (1993: 1).

Butler goes on to develop the concept of performativity through which bodies are materialized through time. This is not a static process but an 'iterative and citational practice by which discourse produces the effect which it names' (Foucault, 1993: 1). This element of Butler's argument draws heavily on Foucault's work, which is discussed in more detail below, but I cite it here because her work is located within a feminist framework and focuses on the instability of gender categories, which are not tied to the body which enacts them. Butler explores the regulation of identificatory practices and seeks out the challenge of

transgression of binary categories, for example through disidenification with regulatory norms. Although Butler's examples relate to sexuality, this clearly has some purchase in other fields of disidentification, such as sport where women might often be seen to be 'doing' masculinity and transgressing the norms; to paraphrase Iris Marian Young (1990), women might be refusing to throw like a girl and want to punch like a boy.

Boxing embodiment: I am my body

Debates about bodies have been located largely within the context of the tension between social constructionist and more materialist views of the body framed within other tensions such as the mind/body split and that between subject and object. There has been an understandable apprehension about the reinstatement of the material body, especially in feminist critiques, given the devaluing of that which is associated with women and with femininity and the over-valuation of masculinity in all its guises. However, such differences are part of the processes through which identities are reproduced. Merleau-Ponty's understanding of 'embodiment' is seen as particularly useful in overcoming the problem of binaries, especially that of the mind/body split and as contributing to Pierre Bourdieu's approach to embodiment. This concept of embodiment can encompass the active construction of identities within sport within the context of investment in cultural capital and in the case of boxing, physical capital.

Merleau-Ponty's 'Phenomenology of Perception'

Merleau-Ponty's phenomenology of perception challenges the Cartesian dualism of mind and body by claiming that the body is not only composed of perceptible qualities; it perceives, that is, it is seen and it sees. Perception is not an inner representation of an outer world but it is an opening onto the world. The articulation of mind and body precedes objectivity and perception and is always located in and through the space of the lived, material body. We do not reflect on our bodies, as if we were outside them; we live them (Merleau-Ponty, 1962). Thus Merleau-Ponty's understanding of the body is as animate, sensible, sensuous (although he gives primacy to visibility and the visual over the other senses) and sentient (1968). This phenomenological approach seeks the meaning of experience as it is embodied and lived in context rather than looking for essences so that the subjective and objective merge, thus emphasizing both the primacy of people's own experience and the routine practices in which the embodied self engages. It is not surprising that it has been developments of Merleau-Ponty's theory of embodiment that have been most influential in sociological accounts of boxing.

Feminist work, such as Young's, in developing an understanding of how the lived body is gendered, has drawn upon Merleau-Ponty to challenge dualistic conceptualizations of the relationship between the mind and the body. However,

Young challenges the universal account of the gender neutral body implied by Merleau-Ponty and claims that the female body is not simply experienced as a direct communication with the active self, but it *is* also experienced as an object. She suggests that there are distinctive manners of comportment and movement that are associated with women (hence 'throwing like a girl' as the title of her work). Young attributes these different modalities, first, to the social spaces in which women learn to comport themselves. In terms of sport this involves constraints of space and learning to act in less assertive and aggressive ways than men. Second, Young suggests women are encouraged to see themselves through the gaze of others including the 'male gaze', as developed in the work of Laura Mulvey (1975), which is explored in more detail in Chapter 6, and to become more aware of themselves as objects of the scrutiny of others. The idea of modalities, which is similar to Erving Goffman's concept of the 'body idiom' (1963) arises out of objectification which is then consolidated as habit, that is the practices that are performed repeatedly, like Butler's concept of performativity or the dispositions associated with Bourdieu's concept of *habitus*, discussed in Chapter 3. This usefully brings together the material body, which is reified as gendered and its practices and dispositions within the social and culture context. As Nick Crossley acknowledges, this can contribute to an increased self consciousness and an alienation of the self which can lead to social disempowerment and, limited agency (2001). It is, however, worth noting, although it is not surprising, that it is not the feminist re-workings of phenomenology which have been taken up by the sociologists who have done most to progress Pierre Bourdieu's understanding of Merleau-Ponty's work, in sport, especially boxing, although there are affinities with the work of different feminist scholars.

Bourdieu, physical capital and illusio

Loic Wacquant makes particularly interesting and relevant use of the work of Bourdieu in relation to the routine practice of boxing, that is the embodied experience of pugilism both in the gym and in the ring in explaining how it is that the boxer takes the punches and continues to deliver them in spite of the distress and pain he (or presumably she if the theory is transferable) is feeling. The social classification of boxing and its associations makes Bourdieu's analysis particularly relevant. Are boxers in any sense compelled to participate in the sport because their choices are so limited? Are they deceived by the promises of reward and success? If they are, then this identification not only involves mis-recognition, it also implies a state of false consciousness. Bourdieu's work offers one approach to addressing these problems which arise from the relationship between social economic structures and embodied selves.

Bourdieu's theory of practice permits a strong sense of the role of the body in relation to social structures through his use of *habitus* and *illusio* which are set within the wider context of fields which extend beyond the outward appearance of the body and locate the agent. Bourdieu's work is relevant in a number of ways. First, his concept of cultural capital is particularly useful in explaining sport, developed through his notion of taste as the marker of distinction. This is especially appropriate to boxing with its association with the working-class participant. Cultural capital can be used in exchange, rather as financial capital can be deployed as an investment to achieve further returns. It is in a sense metaphorical in that cultural capital is not lost at the point of investment, for example educational achievement is a form of cultural capital which the individual can continue to capitalize upon; it is not lost at the point of being invested. Similarly the physical capital which the boxer has can be invested to obtain financial returns and other social and cultural advantages. Physical capital is largely a distinctly male, working-class form of capital. Whilst the working-class man who is attracted to boxing may have limited access to any other form of capital he does have a body which he might be able to use to his advantage, even if this is his only capital. Bourdieu's use of capital and his model of class based on the movements of different sorts of capital through social space provide a means of exploring the details of power relations and inequalities, which are reproduced and renegotiated through symbolic struggles. It provides another route into addressing questions of agency and deception in the formation of identity, especially embodied identity. Loic Wacquant develops Bourdieu's definition of capital as,

> accumulated labour (in its materialized form or its 'incorporated' embodied form) which, when appropriated on a private, i.e. exclusive, basis by agents or groups of agents, enables them to appropriate social energy in the form of reified or living labour (Bourdieu, 1986: 241) to focus on the specificities of investment in physical capital by boxers.
>
> (Wacquant, 1995a: 66)

The concept of cultural capital is also an immensely useful metaphor for the exploration of differentiation, especially class differentiation. Different kinds of capital are interconnected and it is often difficult to disentangle these. For example the social networks that facilitate attempts to maximize cultural capital investment and the alliances between economic and cultural capital are widely enmeshed. The metaphor of cultural capital permits a focus upon inclusion and exclusion through investments that are made in terms of the body, the objectified state and the institutionalized state, most frequently translated into educational qualifications. Sport offers a site, acknowledged by Bourdieu (1986, 1990b) as one in which different kinds of capital are invested, although the understanding of cultural capital in sport has often been weighted more upon the embodied state and physical capital than on the objectified state of cultural goods or institutional aspects such as education. A sport such as boxing clearly illustrates the importance of bodily attributes operating as currency and the necessity for those involved to engage actively in making their own bodies through training activities in order to maximize their returns. Wacquant goes further and describes boxers as 'entrepreneurs in bodily capital' (1995b: 66). This is used most effectively in his ethnographic studies of boxing, where he offers both extensive detail of the techniques which boxers employ in 'preserving and making one's bodily capital fructify' (2004: 128) and insider knowledge, as a practitioner himself, of the imbrication of the physical and mental states, where 'the mental becomes part of the physical and vice versa' (2004: 95). This is not a body viewed from the outside; we *are* our bodies in Bourdieu's account of embodiment (1986), which Wacquant deploys. Bourdieu's approach has shown the importance of the possibility of focusing upon the kind of capital which participants in sport bring to the activity as well as the ways in which they are able to build upon their investment and the class inflections of the processes that are involved. Men's bodies which engage in boxing are expressive of masculinity as a form of cultural capital, but not all masculinities provide the same scope for capitalization and they are not all equally weighted assets. The body practices of sport occupy other axes of differentiation. For example, they are clearly racialized and gendered processes too are played out in different contexts.

These contexts constitute fields which encompass different divisions operating in society. Whilst capital, class and domination make up the 'vertical' differentiation of societies according to Bourdieu, they are also equally differentiated along 'horizontal' axes which constitute fields, which are the social spaces of networks of objective relations between positions (Bourdieu and Wacquant, 1992). Positions in fields, which may be taken by individuals, groups of people or institutions are shaped by the concentration of capital (in all its different forms) and power. Each field, or social space, of which boxing is one, has its own logic. Bourdieu's account of fields is linked to his concept of *habitus*, which relates to the dispositions and competences of participants in the field, which is analogous to a game consisting of resources and players who must understand the game and their own position within it. Thought is not abstract, but involves habituated active engagement with the world and bodily knowledge (Bourdieu, 2001). As Nick Crossley has pointed out: 'Habitus predispose agents to act in particular ways without reducing them to cultural dopes or inhibiting their strategic capacities. Like game-playing skills, the structures of the habitus facilitate the competent pursuit of specified goals' (2001: 94).

Thus, there is a conscious, active engagement in the field. However, agents' actions are shaped by their *habitus* which consists of dispositions, competences, forms of knowledge all of which shape perception, not necessarily at the level of consciousness. 'The schemes of the *habitus*, the primary forms of classification, owe their specific efficacy to the fact that they function below the level of consciousness and language, beyond the reach of introspective scrutiny or control by the will' (Bourdieu, 1986: 466).

Bourdieu includes discussion of unconscious forces although his understanding of the unconscious, whilst drawing on psychoanalytic theory tends to be rather general and is rarely based on a detailed analysis of the structure and logic of the unconscious. Others have made more explicit use of psychoanalytic theory in attempting to theorize the thinking body as 'being in the world, representing the body's 'mindful' relationship to the world which precedes thought and representation (Burkitt, 1999). Burkitt stresses the material, active relationship between the body and its environment, which exists before there is conscious contemplation. Knowledge of the world is developed through people's own perception of it. Bourdieu's concept of *habitus* has been developed more fully to incorporate the interconnections between physical, mental and emotional life (Burkitt, 1999).

Second, Bourdieu's idea of *illusio* offers a way into understanding what is happening in the actual experience of boxing, in what Burkitt calls 'being in the world' (1999: 74) or indeed of any such sporting endeavour. Wacquant uses the concept of *illusio* to address the question of why practitioners actually engage in the work of boxing with its often violent and distressing outcomes as well as the hard work of the routine practice of the gym. The notion of *illusio* as 'the shared belief in, and collectively manufactured illusion of the value of the games (real) men play becomes progressively instilled and inscribed in a particular biological individual' (Wacquant, 1995c: 173). The pugilistic *illusio* is 'the *unconscious fit between his (pugilistic habitus and the very field which has produced it* (Wacquant 1995a: 88, italics in the original). This is what constitutes masculinity in this field.

Illusio operates at the level of the unconscious. The main strength of this concept is its role as a means of explaining how gendered identities, in this case boxing masculinities, are experienced and enacted through an embodied self. Bourdieu's work on masculinity is most clearly developed in *Masculine Domination* (2001), which draws upon much earlier work, for example on the Kabyle as well his textual critique of Virginia Woolf's *To the Lighthouse*. This work is cited by Wacquant as offering insights into the operation and practice of masculinity in very different contexts by transferring an analysis of upper-class Bloomsbury to a contemporary context. Although the move from early twentieth-century Bloomsbury to a boxing gym in Chicago may seem somewhat far-fetched, there is some logic in the argument which seeks to demonstrate the persistence of particular forms of masculinity and the mechanics of their operation and iteration. Wacquant uses the concept of *illusio* to address the question of why practitioners actually engage in the work of boxing with its often violent and distressing outcomes as well as the hard work of the routine practice of the gym. Wacquant's description of the way in which the subjective state of the boxer is both constituted through and constitutes the objective preconditions of the field is particularly powerful in his earlier work in Chicago (1995a, 1995b) and in more recent experience as a competitor himself (2004). Crossley cites this earlier example as the best he has encountered. Here 'practical belief' is not a state of mind but rather a 'state of body' (Bourdieu, 1990a: 68).

> The boxers' *desire* to fight flows from a *practical belief* constituted in and by the immediate co-presence of, and mutual understanding between, his (re)socialised lived body and the game . . . The boxer wilfully perseveres into

this potentially self-destructive trade because, in a very real sense, he is inhabited by the game he inhabits. A veteran middleweight who has 'rumbled' on three continents for over a decade and who reported breaking his hands twice and his foot once, persistent problems with his knuckles (because of calcium deposits forming around them) as well as a punctured ear drum and several facial cuts necessitating stitches, reveals his doxic acceptance, made body of the states of pugilism when he fails to find cause for alarm in his string of injuries: 'Sure you do think about it, but then you regroup yourself, start thinkin', you can't, *it's in your blood so much*, you can't, you been doin' it so long, you can't give it up.'

(Wacquant, 1995a: 88)

This is what constitutes masculinity and its particular manifestation through a gendered *illusio*, from which there seems to be no escape. The concept of *illusio*, as deployed by Wacquant is gender specific. The *illusio* which is constitutive of masculinity appears to afford no ambivalence, resistance or alternatives. For Wacquant, boxing itself makes up the identity of the practitioner of the 'manly art'. His claim that boxing is 'in your blood' (Wacquant, 1995a: 88) indicates a notion of embodiment which, Nick Crossley argues, is complex and multi-layered (2001: 108). So powerful is this process that boxers do not retire, 'they quit' (Wacquant, 1995a: 87). Wacquant's celebration of the bloodied heroism of the boxer in the face of unequivocal risk and danger and the refusal of the boxer to 'give up', is not only clearly located within a particular, gendered discourse, it illustrates the layers of embodiment embedded in the *habitus*. The field demands body practices, active engagement and training in order to participate, which generates labour. Both Crossley's and Wacquant's approaches suggest that this indicates the role of *illusio* in rationalizing the practice.

The matter of over determinism is acknowledged by Crossley, but he argues that nonetheless 'the agent is wholly active here constructing an inductive picture of the world, even if their construction is relatively fatalistic' (2001: 112).

This raises questions, not only about agency and the nature of reflexivity but also about how the concept of *illusio* is gendered. Bourdieu's work on sport concentrates much more explicitly on the distinctions of class and the working-class hero than on gender differentiation (1993). He suggests that the 'working-class cult of sportsmen of working-class origin is doubtless explained in part by the fact that these "success stories" symbolize the only recognized route to wealth and fame' (Bourdieu, 1993: 127). This brings together his thesis about the unity of dispositions of the *habitus* from which engagement in sports is generated and the public distinctions afforded to different sports. Bourdieu's account is based on a conceptualization of heroic working-class masculinity which has considerable purchase in media sport narratives. However, his argument about the processes that are involved in taking up these identities of masculinity through the games men play (whether literally as in sport or through the routine exchanges of everyday life and the 'games' that are constitutive of social existence) suggests a '*collective collusion* [which] endows them with the necessity and reality of shared experiences' (2001: 75, italics in original). Are there gender specific operations of *illusio*, for example, in the case of women boxers is the process which Wacquant describes for men the same?

Yvonne Lafferty and Jim McKay, in their study of the interaction between Australian women and men boxers, draw upon Wacquant's interpretation of *illusio* as 'collective misrecognition' (Wacquant, 2001: 10) and 'collective bad faith' (Wacquant, 1995a: 86). Wacquant suggests that *illusio* is a means of demonstrating that boxers are not deceived by an exploitative system which compels them to sell their bodies to the pugilistic trade but that they are enmeshed in a powerful belief system which holds onto the honour and nobility of boxing. It is hard to see how women could be similarly implicated since the *doxa* of boxing is one that manifests little cultural tradition of women in kinship groups and social networks having boxing 'in their blood', although individual women may give voice to such commitment. Lafferty and McKay cite a statement by an Australian amateur boxer, Mischa Merz, to support their claim that the concept of *illusio* works for women too (2005: 273) and can be applied in the same way as Wacquant does. Another alternative explanation of Merz's statement that boxing is 'in the blood' could be that she is invoking the language of men's boxing in order to be positioned within a discourse which accepts and reinstates the total commitment of the boxer. She is attempting to buy into the language of boxing and to reclaim some of its heroic subject positions in order to be accepted and to 'do' masculinity. There are different cultural meanings attached to women's engagement in the sport which suggest that this could be a gendered *illusio* which is specific to the participants in the context of the wider field in which these meanings are forged.

Some of the difficulties arising from these developments of Bourdieu's theories can be identified as, in the first case, relating to the construction of masculinity which is assumed and could be seen as over-deterministic. Another is its failure to include contradiction and ambivalence, especially as manifest in the anxieties that men have to manage. Judith Butler has argued that Bourdieu assumes that the field is a precondition of the *habitus* and that ambivalence is outside the realms of practice (1999), which could certainly be said to be the case for boxing. In the second case, in terms of the construction of femininity in relation to masculinity, the theoretical framework is largely configured in the context of an assumed norm that is masculinity.

Crossley has drawn on Merleau-Ponty in his work on gym culture to address some of the problems of over-determinism in Bourdieu's work. However, there remain significant criticisms that can be made. Whilst the re-workings of phenomenology discussed above effectively challenge the Cartesian dualism of mind and body they can retain a determinism that cannot account for a sociological analysis of 'action' and 'control' (Howson, 2005: 31). As Young has demonstrated, power relations, especially those based on gender and racialized differences, are under-theorized in Bourdieu's work (1990) in spite of its focus upon social class.

There seems little scope for transformation, especially within the wider arena of social, economic and cultural life within these accounts. However, there are significant advantages in the primacy that is given to everyday experience and detailed accounts of embodied practice, especially in gendering the body. Power relations are implicated in the articulation of gender, 'race' and sexuality in the sporting body and the racialized body has been a particular target of regulation and resistance, especially in boxing, with its long history of attempts to undermine white supremacism, dating back to Jack Johnson's world championship defeat of Jim Jeffries, the 'Great White Hope' and Joe Louis's transformation into a heroic figure for white as well as black fans in the 1930s (Harris, 1998).

Techniques of the self: inscribed bodies?

Where might a critique of power be offered? An approach to the body which does foreground power which has useful applications within the field of sport is developed in Foucault's critique of the power–knowledge relationship. Foucault approaches the embodiment of agency through the relationship between power and knowledge and this has particular relevance in the field of sport in the treatment of governmentality, which examines the power of discourse to produce the body (Foucault, 1972) through social practices associated with surveillance. Foucault's work moved from a focus on surveillance towards an emphasis on techniques of self regulation, which could be seen to accord more agency to the subject. As a sport, boxing is subject to techniques and practices which have established control over the body through regulatory and disciplinary power. These techniques involve the 'practical rationalities' which Nikolas Rose defines as: 'regimes of thought, through which persons can accord significance to aspects of themselves and their experience and regimes of practice, through which humans can "ethicalize" and "agent-ize" themselves in particular ways . . . through their associations with various devices, techniques, persons and objects' (1996: 173).

The concept is useful for exploring some of the processes through which identities are forged within a wide range of interventions. For example, in sport these include medical discourses, regulatory practices such as those of bodies like the WBA as well as those of legislation and, of course, the techniques of training and the practices of the gym; that is, the techniques of production. Embodied masculinities produce and reproduce themselves through these technologies and interventions. The focus on the dynamics of the processes is particularly apposite to an exploration of the embodied identities. However, there are points of resistance as well as failure in what Rose calls the regimes of subjectification, which, in spite of his protests to the contrary (Rose, 2000), seem more akin to the Frankfurt School suppression of agency. As Stuart Hall has argued, in relation to Foucault's notion of subjectification upon which Rose draws, such an approach had the advantage of drawing attention to the specific historical and institutional sites at which identities are formed (Hall, 1996). The notion of 'practical rationalities' focuses on the specificities of discursive practices and formations which are the technologies through which gendered bodies are reproduced and transformed. As was demonstrated in Chapter 3, these technologies do include space for the production as well as the domination of knowledge, although there remains a strong emphasis upon the success of such regimes. Rose argues that technologies of the self permit a conceptualization of the self as both agentic and knowing; as a subject who acts and is acted upon.

Retaining some agency, especially collective agency, is also important for a conceptualization of identity which permits change and a politics of location and resistance. This Foucauldian approach avoids the limitations of essentialism and allows space for transformation as well as the reproduction of selves. This version of identity as associated with identity politics was characterized by differences, including those of 'ethnicity' and 'race'. The sporting body is also inscribed by racism and racialized characteristics. This particularly striking in what Connell suggests, in a white-supremacist context, involves black sporting stars acting as 'exemplars of masculine toughness, while the fantasy figure of the black rapist plays an important role in sexual politics among whites' (1995: 80). The black athletic body is simultaneously inscribed with athletic prowess and sexual threat, which has at times been embodied in black boxing stars. The social construc-tivism and historical specificities of Foucauldian theory lend themselves well to an exploration of these processes of inscription on the racialized body. Paul Gilroy has addressed the role that scientific disciplines have played in establishing 'race', drawing on a Foucauldian approach, although not without severe misgivings, to address the assumption that 'race' pre-exists its figuration through the operation of the technologies which sustain it. Gilroy argues that the racialized body and 'race' as a category are always mediated by technical and social processes. Ontologies of 'race' are not natural and rooted in anatomy but this still creates questions about what is meant by 'natural' and how far the natural is equated with the anatomical body. Gilroy argues that, although it is very useful to employ Foucault's historical explanatory framework, Foucault's own account falls short in failing to accommodate the continued marginalization and devaluing of African bodies (1998). 'Race' too is an object of knowledge, which was inscribed onto the body within discourses of colonialism and science which became intertwined in embodied narratives of nationalism. Gilroy notes the shift from natural science to biology, which is more marked by digital technologies and molecular biology in the contemporary world. Sport, along with other fields, is not only characterized by bodily risks and the concomitant medical interventions that are thus required but also by regimes of performance enhancement, within the parameters of the law as well as, sometimes, outside them, which have material consequences for the bodies involved. New technologies, risk awareness and the creation and regulation of dangers, including those of pharmaceutical interventions constitute contemporary regulatory practices.

Gilroy poses questions about whether Foucault's understanding of biopolitics can be applied to the contemporary world. He suggests that particular applications of biopolitics are undermined by Foucault's insensitivity to the struggles over the unity of mankind that attended its emergence and that Foucault appears to have been uninterested in the meaning of specifically raciological differences in the context of anthropology's presentation of the species as a unified object of knowledge and power' (Gilroy, 1998: 841). The racialized body has been subject to the techniques of visualization and what Frantz Fanon called epidermalization (1967) but also to a whole set of invasions that are constitutive of that whole body and also operate within a framework of scientific and technoscientific discourses, none more so than in sport where sexuality, gender and 'race' not only articulate together but collide.

Criticisms of Foucault and developments of his work in relation to the body are largely contained within two lines of argument. The one suggests that there is too limited a scope for opposition and subversion, for example of the devices of governmentality and the ensuing techniques whereby we govern ourselves. The apparatuses of governmentality may be so effective that there is no space for resistance. Foucauldian approaches can address the social body as a target but have more difficulty in theorizing the actual body as a local space in which knowledge could be transformed (Gilroy, 1998). The second claims that this body is a very immaterial body, if not an absent body; the discourses of culture inscribe the body, but there is no body there. The 'lived body, consciousness of it and its capacities as a space of transformation are obscured' (Howson, 2005: 24), because the body is a cultural object rather than one upon which experience is grounded. Although the power–knowledge conceptualization creates a way of theorizing the links between body practices and self-regulation in the transformation of subjectivity (Rose, 1996) it can be argued that this discursive body remains *dis*embodied, rather than a living, breathing, material body (Segal, 1997a; Connell, 1995). The Foucauldian body is discursively produced and not a living breathing material entity, which is still a 'docile body', understood textually and inscribed by culture. This is supported in another sense by Luce Irigaray, who has argued that one way of questioning the discursive production of meaning is to examine materiality, in which she includes the embodied, speaking, feeling subject who is represented, reflected and reproduced (1991). However, Irigaray's focus has been on other senses, including touch, arguing that phenomenological accounts concentrate too much on the visual aspects of embodiment.

Nonetheless Foucault has been enormously influential in the progression of diverse theorizations of embodiment, although many of his followers have noted lacunae in his theoretical framework. Judith Butler argues that Foucault needs psychoanalytic theory to explain both the psychic investment of subjects in identity positions and the failure, ambivalence and resistance that might also be involved in the processes whereby subjects are recruited. She claims that any 'theory of discursive constitution of the subject must take into account the domain of foreclosure, of what must be repudiated for the subject itself to emerge' (Butler, 1993: 190). Bob Connell, whose very influential work on masculinities is considered in the next section also draws on Foucault but suggests that what is missing in the power–knowledge discursive account is the living body (1995).

Body practices and practised masculinity

Boxing is all about body practices. Given the centrality of the body in boxing and the vital importance to the boxer of attaining the highest standards of fitness it does appear that the major investment made by the boxer is in body practices. Bryan Turner proposed the idea of 'body practices' as individual and collective ways in which social labour addresses the body (1984). For example, the multiple exercise regimes undertaken by the boxer, as by all athletes, are designed to produce gendered bodies. Bob Connell suggests that such an analysis might imply that the body is a 'field on which social determination runs riot . . . the body is surface to be imprinted' (1995: 50). Connell's work on embodied masculinities offers one of the most useful counterarguments to the excesses of social constructionism, reinstating the body that lives and breathes (and dies) rather than being a canvas upon which culture inscribes meanings (1995). Connell engages with both material bodies within their economic, social and cultural context as is illustrated by his conceptualization of hegemonic masculinity and with what could be described as the problem of agency, which in phenomenological accounts is often situated within debates about the mind/body split.

Connell's work, unlike other accounts, such as Crossley's (1995a, 1995b, 2001) and Wacquant's (1995a, 1995b, 2004) development of phenomenological understandings of embodiment (although they do both mention gender), foregrounds gender and focuses upon masculinities. Not only does the body situate us in the present, it constitutes our identities through the bodily experiences that are 'often central in memories of our own lives' (Connell, 1995: 53). Narratives of sport are often closely implicated in the bodily experiences through which they have been produced and whilst the body occupies a central role it is not a passive part that is played; the body exercises agency in these pivotal moments. Some of the ways in which gendered identities are produced through both public and private stories are the concern of Chapters 5 and 6.

Connell's version of social embodiment suggests that: 'Bodies have agency and bodies are socially constructed. Biological and social analysis cannot be cut apart from the each other . . . Bodies are both objects of social practice and agents in social practice' (2002: 47).

Connell compares bodies to Banquo's ghost in Shakespeare's play, *Macbeth*. The ghost refuses to stay outside in the realm of nature and comes to 'reappear uninvited in the realm of the social' (Connell, 2002: 59). This has resonance with Gilbert Ryle's notion of the 'ghost in the machine', which Nick Crossley uses in his critique of the *Social Body* as part of his argument about the limitations of the Cartesian dualism of mind and body, which privileges the body. This analogy is used to demonstrate the distinction made by Ryle between the mind as ghostly material that is not substantial or physical, which is contrasted with the body. In Rene Descartes' *Principia Philosophica*, published in Latin in 1644 (Descartes, 1988), this is 'meat', 'emphasizing its sheer physicality and absence of human characteristics' (Crossley, 2001: 11). This is what Ryle posits as a machine 'akin to a clockwork object or gadget' (Crossley, 2001: 11). Connell's use of *Macbeth* is more troubling as it refers to a more material haunting. Connell argues that theories of discourse have not put the troublesome ghost of this dualism to rest, but have merely made bodies the objects of symbolic practice and not participants in the process of making gendered identities. The problem of agency has a special place in boxing, especially given the dominance of determinist arguments about why people, especially men, engage in the sport. Are they the dupes of a culture which offers an aggressive, physically powerful black masculinity as the only means of attaining recognition? Is it economic factors which drive working-class men to participate in the sport? In what sense do they choose to put their bodies at risk? Connell offers some strategies for dealing with these questions in his discussion of body-reflexive practices.

Body-reflexive practices

Connell poses the concept of body-reflexive practices as a means of challenging an over-social constructionist notion of the body, but with an understanding of the body which nonetheless retains its social dimensions. He uses this concept to put the body back into the social, whilst retaining the social in the body in order to accommodate an understanding of bodies as agentic. Thus the body is both agent and object of practice and it is through these bodily practices that the structures within which bodies are formed and made meaningful and embodied identities are forged, are defined and organized. Bodies and embodied identities are constitutive and constituted. Through 'body-reflexive practices more than individual lives are formed: a social world is formed' (Connell, 1995: 64). The idea of body-reflexive practices permits an understanding of the body as implicated in and addressed by social, temporal processes, without it ceasing to be a material body. Bodies are not matter in the world, individualized as representing the unique boundary of the self; they are the world and are part of what makes social relations meaningful.

The pugilistic bodily activities that constitute boxing are made meaningful and create a social order aligned with a particular version of masculinity through a set of practices. Boxing appears to be a limited space, albeit one which includes the most traditional and expected of the practices associated with masculinity. These practices include those which involve strength, aggression and the ability to inflict pain upon one's fellow combatant and to withstand or avoid pain oneself. However, these activities still operate within the wider social field and relate to other masculinities and other dimensions of masculinity. For example, hegemonic masculinity might be associated with heterosexual assertiveness (Connell, 1995), but boxers, like most competitive sportsmen, are discouraged from engaging in sexual activity in the period before competition. The practice of refraining from sexual activity can be accommodated within hegemonic masculinity through the bodily practice of abstinence along with the explanation that the aggression of the libido is then translated into aggression against the opponent in the ring.

The heterosexuality of this masculinity is uncompromised; its force is unrestrained and even re-confirmed. The energy of this heterosexual masculinity is just re-channelled into the activity of boxing. The punches directed at the targeted areas of the opponent's body are body practices that are part of the repertoire of the boxer which are situated within a framework both of understandings of masculinity and the regulatory apparatuses of the sport, which, for example, permits hits on the head and upper body but not below the belt. A fight includes the bodies of those in the ring and those of the spectators who perceive some greater authenticity in being physically present rather than as television viewers of a disembodied, sanitized event (Oates, 1987), but who are not engaged in the corporeal conflict itself. The corporeal techniques that are practised in the gym and in sparring and form the public presentation of boxing in the ring and in its representation constitute embodied meanings about gender that extend far beyond the ring itself. The physical regime of training with all its privations and routines involves external factors, such as the advice of the trainer, the competitive spirit, including the encouragement to think and act antagonistically towards the opponent, even to the extent of hating him. These often involve the ability to control the pain and to exercise discipline and self-control, which operate not only internally but that are part of what constitutes this masculinity temporally and spatially. Pain is a large part of the experience of the boxer, especially in the training regime, largely because of the pressure under which athletes are put when they seek to achieve success in their sport. Bodily reflexive practices are not only internal to the individual boxer; they include social relations and institutions such as the regulatory bodies of the sport as well as its whole culture and tradition. Bodies which are damaged and injured and just worn, as well as those that are honed specimens to which all participants aspire, are substantially in play in the practice of sport.

Reflexive body practices mean that 'with bodies both objects and agents of practice and the practice itself forming the structures within which bodies are appropriated and defined' (Connell, 1995: 61) it is necessary to look in more detail at the spatial and temporal dimensions of these practices. The practices and the identities produced within and through them are subject to ambivalences and contradictions and to historical disruption. Connell proposes a three-fold model of the structure of gender which can be illustrated by Lafferty and McKay's study of the interactions between women and men in a boxing gym. Connell uses this three-fold model in order to bring in the interplay between the different elements implicated in body-reflexive practices. First, *power relations* incorporate the structure identified as patriarchy, albeit somewhat simplistically. Sometimes in boxing this is expressed simply, for example in the explicit exaltation of men as 'warriors, thereby "proving" their biological superiority over women' (Lafferty and McKay, 2005: 256). Second, Connell uses the structure of production relations which includes the division of labour. In the gym, labour is illustrated by the lack of resources which women boxers are able to access in order to improve their competence and the association of women with 'soft boxing' and men with the transformation of the body into a weapon (2005: 256). Cathexis, or emotional attachment, is Connell's third structure which Lafferty and McKay use to locate the highly sexualized status of women in the sport, as card girls for example. In a mixed gym, they argue, women are presented as sexually tempting to men (Lafferty and McKay, 2005) which accords with much of the literature on boxing of women being excluded from gyms (Sammons, 1988; Sugden, 1996; Woodward, 2004). However, in this instance women are permitted to participate but are still subject to the same regimes of marginalization and sexualization. Lafferty and McKay suggest that representation, which relates to the glorification of male boxers (in the gym as well as in the wider world outside) is an additional structure which informs their analysis. This is a useful way of demonstrating how boxing is a gender regime, especially in showing how sport can accommodate "difference" while not making any changes to its hyper-masculine structure (Lafferty and McKay, 2005: 274). More importantly, for my purposes, it demonstrates the possibility of synthesizing routine body practices, representation and the wider cultural terrain in providing an understanding of how identities are forged within the sport. There is, however, limited interrogation of that wider cultural field in which such meanings are articulated.

Bodies in the gym are the sites of these exclusionary practices of a gendered regime. However, the separation of the structures through which the regime is practised as deployed by Lafferty and McKay might be somewhat artificial and underestimate the cultural terrain which informs the body practices of the gym and this regime allows very little scope for agency. It does raise questions about how women might be able to perform masculinity. If it is not the physical body which prevents wider and more successful participation in the sport, then the continuance of masculine domination has to be attributed to the gender regime and primarily to its cultural and social hold. The wider field brings in other routines and body practices, such as those in which participants in boxing net-works engage. The dominance of men over women persists in spite of multiple challenges and points at which it has been disrupted. Boxing is a site at which there have been limited disruptions although boxers occupy the wider social and cultural terrain and, as a traditional sport, it is widely enmeshed with traditional masculinities and regimes of gender exclusion, although as some research has indicated, even in boxing gyms there are men who are also performing different masculinities in the rest of their lives (de Garis, 2000). Rather than multiple identities, these identifications with masculinities as subject positions within boxing are contradictory, fragmented and multi-layered.

Conclusion

Bodies may be central to boxing but the discussion of how the body might be conceptualized and the problems that are raised when thinking about embodiment in relation to boxing have a much wider remit. The very primacy of the body and of body practices in a sport like boxing raises some big questions about the relationship between bodies and the diversity of bodies that are, as Nick Crossley argues, experienced, active and acted upon (2001). Much of the work that has been undertaken on embodiment in boxing has engaged with the problem of what has been called the Cartesian dualism of the mind/body split, a binary that has been a major concern of feminist critics too. This arises from the importance of evaluating, not only the higher priority that might be accorded to the mind in the mind/body split but also other differential weightings in relation to bodies, for example in terms of gender, 'race', disability and impairment. Bodies are damaged as well as beautiful and there are different meanings and statuses attributed to different bodies in terms of their social and cultural meanings. An understanding of bodies and their relationship to the social world and its power relationships both invites more detailed empirical analysis of the routine practices, especially the body-reflexive practices through which identities are constructed and through which people make sense of their lives and of who they are.

A focus on boxing offers a useful route into reinstating the material body into more discursive and social constructionist approaches which have been criticized for their over-emphasis on the body as an inscribed surface, rather than as a sub-stantial and agentic material entity. However, whilst boxing, as so predominantly and traditionally masculine a sport invokes essentialist claims to the centrality of a biological body, the discussion in this chapter has demonstrated the much wider application of debates about the relationship between mind and body and between social and cultural inscriptions and fields and the material body itself; not that the body can ever be neutral as 'it' because the body remains firmly gendered, often in a female/male binary. The intransigence of dualisms are highlighted by the analysis of embodiment.

By bringing together routine practice, individual and collective agency and the social frameworks within which power relations circulate, it is possible to provide theories of embodiment which avoid the criticism of over-determinism. Connell's work on body-reflexive practices goes a long way towards accommodating differ-ent dimensions of identification. There may be particular sensitivities to claims that selfhood is constructed only in relation to economic, social or cultural factors in boxing but the question of agency is central to all discussions of identity. Feminist critiques, although very rarely incorporating an analysis of the field of boxing into their remit, have a great deal to offer in deconstructing the value-laden dichotomies through which embodiment has been constructed and to point to the social and cultural meanings that are complicit in the configuration of embodied identities.

The concerns of embodiment have frequently been located within a discussion of routine practices. Routine masculinities extend beyond the gym, however. Nonetheless the embodied practices through which masculinities are made and re-made have given more emphasis to the corporeal practices of the sport than its spectatorship. At points the desire to reinstate the body into theories of identity and into intellectual inquiry as a whole, might have led to a marginalization of the symbolic. Boxing bodies, especially those of the black male stars of the sport such as the super-athletes in the heavyweight category, are so highly visible that bodies become indistinguishable from their representation. This aspect of embodied identities is the subject of Chapters 5 and 6, which will pick up on the possible underestimation of the symbolic status of the body, especially for those whose bodies are inscribed as outsiders, or reduced to their biology by theories which focus on the reinstatement of the actual body. The symbolic can be used to provide a link between the private stories of embodied practice in the gym and the public stories in which gender, 'race' and class combine to articulate different dimensions of fantasy and aspiration along with routine body work in visible narratives of the sport.

Chapter 5

Public stories, personal stories

Heroes, celebrity and spectacle

Introduction

Boxing is highly visual. The sport offers opportunities for the display and performance of masculinities that are both visual and visible. The discursive field of the sport presents publicly, often spectacular versions of gendered identities through which attempts can be made to secure boundaries to the self. This chapter explores how boxing brings together public and personal stories in the reconstruction of masculinities. From the spectacles that take place in the ring and through television coverage to the displays in the gym and at local clubs and different venues it offers a site for research which is characterized by the spectacle of performance and the legends and stories of celebrities and heroes which shape the understanding of those who participate, those who watch and the wider community. Boxing offers an example of representational processes in play in popular culture, illustrating well the constitutive dimensions of representation, bringing together different symbolic and discursive systems. David Chandler, in his introduction to the *Anthology of Boxing and Visual Culture* cites Joyce Carol Oates' statement that 'each boxing match is a story' (1987: 8) and adds, 'it is also a picture' (1996: 13). This chapter brings together different symbolic systems, including stories and pictures, in the making of identities.

Personal stories told in the gym elide with the public representations expressed through media stories and the images and mythology which permeate the sport at all levels. Identities are forged through regulatory practices and mechanisms and through apparatuses of inclusion and exclusion that are implicit and explicit within boxing and through the investments that are made and re-made in attempting to find stability and some sense of belonging through narratives of continuity in a world increasingly characterized by change and uncertainty (Bauman, 2004). The myths and legends of boxing provide both stability and excitement in creating a sense of location as well as security. The chapter includes a discussion of the contemporary phenomenon of celebrity, as one of the most visual and visible aspects of contemporary sporting cultures and some of the ways in which the spectacles of boxing illustrate the Bakhtinian notion of carnival with its display and excess. Boxing is marked by the elisions and tensions between public and personal stories, between discipline and control on the one hand and excess on the other and between beautiful bodies and the damaged bodies which, as a very real possibility, haunt those who participate in the sport. The spectacles of the ring and the public stories of boxing often feature the materiality of these damaged bodies, as was demonstrated in Chapter 4, just as the gym is the site for the painful ordeals of rigorous preparation that are all part of the experience of this sport.

Boxing brings together images and stories which combine narratives of the spectacular with spectacles inside and outside the ring and particular experiences of spectatorship. Chandler suggests that boxing lends itself very well to analyses of representational processes; 'the boxing match is neatly framed, squared-off by the ring; it is a set piece to be deciphered, a tableau' (Chandler, 1996: 13). This framing informs my analysis of the meanings that are reproduced and the identities that are forged and bounded through representations of boxing in this chapter as well as the boxing films which are the subject of Chapter 6. The synchronic moment of a visual image condenses both the public and private stories that create that moment and, the moment itself, its past and the dreams and aspirations it feeds in the future.

The ring as frame

The ring is crucial to the setting of the visual narrative of boxing and this image of the famous Ali–Foreman fight in Kinshasa Zaire in 1974 has become

Figure 5.1 The ring as frame, Kinshasa, 1974 (Photo: © Empics)

one of boxing's most visible and memorable moments. The ring carries a whole range of meanings bounded, like a photograph itself within the frame of the ring. I have chosen this image to introduce this chapter because it features one of boxing's greatest heroes, Muhammad Ali, who has become the focus of a set of public narratives which inform and merge with the private stories of those who enter the sport as well as demonstrating the power of boxing legends way beyond the confines of the sport itself. Boxing masculinities are constructed through heroic narratives and Ali plays a large part in many of these stories.

The ring is a metaphor for the rule-governed practices that are bounded by the ropes and the stage upon which the art of boxing is enacted. Chandler goes as far as to suggest that boxing has 'evolved into a form of representation' (1996: 13) and traces this genealogy from the implementation of the Marquis of Queensberry's rules in Britain in the 1860s. This significant moment in the history of boxing involved the implementation of mechanisms to regularize the sport, transforming it from side-show fighting and street brawling into a highly regulated, largely upright contest, with gloves and set within a specific temporal and spatial frame, with three-minute rounds interspersed by one minute rest periods in a reconfigured time-frame; a ring elevated on an indoor stage, rather than pitched on the grass outside. The contest is set in time by the duration of the rounds and by the count down of ten. Being knocked out, 'KO'd', does not necessarily involve being rendered unconscious; it means that you are knocked out of time; 'while the standing boxer is *in time*, the fallen boxer is *out of time*' (Oates, 1987: 15). The ring and the new rules made boxing a new sort of commercial spectacle and legitimated particular forms of fighting, with some fighters rather than others as the participants in the new spectacle.

The implementation of these rules had an impact upon women's participation in the sport. Women continued to fight as prizefighters, as they had for some time, but this led to the association of women boxers with the circus, the fairground and the travelling booths and a different kind of spectacle from that instated for men's boxing. As was demonstrated in Chapter 3, however serious women might have been about their sport 'because of its low-class, disreputable image, it remained "underground" or at best marginalised' (Hargreaves, 1996: 127). Thus the gendering of representations of boxing and of its spectacles, for example in the sexualization of women's fighting, has its roots in historical practices and interventions and in regulatory practices which created particular versions of gendered identities which are closely linked to the ways in which they are represented in sporting spectacles and through visual images. These apparatuses of intervention, including the establishment of regulatory bodies and processes of legitimation which have contributed to the exclusion of women are all part of particular discursive regimes within sport and make up its legends and myths. Women's boxing only became recognised as a professional sport in a few states of the US in the 1970s and it was not until 1995 that there was a legitimate Women's World Championship.

The implementation of new rules did not make boxing any less violent for men though, but it made the ring more accessible to the entertainment industry and to mass commercial spectacles (Gorn, 1986). Promoters could make admission charges, organize and police spectators through a new set of regulatory and disciplinary practices, but the sport itself became characterized by a much faster pace and short sharp punches (Gorn, 1986). These changes shifted the perception and understanding of boxing, especially men's boxing, from its rural heritage in the fairground to a new space, marked by wider commercial interest and popular spectacle.

Boxing masculinities are widely enmeshed with its visibility, as well as with its visual aspects. The conflicts and crises that beset boxing often occupy a central position in the public space where the morality of fighting is contested. This dimension of visibility, associated as it is with disputes about the health risks and safety of boxing as a sport carries particular resonance. Such tensions carry over into media coverage of boxing's 'bad guys', who may get an even worse press than those who transgress in other, less controversial sports. The image of the 'bad guy' in boxing is often implicated with the sport itself, for example in an excess of violence in the ring as well as transgressive behaviour outside it. The sport's visibility has also been greatly augmented by the transformation of boxing into a virtual spectacle broadcast on television as 'the world's most popular spectator sport' (Chandler, 1996: 17). The drama of the ring is now mostly experienced through the medium of television, although, of course, big fights continue to attract vast audiences. Boxing, like soccer, is a truly global sport and this shift has led to a transference of the sport, its representation and localized affiliations from some of its grass roots' cultural heritage and created problems for the construction of the heroic figure of the boxer and the individualized courage and honour of this existential figure. Personal narratives of rags to riches persist as does the aspiration of achieving glory in the ring, but the image of the boxer is also troubled and contradictory.

Representations of boxing in the contemporary world largely occupy two spaces which reflect and create the meanings and practices of the sport; the ring and the gym. The ring is in the spotlight, featured on television and in the media, whereas the gym is the private world of boxing, often located, not only out of the limelight, but in the darker reaches of the city, well outside the mainstream of urban life. Hence there is some perpetuation of the associations between boxing and 'low-life'.

Boxing can also create invisibility, for example in the history of white racism in the US early in the twentieth century. Identities are constituted through visibility, but they are also marked by invisibility. As Ralph Ellison notes in the introduction to *Invisible Man*,

> despite the bland assertions of sociologists, 'high visibility' actually rendered one un-visible – whether at high noon in Macy's window or illuminated by

flaming torches and flash bulbs while undergoing the ritual sacrifice that was dedicated to the ideal of white supremacy.

(2001 [1974]: xxxiii)

Ellison uses the example of a fight at the start of his novel which relates the invisibility of the protagonist, unseen because people refuse to see him. In the opening scenario a young African-American man is forced to participate in a collective free fight with other black youths for the entertainment of white businessmen, before he is permitted to make the address he had been expecting to make. Invisibility becomes both the mark of the black men in a racist society and a strategy for survival. Visibility is also gendered.

Women: now you see them, now you don't

Masculinities may be central to boxing but the sport is not and never has been only for men and about men. How do identificatory processes work for women in boxing? Women box and the sport is becoming increasingly popular, especially, for example, in the US (WBAN, 2005a). There are champions and a growing interest in the sport at all levels, including the gym, where skills are developed, even if, like many men who go to a gym, many women never fight competitively. The Women's Boxing Archive Network (WBAN) lists coming fights and provides evidence of a growing interest in all aspects of women's boxing, including some discussion of mixed bouts, which are acknowledged as problematic and seem on the rare occasions they take place to involve significant mismatches, sometimes with very ill-prepared men. The internet provides a liberatory space for the representation of women's involvement in boxing, although the extent of liberation is debated. There is also evidence of increased participation by women in the sport in different parts of the world, for example in the UK, with some interest being expressed by students and inter-university competition among women (Randall, 2004). However, within the context of this chapter my concern is with the representations of boxing and its heroes. Women's exclusion from the sport at different points historically and their marginalization, is not, as the received wisdom of many men who box claim, a matter of weight, size and competence (Woodward, 2004), as much as their absence from heroic narratives and relative lack of celebrity status. Interpellation into gendered identity positions in the sport is more problematic for women than for men. Women are not only excluded from the discursive field but lack the psychic investment in versions of the self which address gendered insecurities for men more so than for women. Women feature in the spaces reserved for coverage of women's sport but not so frequently in the mainstream, for example on prime-time TV. The images of women boxers remain sexualized in the poses they are seen to be adopting, especially women not in the heavyweight categories, for photo shoots, as displayed on the WBAN website. There are exceptions, of course, and Laila Ali is clearly emerging as a strong woman with heroic status, although some of her earlier prominence must have been due to her being Muhammad Ali's daughter, which has enormous potential for the re-articulation of gendered identity. The link with her father opens up some positive political associations with resistance to racism and empowerment, all of which indicates the emergence of a new subject position for women in boxing. As Mike Marqusee demonstrates in his biography of Muhammad Ali (2000), although Ali might have become incorporated into the US establishment, symbolized at the 1996 Atlanta Olympic Games, at a time when Ali was 'hailed as an "American hero"' (Marqusee, 2000: 3), his role in the 1960s was very much as an icon of Black Power, resistance to racism and opposition to the Vietnam war. Boxing might afford the possibilities of newly constructed gender identities that could embrace women boxers as well as men. Jennifer Hargreaves quotes women who enjoy boxing and see it as a means of enhancing rather than diminishing femininity; they relish the excitement of physical aggression and see the dangers as minimal (1996). Laila Ali presents a contemporary version of a woman who is able to take on an heroic identity without the undertones and overtones of misogyny and racism and avoiding the necessity of 'doing' hegemonic masculinity through excess of aggression and threat as might be the case in the version of masculinity performed, for example, by Ann Wolfe.

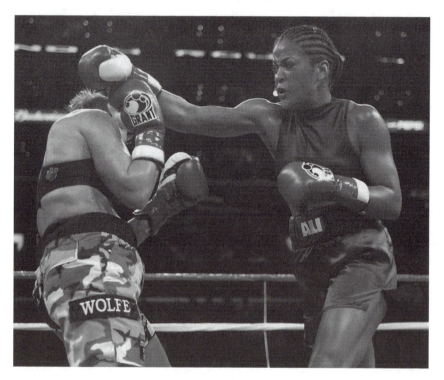

Figure 5.2 Laila Ali in action, 2003 (Photo: © Empics)

There are key moments in the history of women's boxing, but it still carries the memories of its earlier associations with unrestrained combat at fairgrounds and even less salubrious sites. In this field, as in so much of the visible cultural terrain, femininities have to accommodate the tensions between the Madonna and the whore. The alternative is invisibility. Women's boxing, like so much of women's sporting engagement has been hidden from history (Hargreaves, 1994, 1996). What is invisible is unstated and includes both a silence about women's achievements and endeavours and a failure to articulate and express assumptions about sexualized understanding of good and bad. The WBAN chronology of women's boxing, a site in all senses for communication about women in the sport, note 1720 as the historical point at which there are records of women's boxing bouts. Jennifer Hargreaves suggests that there were famous women fighters, such as, in the eighteenth century, The Famous Boxing Woman of Billingsgate, Bruising Peg and The City Championess. Women were clearly not accorded champion status but marked by their gender. Billingsgate would have had particular significance in the eighteenth century as Bakhtin notes. These names are not part of the common currency of boxing greats, although it is likely that male prizefighters of the time are not either. It is, however, evidence that women fought, even if at the time for women, as for men: 'the contests were vicious free-for-alls, either topless or in tight-fitting jackets, short petticoats and Holland drawers. They involved punching, feet and knee kicking to all parts of the body, mauling, scratching and throwing and usually resulted in serious injuries' (Hargreaves, 1996: 125).

With increased attempts at regulation prizefighting became less common, although Hargreaves notes that it did continue in Britain and in the US with particularly vicious fights including mixed competitions between women and men (Hargreaves, 1996). Barbara Buttrick, 'Battlin' Barbara', the first woman fighter to appear on television, although initially an unlicensed boxer, became 'the undefeated World Fly and Bantam Weight Boxing Champion from 1950 to 1960' (Eskin, 1974: 30) and gained a reputation both as 'a little toughie' and a disciplined practitioner of the 'noble art' (Eskin, 1974). There are some women who are performing this version of masculinity, but heroic figures are few and far between and, in spite of the growing interest in boxing among middle-class, professional women, there are difficulties which women face when attempting to situate and reconfigure their own gender identities in boxing.

Problems remain in constructing heroic narratives that bring together women and violence. For women there is a legacy of fear and danger which is largely not articulated with a heroic project of overcoming the anxiety within and the danger without, but is enmeshed with ethical discourses drawing on repertoires of the apparent immorality of women's fighting historically and the apparent vulnerability of women, both physically and emotionally that is part of the relational construction of masculinity to which femininity is counterposed. Heroic masculinity is possible through physical endeavour which could include pugilism; heroic status is much more problematic for women who seek it because they have more to fight than their opponents in the ring.

Heroes and legends

Those stories which become incorporated into a culture and attain the status of legends are usually characterized by a heroic central character. The hero is the figure who is 'larger than life'. Heroism, which is not linguistically gendered in English as both women and men can commit heroic acts, whereas the individual who commits the heroic act, is either a 'hero' or a 'heroine', although the latter is more rarely used now. This gendering draws upon traditional repertoires that equate heroism with glory and often with military success and acts of honourable pugilism. Heroes are situated within a moral framework and the battles fought are often between good and evil, with the heroic triumph of the former. Sporting heroes have a long history, one strand of which in the west reproduces Ancient Greek concepts of heroes who were capable of amazing, superhuman acts of bravery achievable through their divine ancestry. For example, these acts could be Homeric triumphs in battle or struggles against the supernatural; all are characterized by excess and an individualized glory framed within a discourse of honour. These legends are also distinguished by pivotal moments or points of great significance in the story, whether it be battles or particular conflicts that are recorded, retold and embellished as the legend grows. Sporting stories demonstrate similar features, with 'great moments' occupying prime positions in more recent sporting legends. The classical inheritance also attributes elements of this heroism to sporting achievements, especially athleticism at the games, of which the Olympic Games are the most significant. Whilst the Ancient Greeks accorded heroic sporting status to young male aristocrats who engaged in a range of athletic pursuits, including wrestling and boxing, paeans of praise were written to these sporting heroes, including those who engaged in pugilism (Pindar, 1997). Roman gladiatorial combat however, might have more resonance for boxing in the modern world. Gladiators were predominantly enslaved people (of whom the vast majority were men), not aristocrats, but could achieve freedom through success in the arena, although, of course, their viability in the face of such fierce opposition was unlikely and the life of a gladiator was very short.

Sport does feature in heroic legends not only in conjunction with military exploits, especially in modern times. These legends inform contemporary understanding. The structure and ethos of such legends are patterned by gendered expectations, almost universally coded male, imbricated with military honour and often drawing on the superiority of class hierarchies, as argued in Chapter 2, although with the space for an escape through sporting prowess and heroic achievement for escape from oppression. Whilst I am not suggesting that these traditions present closed impermeable systems, there are more than evidential traces of ways of thinking about heroism which do present some limits about who can be included in such stories and especially those that become legends.

Representation of the heroic in boxing, as with most sports, is an embodied heroism, drawing on Platonic ideals which synthesize beauty and goodness, although the violence of boxing and the corporeal contact create a problematic synthesis. Goodness is a troubled concept in boxing and might be more usefully construed as honour, but as was illustrated in Chapter 4, the beautiful body occupies an important space in the sport. Heroism in sport involves corporeality and success, the somewhat bizarre British concept of the 'plucky loser' notwithstanding. Success may be against the odds and this is nowhere more marked than in the rags-to-riches narratives of boxing. There is a strong argument that boxing is more about losing than about winning. In the one-on-one context of the fight one person has to lose and this is the lesson of boxing: how to lose. Losing can be as iconic as winning. One lost fight invokes memories of others in the annals of the sport. Boxing heroes are reconstructed through the reiteration of past encounters. As the journalist Paul Hayward said of Kostya Tszyu's failure to move from his stool after the eleventh round of his light welterweight championship fight against the British hero Ricky Hatton,

> Nothing will ever quite beat Roberto Durran's surrender to Sugar Ray Leonard in the eighth round of their rematch: 'No mas, no mas' No more, no more. But through the throng of bodies extending sympathy to Tszyu, Hatton could see the scale of his conquest and the brutality of his trade.
>
> (2005: S1)

Losing can put your name in the history books, too, as Joe Frazier was assured at the end of the fourteenth round in the 'Thriller in Manila' against Muhammad Ali in 1975.

Boxing abounds with legends and myths; stories of fights and fighters, which constitute a particular form of heroic masculinity and, as Joyce Carol Oates has argued, boxing holds on to its legends. 'An observer is struck by boxing's intense preoccupation with its own history; its continuous homage to its own heroes – or are they saints?' (1987: 108). However, it honours very few, but 'so enshrines them in the glamour of immortality . . . As in any religion, present and past are magically one' (Oates, 1987: 109). Repertoires of magic, legend and religion combine to construct boxing myths. The application of a Barthesian notion of myth, not as distorting but as presenting the truth within the sport and its discursive field, to 'authenticate its own sense of being, i.e. the very fabric of its system of meaning' (Hawkes, 1988: 131) has a special resonance within boxing. The idea of myth has common currency in the sport and assigns its main protagonists heroic status. Boxing has its kings and princes perhaps more than any other sport, the most notable, of course being Muhammad Ali, with the 1970s cited as 'life at court when we were kings' (Jones, 2004). Ali, who could be seen as one of the most visible figures in the sport, was central to the heavyweight division which had never been inhabited by such an array of talent as it was in the 1970s, including Joe Frazier and George Foreman as Ali's most formidable opponents.

Thomas Hauser echoes this view of a golden age of heavyweights and bemoans its passing and the current lack of major heavyweights in the US which he attributes, at least in part, to the higher salaries available to the stars of baseball and American football (2004). Money is a key component in the creation of sporting royalty and to contemporary constructions of celebrity, but celebrity is a more recent phenomenon, especially in its contemporary postmodern configuration. This may also be a construction of celebrity that is particularly individualized, perhaps most especially in the misdemeanours of celebrities and the construction of the infamous, that is the 'bad guys', rather than the heroes.

The mythology of kingship pervades boxing, although pretenders to the title might only manage to aspire to be princes, especially if they are not heavyweights, like the British boxer 'Prince' Naseem Hamed. Donald McRae describes meeting Naseem Hamed before his bantamweight title fight with Vincenzo Belcastro in 1993, and Hamed informing him 'I'm gonna be a legend' (1996: 140). Boxing deploys the language of legends and constructs its own mythological heroes. However, the mighty also fall, as has Hamed, who latterly has attained more media visibility for driving offences than for any boxing success. Media coverage of 'Iron Mike' Tyson has also frequently deployed the notion of the 'lights going out' and the myth destroyed (Berbick, 2004). In June 2002, Lennox Lewis 'destroyed the myth of Tyson' according to the *Guardian* newspaper (10 June 2002). Boxers constitute the myths in which they are the heroes. They may indeed be, as Paul Ricoeur has suggested, the heroes of their own stories but not the authors (1991) and Tyson's story offers good illustration of this. As the writer and academic June Jordan writes in her critique of Tyson's conviction for rape, 'Requiem for the Champ': 'He felt the stigma of a prior hatred and intentional poverty. He was given the choice of violence or violence: the violence of defeat or the violence of victory' (2002: 164). Tyson's story offers a particularly good illustration of the tensions between success and failure and 'good' and 'evil'.

Although, as I shall demonstrate below, boxers often cite famous pugilists as their heroes and role models, in boxing mythology 'bad guys' are also linked together in the popular imagination and, even more, in the popular press. For example, Mike Tyson, who had mistakenly, but not surprisingly, been rumoured to have been Sonny Liston's nephew (Hennessy, 1990) became linked to Liston, the 'baddest of the bad black heavyweights', as a terrifying, threatening figure; a real 'bad guy' who was violent and had been in prison on several occasions; an example of infamous celebrity within a framework of racialized individualization. Tyson was claimed to have replayed Liston's role as 'the personification of the urban nightmare' (Piper, 1996: 77). However, such associations go back further in the genealogy of racialization of the good and the bad in boxing, for example to Jack Johnson's inflammation of white supremacy at the start of the twentieth century. However, Keith Piper argues that Tyson does not lie directly in the tradition of Jackson and Ali whose dissent against white power lay more within the arena of making visible black oppression and exclusion. Both Jackson, who not only defeated his white opponents in the ring but clearly enjoyed doing so and Ali who refused his slave name of Cassius Clay and went on to refuse to fight in Vietnam, employed bravado and extrovert expression in a direct challenge to white supremacy. Piper claims that Tyson departs from this tradition, although the Tyson narrative parades a number of key themes which operate around 'race', power and sexuality, of which criminality and imprisonment is one, through which racialized 'bad guys' are constructed in boxing. He suggests that Tyson's representation is one which feeds directly into 'the demonization of black masculinity in contemporary society, and which reinforces the dominant white male ideologies which continue to bombard us' (1996: 79).

There are many versions of the Tyson story and different interpretations of his rise and especially his fall (O'Connor, 2002), but I have cited this dimension of the story here as an example of a construction of celebrity and the primacy of the visible in the reconstruction of the central characters in boxing narratives. Tyson has been described variously as 'a prehistoric creature rising from a fearful crevice in our collective subconscious' (Oates, 2002: xiv) and by George Plimpton as 'yet another in a line of colourful characters going back through Muhammad Ali, Archie Moore, Sugar Ray Robinson to Jack Johnson' (2002: xiii). Tyson's story of individual redemption and condemnation could have been designed to re-affirm the possibility of a meteoric rise to fame, through boxing, as part of the American Dream. As Piper argues,

> Tyson became the symbol of the supreme 1980s professional because he emerged as raw material to be moulded into an invincible fighting machine by the white father figure [Cus d'Amato, his trainer]. When the civilising influence of American paternalism was stripped away, he was left at the mercy of new postmodern nightmare.
>
> (1996: 79)

Tyson's celebrity status has persisted, right up to his defeat on his stool in his last fight in 2005 and his heroic status has not been entirely lost in spite of his conviction for rape in 1992. Plimpton refers to Tyson's conviction for raping Desiree Washington as 'a most dubious conviction for rape' (2002: xv). Tyson does have his defenders, even in the case of biting off part of Evander Holyfield's ear in the ring (Dunn, 2002). He is still cited as an inspiration to young boxers. As Daniel O'Connor says in his introduction to *Iron Mike*, 'Tyson still commands loyalty in the black neighbourhoods . . . particularly among the young' (2002: xix).

These narratives of celebrity and especially the symbols attached to the representation of heavyweight champions are highly visible in their reinstatement of dichotomies of good and evil and right and wrong. Perhaps it is inevitable that this should be the case with boxing which so confounds taboo and flouts moral prescriptions against killing and inflicting pain. 'It celebrates, not meekness, but flamboyant aggression' (Oates, 2002: 155), so it is only to be expected that its stories are the most dramatic and the most polarized in the presentation of good and bad. Boxing legends and especially its heroes are constituted through moral trajectories. These are the myths which are so powerful in making and reinstating the boxing masculinities through which boxers at all levels of the game make sense of their own experience, especially in relation to their attraction to the sport. Such legends, although often complex and contradictory, are key to the identifications which take place in the sport.

Not only do many of the men in the gym identify with heroes, they seek to create their own legends through fantasies of triumph that have resonance with the traditional mythology of boxing. Such aspirations become part of the training practice and are told and retold in the gym (Woodward, 2004). Stories such as Naseem Hamed's 'I'm gonna be a legend' tale are rehearsed and reiterated by those who train at the gym (Woodward, 2004). After the fight mentioned above between Hamed and Vincento Belcastro in Sheffield, Hamed was accused of going too far in the shower of punches he landed on his opponent. His defence was that he wasn't really there: 'I was in Las Vegas, winning a world title'. The trainer, Brendan Ingle, endorsed this, somewhat apologetically, telling reporters after the fight in which his fighter attempted to humiliate his opponent, that Hamed was lost in a fantasy about being Sugar Ray Robinson outwitting Marvin Hagler at Caesar's Palace in 1985. The masculinities that are implicated in the practice of boxing are about fantasy, mythology and the invocation of legend.

Local heroes, family ties

Boxing legends are local as well as global, although the two interrelate and the apocryphal tales told in the gym, through local networks and in associated activities become established as myths of particular heroes. Narratives of kingship are imbricated with those of kinship and the 'brotherhood of boxing'. In my own research at Brendan Ingle's gym in Sheffield the notion of a boxing hero was frequently cited as a key reason for entering the sport (Woodward, 2004). This was a gym where only men trained and women were not included. These heroes might be less public figures, such as the boxer's own brother, in the case of cruiser weight world champion Johnny Nelson, or more visible, global, all-time heroes like Muhammad Ali or more local champion heroes like Lennox Lewis or Chris Eubank. 'Well, it was Ali of course, not just the fights, not just how good he was as a boxer. It was him' (Johnny, black boxer, 1997).

It might be a particular fight, most likely viewed on television, although the boxer might have been taken to a local competition, which has captured the imagination and created the possibility of belonging to this world. It is the 'big fights' that have most resonance in both the excitement they generate through the display and spectacle and the starring roles of the protagonists.

> I first got really interested in boxing when I saw the Bruno Tyson fight in 1989 and I've followed it very closely, ever since, been following most fights.
>
> (Roger, white boxer, 1997)

I were just a skinny kid at school and I used to get bashed around a bit
and pushed about and I wanted to . . . at the same time Tyson were on his
way up and I used to get up at three o'clock at morning and watch Tyson, so
I thought I'd give it a go.

(Dave, black boxer, 1997)

I was working in a fitness studio and Chris Eubank actually came and
opened the fitness studio for us and I was speaking to him and he put me
onto Brendan Ingle and got me boxing so I really owe it down to Chris
Eubank.

(John, white Yorkshire boxer, 1997)

Heroes may be more local and family plays an important part in the identificatory
processes that are implicated in the creation of heroes.

I started boxing because I suppose peer pressure, lot of my friends did it. My
hero, my brother did it.

(Johnny Nelson, black WBO cruiser weight champion, 1997)

There is sometimes an explicit acknowledgement that boxing is 'in the blood' in
the sense of familial genealogies which become part of the construction of legends
in private stories. This is not the 'in the blood' of Bourdieu's gendered *illusio* as
discussed in Chapter 4, but is familial blood ties, which involve recognition of
a genealogy of belonging and identification with a tradition of masculinity that
is not necessarily traditional, or hegemonic masculinity but is part of space–time
and familial heritage. Although whole families and kinship groups are implicated
in these traditions, they are marked by gender. Expressions of continuity and
inclusion by participating in boxing are much less likely to be open to young
women, although women as relatives are part of the genealogy that is expressed
in the public arena, for example with the success of an individual, male boxer such
as Amir Khan the British Olympic silver medallist of 2004 who turned professional in 2005 after beating the Cuban champion Mario Kindelan who had
beaten him to gold at the Olympics. Whilst Amir Khan's image was frequently
located within the context of his family who were depicted waving Pakistani and
British flags at the Olympic Games, heralding a new expression of ethnic diversity,
it was his male relatives who occupied the most influential positions in relation
to his career management. Women occupy a supporting role, legitimizing the
blood ties but outside the frame of action and agency.

Whereas the stories of being small and of being bullied, which nonetheless
often coincide with reference to aspirations to emulate a hero, invoke the
traditional masculinity that seeks to defend the self through embodied practices
of self defence through aggression, appeals to belonging to this tradition are
expressed through place and kinship ties.

Figure 5.3 Amir Khan at the 2004 Olympics with his father (Photo: © Empics)

> I first started boxing aged 13. Me dad introduced me to a guy who used to train. Father used to box and me grandfather before him. It's like we've all done it in our family.
>
> (Chris, white boxer, 1997)

As the trainer at this club himself says:

> Oh well, all my brothers boxed when I was a young lad of two and three and I've been watching it since two or three and I've been at it fifty-odd year. Boxing, boxing and myself trainer and fighter and managing and promoting, marvellous game.
>
> (Brendan Ingle, white Irish trainer, 1997)

Boxing heroes are enmeshed with family and community in the private stories of those who box. Professional boxers are represented as local heroes. When Ricky Hatton won his light-welterweight championship fight against Kostya Tszyn at Manchester's MEN arena in 2005, he was hailed as 'Manchester's boy-next-door' (Rawling, 2005: 16) and an 'ordinary', local lad, celebrating with a few pints with his mates in his local pub. In some ways boxing is the most egalitarian of sports with its heroic figures and key protagonists training at the same local gym as those who just come to spar and those who are unlikely ever to win a contest, let alone a professional bout. The spatial location of boxing gyms, unlike the training grounds and facilities in many other sports, persists in the poorer areas of town. A champion boxer may continue to train at the club where he started because of his trainer, who may also achieve elements of heroic status, with some trainers entering the canon of boxing legends, one of the most notable of whom must be Cus D'Amato in the Tyson story. The Ferrari is parked outside the run-down down-town gym and the ordinary punters have access to their heroes. Thus these aspirations seem more possible and immediate, however unattainable they must be for the majority of those training at the gym.

Boxing stories: boxing networks

Boxing's myths and legends are constitutive of gendered identities with particular resonance for masculinity and those who invest in these masculinities. The subjects positioned within the field are not only those who engage in the pugilism of the sport, although, as was indicated in Chapter 4, corporeal practice and engagement is especially powerful in the embodied identifications in such masculinities. Those who are part of boxing's networks are eager to establish their own credentials through expressed knowledge of the myths through which the culture of boxing and its heroic figures are reconstructed and articulated. For example, sports journalists and academic researchers enhance both their own credibility and their media narratives through detailed accounts of events that are to become boxing myths, as well insider stories about the minutiae of boxing life and associated activities, some of which are not as regulated as the sport itself. As discussed in Chapter 3, this is a feature of much of the academic work that has been written about boxing, for example in the ethnographic participant observations of sociologists like Wacquant. However, scholarship and journalism elide in sport. For example, social psychologist Geoff Beattie produced an 'insider' story of Brendan Ingle's gym in Sheffield in which he details his immersion in the life of the gym, not only training and sparring, but engaging in some of the extramural activities (1997). These range from travelling to a fight with frequent toilet stops to get the boxer's weight down, through drunken nights at clubs, to witnessing bare-knuckle fights and other illegal, associated events. The author's credibility and insider status is achieved through his identification with the masculinities that are enacted at the gym and in its linked activities. The ties of kinship and of belonging to a tradition are mostly not available to those to occupy the public arena of story tellers, so other strategies must be adopted to establish connections with the masculinities that dominate this space. If biographies of belonging are not possible, then engagement with the activity of fighting may be another alternative. The collusion is sealed by some actual engagement in pugilistic combat. Fighting is not always possible of course and there are other means of establishing a colluding masculinity.

In his famous account of the 'Rumble in the Jungle' in Zaire in 1974 (1975) in which he describes himself in the third person, Norman Mailer advances the narrative and expresses the intensity of his feelings, by moving from referring to himself as 'Norman', then 'Norm', as the book progresses, with the occasional more formal 'Norman Mailer'. We read that 'Norman went back to the States' (Mailer, 1975: 30) as Mailer has decided to use his first name because 'everybody else in the fight game' does and 'the only alternative was to do a piece without a name' in order to acquire an 'anonymous voice' (Mailer, 1975: 32). The effect may be to implicate Mailer himself more strongly in the masculinity of the fight culture, rather than to distance him from the narrative. 'Norm' is one of the party and not an onlooker. Collusion operates by invoking other such masculinities and heroic narratives. Just before Ali goes to his dressing room before the fight, Mailer describes his own emotions:

> If ever a fighter had been able to demonstrate that boxing was a twentieth-century art, it must be Ali . . . What could be of more importance to Norman? He knew some part of him would have to hate Ali if the fighter lost without dignity or real effort, even as part of him could not forgive Hemingway because of the ambiguity of his suicide.
>
> (1975: 162)

Art, heroic masculinity and pugilism coincide and Mailer is implicated through his own association with Ernest Hemingway, who occupies an iconic status in relation to a particular version of masculinity as rugged, adventurous and hard-drinking with which Mailer seeks to collude. Hemingway, whose fictional work includes tales of bull-fighting and deep-sea fishing, was also a participant in the hunting, shooting and fighting that are the practices of this version of masculinity. As a writer too, Mailer is able to establish a gendered collusion through his status as a privileged observer and commentator. Hemingway's masculinity is also one that is constructed within a particular coding of winning and losing that lends itself so well to sporting endeavours; losing but not losing. Although Hemmingway did not write a great deal about boxing, he did pick the sport in order to explore the issue of losing. The honour and dedication of the unsentimentally heroic masculinity, which concerned Hemmingway involves picking yourself up off the floor. The former England cricket captain, Michael Atherton speaks of his admiration for Hemingway, especially citing the short story 'Fifty Grand' (Hemingway, 1936), telling how an aging boxer throws a fight for $50,000 (Atherton, 2005). So powerful is the collusion between athletes that is implicated in this masculinity that there is no perceived irony in the empathy and praise for a story which is ultimately, however sympathetically told, about unfair play and deception in sport however tragic the circumstances may be. What is more important is the identification with the dilemma of losing and failing and the recognition that masculinity in sport is about losing as well as winning; maybe even more so. Part of being included and demonstrating insider status is achieved by knowing the stories and being part of their fabrication and thus buying into the myth. Heroes, histories and narratives of public stories about heroes interweave with the private aspirations and these legends and the networks in which they circulate form a large part of the narratives through which masculinities are constructed within boxing.

Boxing as carnival

Although public stories are retold in local spaces and through local networks they increasingly occupy a global stage. Boxing is increasingly global entertainment. Its most public stories are told at places like Madison Square Garden or Caesar's Palace where vast resources are spent on providing spectacle and which are transmitted to television screens across the world by satellite so that millions of people can share the experience. Light is cast on the elevated ring which is surrounded by the darkness of the watching crowds awaiting the violent combat. The gym, in contrast, might be a much gloomier venue: located in an impoverished area and characterized by banal and tedious routine. However, the gym, too, has its element of performance, display and psychological tension, even if it accommodates a more collective environment than the individualistic stage of the ring for competitive fights. There are elements of the carnivalesque in boxing, which is characterized by excess and even by parody. Joyce Carol Oates suggests that the woman who boxes is a parody: 'raw aggression is thought to be the peculiar province of men, as nurturing is the peculiar province of women. (The female boxer violates this stereotype – she is parody, she is cartoon, she is monstrous.)' (1987: 73).

It is not entirely clear where Oates herself as the woman spectator and aficionado of the violence of boxing is situated in this polarized scenario of gender stereotypes. However, she suggests that women's interest in men's interest in boxing which is complemented by their more familiar repugnance for the sport itself is the source of their involvement. Women, coded as heterosexual in the case of men's boxing cited here, are thereby seen as attracted by men's interest rather than the sport itself, in which any actual physical involvement would be, according to Oates, absurd and parodic. Women's exclusion from much of the boxing mainstream makes their endeavours more likely to be serious and straightforward than parodic and certainly not ironic. Men's boxing presents more scope for parody. There is also an element of transgression in the performance of masculinity by men in boxing which involves display and spectacle as well as what may at times appear to be a parodic masculinity in an exaggeration of an aggressive masculinity which defies more recent transformations and the emergence of figures such as the 'new man' (de Garis, 2000). Boxing masculinities challenge what might be becoming new orthodoxies of caring, democratic and empathetic masculinities.

Richard Giulianotti suggests that the term 'transgression', in its anthropological sense of contravening the social order and breaching moral imperatives, is preferable to the concept of resistance, because 'resistance implies intentional social opposition, transgression focuses upon consequences of actions' (2005: 56). He goes on to link cultural transgressions with carnival and folk culture's carnivalesque. Cultural transgressions are frequently discerned in carnivals and the carnivalesque of folk culture, in which boxing has its roots and is a good example of the carnivalesque, in its display and parody of masculinity. Bakhtin uses the term carnival to describe hedonistic activities characterised by excess and the symbolic overthrow of hierarchies and social order, such as were experienced in medieval fairs. Such activities included overt sexual displays and excessive consumption of food and drink (1984). The display of the fight with the associated trappings of popular culture present an activity that could be construed as contemporary carnival in its excess, if not in its lack of control. It may be that Ali's display of showmanship could be categorized as carnivalesque on occasion. Ali's sayings are memorable; not least his repudiation of the draft to fight in Vietnam and assertion that he had no quarrel with the Vietcong (Marqusee, 2000). There is subversion in the parody which he noted, quoted in different ways at different sites, including in Ali and Durham, that 'boxing is a lot of white men watching two black men beat each other up' (1975). Ali is famous for his entertaining, confident chants of 'float like a butterfly, sting like a bee' and claims of 'I am the greatest' and, reputedly, 'I'm not the greatest. I'm the double greatest. Not only do I knock 'em out, I pick the round' (Oliver and Simpson, 2004: 292). However, there are also myriad stories of excess which are not entertaining or subversive, but which result from apparent lack of control in the ring, such as Mike Tyson's infamous World Boxing Association (WBA) heavyweight fight against Evander Holyfield in Las Vegas in 1997, when Tyson bit off part of Holyfield's ear.

Boxing is also an entertainment, which is attended by a high-paying audience, including celebrities in other fields, who sometimes enjoy dinner while they watch the display. This highlights the embodiment of class difference and demonstrates starkly the divide in the investment of physical capital by the largely working-class protagonists in the drama of the fight, which at this particular site is viewed by those who are more affluent. Harry Crews illustrates this well in his account of watching a Tyson fight (against Michael Spinks in Atlantic City) with the celebrity Madonna and the actor, her then husband, Sean Penn (1989). However, popular culture is not only implicated in boxing at the level of celebrities, even sparring in the gym is accompanied by popular music, presenting a display not that far removed from the disco (Woodward, 1997b). The repetitive actions of the boxers engaging in training such as bag work is enacted to the pulsating, insistent rhythms of music more usually part of the dance and club scene, signifying a somewhat ironic elision between the pugilistic practices of the boxer and the movements of the dancer in the context of celebrity popular culture. The music is selected by the gym member with the highest status and prestige and reflects not only personal taste and the hierarchy of the gym but also a synthesis which puts boxing into popular culture (Woodward, 2004).

Celebrity and carnival

Celebrity is demonstrated by the combination of areas of popular culture such as the music industry, film, soap opera and reality TV. Sports stars may have been slower to come to celebrity and celebrities are far removed from the heroes which are intrinsic to the genealogy of boxing. Celebrity is also characterized by failure as well as by success. For example, the fall from grace, the enormous attraction in infamy and disgrace as well as success and heroism of Mike Tyson illustrates this well. Celebrities are spectators and boxing has its celebrities. At an historical moment when the west is star-struck and obsessed with 'the celebrity' there are clearly points where celebrities are not only personalities but heroes. Eliot Cashmore notes the replacement of the sports star with the 'celebrity athlete' (2005: 398), observing that 'their fame might have had its sources in sport, but when they appear in the celeb magazines or on TV talk shows they are indistinguishable from other celebrities' (2005: 398).

P. David Marshall suggests that celebrity is always underpinned by assumptions about individuality and sociality (1997). One of Ali's pronouncements expressed the irony of this in his response to the question of how he would like to be remembered: 'As a man who never sold out his people. But if that is too much then just as a good boxer and I won't mind if you don't mention how pretty I was' (Oliver and Simpson, 2004: 304).

A celebrity has to be recognised, even if it is only for being a celebrity, although it is becoming difficult to keep up with the minor celebrities who populate their very own genre of reality TV. Celebrity has to be visible and one of the ways of being visible in boxing is to be a 'bad guy'.

The phenomenon of the 'bad guy' illustrates some of the problems for the celebrity in boxing as a sport which has so contentious a public image. As Marshall argues, celebrity culture is the site of discursive struggle (Marshall, 1997) and is characterized by a struggle for recognition manifest in the relationship between celebrity and audience which may suggest a space for the reconstruction of celebrity in boxing for women. Is it possible for women boxers to occupy a celebrity space dominated by waifish pop stars and skinny supermodels? Just as boxing masculinities may sit more easily with a more traditional version of the identity and be difficult to accommodate in a field of ambiguity and transformation, the femininity associated with women boxers offers an uncomfortable alliance with the figures of femininity which have such wide contemporary currency. There is some possibility of representations of strong women. Laila Ali's strong figure, including her representation in advertisements, in a virtual fantasy reconstruction defeating her father, Muhammad Ali at his peak is a good example of a reworking of the boxing hero that can redefine gender. Celebrity figures function as fantasy objects and, disputably, as role models. Celebrities, in boxing as elsewhere, engage in conspicuous consumption and are objects of aspiration and desire, which invokes the Lacanian phantasmatic relationship between the wider public and the celebrity, rather than the desire to see oneself perfectly

Figure 5.4 Tyson leaving court, again, 2004 (Photo: © Empics)

reflected in that celebrity whom we might seek to emulate in their pugilistic endeavours. Boxing has its specificities and the notion of celebrity may be insufficiently robust to account for the identifications that take place among the practitioners of the sport. However, for some boxers of whom Muhammad Ali is one of the most well-known boxing figures, it is possible to be both a hero and a celebrity.

Excess and carnival

Boxing is entertainment like no other. Whilst this spectacle is based on rigorous training and the development of high levels of skill and artistry, the aim of the combat is to inflict damage and pain on the opponent; as Joyce Carol Oates says 'to attack another and force him into absolute submission' (1987: 49). It is fighting as well as boxing and could be seen to belong, not just to pre-modern societies but to some primordial, pre-civilization (1987: 49). At an historical moment when western societies are dominated by what Rose calls 'psy' discourses (1996) and people are ever more exhorted to focus on the qualities of the inner person and to seek counselling for any disquiet, the idea of two people hitting each other as entertainment is unsettling. The 'violence' of boxing also flows 'from the crowd

. . . a heightened expression of the crowd's delirium' (Oates, 1987: 50). This is an entertainment of excess and lack of restraint, which can lead to pain and distress, as well as of artistic discipline and the display of the perfectly honed, fit, beautiful body.

An outcome of violence in the ring is the grotesque body of defeat and serious injury, which elide with the broken bodies discussed in Chapter 4. The grotesque body, although not the trangressive, exaggerated body of Bakhtinian carnival which comically and grossly subverts the social order, is nonetheless subversive in its grotesque representation and transgression of the norms of civilized culture and of 'civilized' spectatorship. This is a display of the mutilated, damaged body as spectacle and as entertainment as one of the grotesque, tragic moments of boxing, such as represented in the image of Gerald McClellan breaking down in the ring in his fight with Nigel Benn in 1995 (see Figure 4.1).

This damage is what haunts all boxers, whether they engage in competitive fighting or even if they only spar at the gym, although it is at the level of professionals that this is most powerful, because this is where it is most spectacularly and publicly displayed. In boxing, celebrity is closely tied up with losing as well as winning and with the spectacle of violence that takes place in the ring. This relationship between winning and losing and between the beautiful and the broken body is crucial to the internal dialogues through which masculinities are forged. Failure in the ring can represent failure of identification, especially with the heroic masculinity of success. This is why I argue that losing is as important as winning in an analysis of boxing masculinities. However, these are not oppositions; part of this internal negotiation is related to the matter of how to lose and how to retain honour and selfhood through the realization and actuality of failure. Failure is constructed through success and success through failure.

The interrelationship between success and failure is reproduced in the relationship between high and low cultures. Peter Stallybrass and Allon White, in their analysis of representations of 'low' entertainment and the carnivalesque, suggest that 'high' and 'low' culture are interdependent and 'low life' is instrumentally constitutive in the shared imaginary repertoires of the dominant culture' (1986: 6). In this way high culture 'includes that low symbolically as a primary, eroticized constituent of its own fantasy life' (1986: 5). There is disgust, fear and desire in the construction of subjectivities through the representations of 'low life' and of carnival with all its associations with the ritual spectacles of the vulgar and crude. The carnivalesque is apparent in boxing, not only through its genealogy of associations with fairs, popular feasts and travelling booths, but also through its negotiation of fear and disgust.

Boxing permits what Stallybrass and White identified as a feature of nineteenth-century capitalism, as an 'alarming conjuncture of the elite and the vulgar' (1986: 135) and can be seen as combining what they cite from Charles Dickens as addressing the high–low interrelationship between attraction and disgust, between the bourgeois and the slum as 'the attraction of repulsion (1986: 140). Boxing features such contradictions that are inseparable. It carries the mark of civilization. It is heavily regulated yet it permits an alliance of raw appre-hension, involving flesh-on-flesh, in the most corporeal of sporting contests, with parodic display. Boxing is not a form of entertainment that can be explained and positioned within Bakhtin's notion of carnival, as containing a utopian urge (1987), although there might be liberatory potential in the display of anger that boxing permits. It is more in its expression of that which is largely not per-missible to speak or show, which is outside culture. Carnival displaces the normal social hierarchies. The parodic, excessive displays of traditional, aggressive, corporeal masculinities within the space afforded by boxing and the gym subvert 'new' masculinities and offer some resistance within racialized, classed discourses of masculinity. Carnival is a spectacle that is also gross and vulgar, repressed in bourgeois culture in the modern period, according to Bakhtin, yet there is also voyeuristic pleasure in carnival even if bourgeois enjoyment of the spectacle is voyeuristic and tinged with guilt. Boxing is a spectacle beset with contradictions and ambiguities enjoyed and reviled in equal proportions, probably at the same time.

Joyce Carol Oates claims that boxing is 'real' and not a dramatic, theatrical device (1987). Whilst what constitutes the 'real' and reality is highly contentious, I would want to challenge Oates' rejection of the drama and theatricality of boxing and, in particular of the gendered identities that are played out within the sport. Boxing is self-consciously staged for the entertainment of those who watch rather as gladiatorial combat was in Ancient Rome. There is a show with warm-up acts and razzamatazz. Sometimes it is on a big scale, sometimes it is a smaller venue and more exclusive spectators even have dinner while they watch the 'show'. The process of interpellation is complex, if immediate and identifi-cations are associated with power and control on the part of spectators. This is exercised through the economic power of class dominance, ethnic and racialized distancing and 'othering' and through the excitement and drama of the spectacle itself. The experience of a fight is clearly directed at entertainment for the spectator and reinforces the theatricality of the moment. However, the entry into the ring is marked by the moment of disrobing, of removing the fantasy costume and leaving the 'magic carpet'.

Spectacular effects are achieved not only by the drama of the main fight and any additional bouts, but by explicit acknowledgement that this is part of a field of entertaining practices that require lights, music and frequently attractive young women who are not boxers, but part of the show. Although, of course sometimes women boxers are also part of the show and even, in the case of Christy Martin and Deirdre Gogarty in 1996, the main show, upstaging Mike Tyson, albeit in a somewhat easy fight against Frank Bruno. Women's boxing can also attract television viewers, for example as Laila Ali's fight against Jacqui Frazier's did in 2001, attracting 100,000 pay-per-view purchases. Before claiming a take-over by women it is worth noting that the Ali–Frazier ticket might have been part of the attraction. Women's boxing too, in its public display, still carries some of the ambivalences of the fairground spectacle. For example, media coverage of the

Figure 5.5 Magic shows: 'Prince' Naseem Hamed on the magic carpet
(Photo: © Empics)

Texan boxer Ann Wolfe focuses more on her fights with men and the apparent refusal of female opponents to take her on than upon her performance in the ring (Walters, 2005a). Even Wolfe's knock-out of her opponent, Vonda Ward, in a light heavyweight championship fight in 2004, reputedly the 'best knock-out in women's boxing' (Walters, 2005a: 42) is used more to create a threat, or promise, of frightening aggression, than as a technical triumph. The threat has to be visible and the images of Wolfe adopting a macho aggressive stance and the television coverage of her fights all endorse this version of a woman 'doing masculinity' where violence and damage is routine. The centrality of television and the return of fights to terrestrial television in recent years is all part of both a project to revive interest in the sport and to provide an entertainment which seeks to recapture the excitement of spectatorship by virtual means.

Although the gym may be a dark space almost invariably located in the poorer areas of town and often marked by the lack of resources and the poverty of the actual place, there can be a festive atmosphere instilled by the background beat of contemporary music amidst the gruelling hard work of training through rigorous and demanding effort (Woodward, 2004). The gym, in spite of its hardships, is not exempt from the drama of boxing. Boxing does appear to be about dramatic presentation through the enactment of the spectacle of machismo in a drama that includes the personal management of fears and anxiety. What is indisputably material about boxing is the brutality of some moments in the sport and the actuality of death, albeit rarely, in the ring.

Spectacles of violence

Boxing and violence are linked, not only in the ring in the corporeal combat, but perhaps even more significantly in the representation: in the spectacle in the ring. In the 'noble art' there can be boxers and fighters. Fighting alone is insufficient to achieve success, but however skilful the sweet science, there is both direct contact and the danger of hurt and the promise of violence which draws in the spectators. Trainers distinguish between fighters and boxers, although they are always combined in great boxers, but the distinction is necessary to differentiate between unrestrained, gross acts of aggression and the skill of boxing. This distinction also has resonance for the violence of the spectacle: for the promise of violence. Amateur boxing, although skilful, lacks the drama and excitement of professional fights. Amateurs usually win on points whereas professional boxers are more likely to aim for a knock-out. Protective helmets make for a less primordial combat and exposure to hurt is part of the heroic masculinity of boxing. This applies to combatants and spectators. Boxers and spectators have to accommodate the ambivalences of defence and aggression as embodied in the dangers of the sport. Part of the mythology of boxing masculinities requires courage in the face of injury. Injury is integral to the sport and its practices and display, although it is not inevitable, of course. Watching pre-empts the fear of participating. The masculinities that collude are thus pre-emptive.

Whilst I have focused my discussion on boxing, it has a much wider application, which is threaded through the discussion in this book. Arguments about the extent to which a deconstruction of discursive practices can be seen to explain particular identity positions are challenged in different ways through exploring the interrelationships between embodiment, psychic investment and social and cultural practices. The debate as expressed through boxing is often framed by the tension between essentialist and non-essentialist versions of masculinity. Does boxing persist as a public spectacle and legitimate everyday activity in the gym because it fulfils a desire to engage in violence and to look at acts of aggression? Is this bound up with a version of masculinity expressed by Chuck Palahniuk in his novel *Fight Club*, upon which the eponymous film was based, as one half of a 'real self' within which aggression is instinctive (in Mitchell, 2003: xi)? Alternatively, this phenomenon of the apparent glamorization of violence is an expression of deeper anxieties which operate within the psyche, giving voice to fears, not only of the loss of the heritage of masculinity as Palahniuk suggests, but also of the fragmentation of personhood which defence mechanisms are invoked to redress. The culture of boxing offers a space in which there is some security of identification with a bounded masculinity, however illusionary this might be.

The commonsense discourse of innate aggression permeates the narratives of boxing. In his discussion of the Nigel Benn–Gerald McClellan fight from which McClellan, having been knocked unconscious in the tenth round, never fully recovered, Kevin Mitchell suggest that this violence is elemental and evolutionary (2003). What is most interesting about his book is the acknowledgement of the pull of violent spectacle and the questioning of its attraction. Mitchell is attempting to describe the tension between the tragic and the entertaining, between farce and nobility, reiterated within the folklore of boxing as equating pugilistic masculinity with a Darwinian notion of the survival of the fittest. He also seeks a solution in essentialist scientific explanations of the desire for violence and its glamour, rather than considering what is constitutive and not mimetic about its representation. There might be stability in the notion of essentialist fixity, but it does not address in any way either the role played by such narratives in reinforcing particular versions of masculinity or the internal conflicts which might lead to the identities that emerge and are re-played.

Excess and the unconscious

The internal dialogue of masculinity that is played out in the literature and in the narratives of masculinity associated with the sport are also part of the lives of boxers. Whereas there is a strong case to be made for the aggression and violence of boxing derived from the anger of its participants as in no small part due to their experience of racism and social and economic injustice and exclusion, a simple reading off from inequality to brutality is exaggerated (Jefferson, 1996, 1998). Oates claims that boxing is about anger (1987). Indeed, given the life experiences of some boxers, for example in terms of racialization, economic disadvantage, marginalization and social exclusion, it would be hard not to be very angry indeed. However, there are conflicts and ambiguities which subvert the strength of this thesis. Tony Jefferson, in his analysis of Mike Tyson, surely one of boxing's great 'mixed-up guys', maps his transition from 'little fairy boy' to 'the compleat destroyer' and his fall from grace (Jefferson, 1996). Tyson offers an illustration of an extremely deprived childhood and adolescence (O'Connor, 2002), but Jefferson suggests that it is possible to explore some of the internal, psychic processes that are in play, by using the secondary sources of Tyson's life history that have been made available. Tyson, like so many boxers reports having been bullied as a child, a 'fairy boy' with a lisp who seemed to have no skills or competences and was constantly bullied. Jefferson uses a Kleinian critique of how psychic defence mechanisms manage anxiety. Tyson chose to identify with the 'bad guy' identity which was enacted as a response to his childhood bullying. Jefferson recounts the famous key moment in Tyson's childhood, which has also achieved apocryphal status in boxing mythology, when a bully killed one of his pet pigeons and Tyson fought back, beating the bully (1996: 159). Jefferson argues that Tyson embraced the 'tough guy discourse' (1998: 77) which he sees as enabling a version of agency which victimhood would not. Tyson's '"burning intensity" and the strength of his identification with boxing, is not just about winning, becoming the champ, about "money and power without compromise"; it is also about a set of desires or needs, usually suppressed, that occasionally burst through the conscious motivations' (1996: 164). The working through the contradictions, for example in the case of Tyson, can, of course, be applied more widely to demonstrate that there are psychic roots of the rage that is enacted within boxing which in no way undermines the structural inequalities that can be seen to contribute to some of the anxieties to which anger gives expression.

Whilst Jefferson's account of psychic processes in the management of internal conflict clearly has some purchase in an exploration of the engagement in the sport and its manifestations of violence, it is more difficult to apply his specific biographical narratives to spectatorship. This is not to suggest that there are not psychic dimensions to watching as well as taking part, as I shall show in Chapter 6. The spectatorship of violence, whilst concerning what is represented and what is most material also suggests an excess that goes beyond what can be symbolized, although there is clearly an element of projection of the fears and anxieties of those who watch onto the spectacle being enacted in the ring. Manifestations of the unconscious in boxing, whether in its practice or spectatorship or involvement in its networks and culture, goes beyond assumed routines and taken-for-granted ways of being in the world. The unconscious is apparent in the excess of conflict and in the irrational and troubling aspects of boxing identifications.

Slavoj Žižek develops the Lacanian distinction between the Real and reality and argues that the Real is outside discourse and cannot be accommodated or described within it. Žižek and Dolar argue that 'the ultimate lesson of psychoanalysis [is] that human life is never 'just life': humans are not simply alive but are possessed by the strange desire to enjoy life to excess, passionately attached to a surplus that derails the ordinary run of things' (2002: 107). The notion that there can be anything outside representation is itself problematic. As Stephen Frosh points out, even among those who support the usefulness of a Lacanian Real trying to write about what is not expressible is 'difficult without lapsing into mysticism' (2002: 152). However, the other aspect of writing about the unwritable and symbolizing the unsymbolizable is that where it is attempted it is more often done in the context of the avant-garde (Kristeva, 1987) or of work of some artistic merit (Žižek, 2002) than in relation to sport as an aspect of popular culture. However this is not to say that the extra-discursive cannot be accessed through more popular media. The discourse of boxing is often characterized by dramatic, even poetic language and an attempt to invoke that which cannot be expressed.

Žižek's Lacanian Real is more than a Freudian unconscious. This is a real which is experienced as an absence, but nevertheless an absence which is ubiquitous and dogs our every track. The real is that from which we recoil, illustrated by Sigourney Weaver in *Alien* recoiling from the monstrous figure of the alien 'the subject constitutes itself by rejecting the slimy substance of *jouisssance*' (Žižek 1993: 62); a taking pleasure in that which seems anything but pleasurable and certainly not pleasant. In some of his work Žižek (1992) presents the Real as disgusting; a monstrous entity, which can also be linked to pleasure, but only insofar as it involves the inseparability of revulsion and titillation, by looking at that which is disgusting or humiliating, like turning to look at road accidents or watching violent films or witnessing the violence that can take place in the ring, knowing that this violence can go to extremes. The Real exists only in contradistinction to reality and thus matches the limitations of languages. Sarah Kay suggests the Lacanian trope of describing the Real as something which is stuck to the sole of your shoe and which cannot be removed (2003: 4). Žižek's Real seems more useful in locating disgust and alienation than pleasure, although its ambiguity, which must surely be necessary because it cannot be symbolized, affords a point of entry into that which cannot be explained discursively or which presents disruption to the shared norms of performance.

Boxing identifications are not only reproduced through heroic narratives. The Real offers one route into the instatement of the psychic into the discursive which Judith Butler has agreed is a necessary antidote to Foucauldian versions of the social (1993). The internal conflicts over the identities that are reproduced in boxing for both participants and spectators recruited into its culture and practices suggest that a discursive explanation of the processes that are implicated, is insufficient to accommodate the passion and excess, especially as marked by the 'attraction of repulsion'. Butler, however, forcefully rejects the Real upon which Žižek's whole explanatory framework is based because of what she perceives as its deeply misogynist relationship to gender difference. However, there are some points of consonance which might make Žižek's Real redeemable or even applicable to exploration of such a violent activity so deeply wrought with contradictions. Butler agrees that any 'theory of discursive constitution of the subject must take into account the domain of foreclosure, of what must be repudiated for the subject itself to emerge' (1993: 190). She also points to the problematic of symbolizing what cannot be symbolized although she accepts the usefulness of Žižek's reworking of the Althusserian understanding of interpellation. So much of the culture of boxing and of its stories and recruitment of subjects is framed within a structure of masculinity which associates its violence with that masculinity that it can be argued that gendered subjects are hailed at an unconscious level. It may be safer to explain the violence of boxing as a discursive mechanism of iterative practices which through repetition become stabilized; invoking the unconscious may itself be dangerous. Attempting to explain violence makes one complicit in its practices. However, there are moments, especially in spectatorship where the relationship between what is seen and who sees it necessarily involves some complicity and collusion and acknowledgement of the psychic as well as the discursive dimensions of identification. Unconscious identifications are made with gender, notably masculinity, in a manner that presents enormous difficulties for women in forging a version of femininity that would be recognisable. This is manifest in the discursive practices and apparatuses in the field of boxing and through the particular investments in masculinities which afford some stability however far this involves misrecognition in psychoanalytic terms.

Conclusion

This chapter has explored some of the ways in which the routine and the dramatic combine, along with the personal investments that are made in the public displays of boxing in order to evaluate the extent to which boxing identities, especially masculinities, are discursively produced and reconstructed. The visual images and narratives of boxing and particular aspects of the sport's visibility and invisibility in the public terrain constitute particular, gendered identities. The drama of boxing is distinctive, especially when witnessed live, as opposed to what Oates calls the more 'sanitized matches broadcast on television' (2002: 155). The very purpose of boxing is both dramatic and real and beset by contradictions which demand some acknowledgement of unconscious as well as conscious forces in play and challenge the adequacy of purely discursive accounts of identity formation. Boxing masculinities are not simple stories of heroic endeavour. For example, the status accorded to the sport's more violent protagonists, like Mike Tyson, also reflects and refracts dilemmas and paradoxes of masculinity that are experienced outside the parameters of the ring and the boundaries of this particular sport. Some versions of heroic masculinity occupy prominent places in boxing. The rags-to-riches, ghetto-to-the-mainstream stories are part of boxing's imaginary, and underpin identifications that are made with heroic public figures. However, there is diversity in the identities that are so constituted. Narratives of celebrity are part of the visibility of the 'good guys' in boxing, but 'bad guys' and 'mixed-up guys' also feature in these spaces within representations of boxing and some boxers move from one position to another.

The heroes of boxing are much more likely to be associated with masculinity than with femininity; it is difficult, although not impossible, as I have shown, to find heroic figures with whom women can identify. Whilst women can and also do adopt the subject position of the hero, the dominance and visibility of masculine heroes is a powerful force of exclusion, as is the collusion of those who are implicated in making meaning about boxing and in its visual and visible culture, as well as in the silences that such complicities can produce. Routine masculinities include collusive practices outside the gym and extend into the wider field and the networks through which boxing stories are told.

Boxing stories are neither simple nor framed within coherent heroic trajectories. Masculinities, as represented by the major protagonists of the sport and key figures in its networks, mirror the 'dark trade' (McRae, 1996) of boxing, including its transgressive aspects, as well as its honourable, courageous identifications. The 'attraction of repulsion' of boxing presents versions of masculinity which attract but are not necessarily attractive. Identities have to achieve some settlement of these internal contradictions. Such masculinities have to accommodate fear and ambivalence as well as honourable heroism. The distinctive nature of the violent encounters of the sport and the threat, if not necessarily the actuality of injury and harm, both create and address anxiety. These are pre-emptive masculinities, in which people invest in order to resolve the very problems they generate. The routine masculinities enacted through the networks of boxing present explanations of collusive masculinities, but in their focus upon belonging they underplay the tensions that are implicit in such identities.

The most visible aspects of boxing are associated with men and with a particular version of heroic masculinity, although this heroism takes many different forms and is, as with the beautiful bodies of boxing, haunted by the ghosts of failure; of the broken body and of the fallen hero. The heroes are, however, mainly men and boxing stories are mostly about masculinity. This is changing, even within such a traditional sport. Women are emerging as heroes, often through some association with male stars, like Laila Ali and Jacqui Frazier, but women are beginning to tell their own stories. It is, however, difficult to tell these stories without invoking the discourse of heroic masculinity and to find a space within which women can speak. There are few public narratives, especially of any longevity which inform heroic boxing stories and representations and I have argued that it is through the stories that are told that identity positions become established, if only temporarily or even momentarily.

The elision of 'men' with masculinity arises from the embodiment of boxing identities and the status of the material body in the sport. As this chapter has demonstrated, the gendered genealogy of boxing with its reliance on visible, gendered differences has also played a significant part in the making of masculinities. It will be apparent that there is some slippage here between the use of the terms 'men' and 'masculinity', whereas most of this book has been concerned with masculinities. I have not suggested that women cannot 'do' masculinity or that such a gendered identity is the prerogative of those who are classified as or would call themselves men. However, stories of masculinity that are told and which inform and make up the masculinities as gendered identities which have particular status, are those which feature people who are men and offer to do so by excluding or marginalizing, or even mocking, those who are women. The most pervasive discourse which rationalizes women's marginalization in boxing involves appeals to vulnerable corporeality and an ethics of protection. This makes it difficult for women to 'do' heroic masculinity in this space without adopting the aggression of traditional machismo, either as a boxer or as a spectator and mimicking that version of masculinity. Arguments for greater inclusion and increased recognition of women's boxing are largely phrased in a discourse of equality deploying counter arguments to these claims of women's frailty. Neither of these takes cognisance of the primacy of cultural constructions of gendered identities within the sport and the enormous difficulties which are presented to women in having to 'do' heroic masculinity or find some new version of heroism which permits inclusion and active, agentic participation.

There are pivotal moments in identity narratives at which there may be recognition and identification. The interpellation that takes place in the context of sport offers particularly gendered and racialized inflections, which have to accommodate ambivalence, inconsistency and disruption. Althusser's concept of interpellation highlights the ways in which people are recruited into subject positions, especially when considered in conjunction with the narrativization of the self that is made possible not only through the individual's life course experience and imaginings, but through the public symbolic, discursive space in which meanings are made and in which sport plays a major role. By focusing on the interrelationship between public and personal stories and the ways in which visibility and invisibility are configured, I have argued for an understanding of identity and identification which is synthetic. Subjects are made and re-made through making investment in identities which offer some stability and sense of belonging, however momentary this may be. Cinematic representations offer particular cultural moments within the wider arena, outside specifically sporting boundaries, for making such investments and for recruitment into identity positions, and boxing occupies a special place in film, which is the subject of Chapter 6.

When the going gets tough
Going to the movies

Introduction

Films engage with and reconstruct dreams, fears, aspirations and dramas that are woven into the routine of everyday life, none more so than in 'boxing films'. Cinema offers a field for the exploration of the discursive production of masculinities and the psychic investments that are made through the processes of identification. Technologies operate within specific material circumstances and create new modes of understanding. As Walter Benjamin argued, film provided a transformation of perception akin to that of psychoanalysis:

> The film has enriched our field of perception with methods which can be illustrated by those of Freudian theory . . . the film, on the one hand, extends our comprehension of the necessities which rule our lives; on the other, it manages to assure us of an immense and unexpected field of action . . . With the close-up, space expands; with slow motion, movement is extended . . . slow motion not only presents familiar qualities of movement but reveals them in entirely unknown ones . . . The camera introduces us to unconscious optics as does psychoanalysis to unconscious impulses.
>
> (1999 [1936]: 77–8)

Benjamin was writing about the early days of film technologies and his ideas have been developed in diverse ways more recently, for example in relation to the impact of technoscience (Haraway, 1991) and in the gendering of cinematic representations (Humm, 1997). The point remains that technologies are implicated in the transformation of perception and subjectivity. Films are a key component of visual culture and offer a most useful vehicle for the exploration of the privileged cultural status of the visual in a medium which is particularly marked by gendered differences. The cinema and films, which are increasingly viewed on DVD in the home, offer a space in which the fantasies that make up identity formation and the processes through which selves are created and reinstated can be located. A film like *Fight Club*, which embraced new developments in film-making, depends heavily on the rapid interspersal of images for delivering its message of the complex interrelationship between the narrator and his alter ego, Durden. This was made possible by technologies that permit the possibility of pausing and freezing frames and facilitate the deconstruction of what might appear to be subliminal messages.

Although boxing is a high-profile sport with massive investment which still retains a strong following, it does not occupy so mainstream a position as do popular sports such as American football, baseball and basketball in the US and football, in Europe and South America, for example in news and sports media pages and on television networks (especially terrestrial TV). One of the most positive celebratory points at which boxing moves centre stage is through the spectacle of film. However, although boxing films have a long history, the cinematic depiction of combat in the ring does involve a set of aesthetic and ethical relationships which might be antithetical to commercial movie making. Films are part of the wider cultural terrain in which these tensions and their implications for the reconfiguration of identities are played out.

This chapter explores some of the ways in which masculinities are made and remade through the representation of films, for example in the fight film genre and what could be called 'boxing films'. It is worth noting, however, that many films are either only tangentially associated with boxing or, even if they do purport to be 'about boxing' 'are always about so much more, especially, they are about social commentary more or less bound up with issues of masculinity' (Buscombe, 2005: 67). The archetypal boxer in film has traditionally been portrayed as a singular heroic figure of troubled masculinity. This figure is 'a romantic-modernist representation of existential man in all his bleak grandeur [who] attained definition in Hollywood post World War 11, but also in other visual and textual arts' (Mellor, 1996: 81). In the twenty-first century the trope of the heroic triumph over adversity and especially economic disadvantage, persists, for example with *Cinderella Man* in 2005. In this film, cited in the Introduction to this book, Russell Crowe, of *Gladiator* fame, plays the impoverished ex-prizefighter James Braddock who, down on his luck, along with vast numbers of other Americans during the Great Depression of the 1930s, having lost money in the Wall Street Crash, returns to boxing in an attempt to save his family. Familiar narratives of honour, desire for respect and self-esteem combine to repeat a story of honour whereby a fighter retired form the ring, against the odds, is able to take on Max Baer, the then heavyweight champion of the world and lift the title.

The cinema presents and re-presents particular versions of the narratives of heroic masculinity which resonate with those forged at other sites and through different stories. For example Muhammad Ali's heroic status, reconstituted at different points in his biography and is manifest at so many sites, including cinema. The heroic masculinity of the champion of civil rights such as Ali is one version which collides with the 'bad guy' heroes and anti-heroes, who are also always present in boxing stories and the 'mixed-up guys' whose 'bad guy' status at particular moments can be understood within the specificities of their biographies of disadvantage and oppression. Ali's own biography has involved troubled moments in his relationship with the state and mainstream white culture.

Boxing films are frequently implicated in the representation of violence in the cinematic context. This invokes associations of violence within boxing, which Kevin Mitchell calls the 'glamour of violence' (2003). One of the most highly rated boxing films ever made, Martin Scorsese's *Raging Bull*, has scenes of violence that are resonant of the experience of witnessing a fight and of 'being there'. Scorsese's hallmark themes of violent men in crisis and his 'signature directorial style with flashy, imaginative visual flourishes, long and complex takes and pervasive pop music in the background' (French, 2004: 125) lend themselves well to a powerfully intense portrayal of boxing and the elision of anger, corporeal contact and aggression. The intensity of the spectacle invokes anxieties about voyeuristic spectatorship which are integral to the practice as well as the representation of boxing. As I have argued in this book, boxing is beset by ambiguities and contradictions and this chapter also examines the ambivalences in cinematic representations and the contradictions they reproduce, all of which contribute to the development of theories which offer explanations of the enactment, representation and experience of masculinity in the context of accommodating disruptions and managing anxiety.

Boxing films, like so many in the mainstream of cinema, which is a medium that trades in fantasy, may also appear to represent hyperbole and excess. Mitchell, following the claims of the boxing writer Richard Hoffer about the melodrama and hyperbole of the sport, argues that such films are not required to exaggerate; characters such as Don King, Mike Tyson and Jake La Motta are already personalities writ large (2005c). This raises questions, however, about the relationship between what is real and what is artifice and between the actual pugilist and the actor who plays him, or, more rarely, her. There is some illustration, in the discussion which follows, of how boxing films and boxing itself are subject to exaggeration and hyperbole in some respects, and that it is boxing which aspires to magnification. Actors are expected to become caricatures of themselves, just as some actual boxers enact an excessive version of masculinity. Boxing and boxing films, especially, illustrate well the manifestation of excess and the complex relationship between authenticity and deception and between fantasy and reality.

Hyperbole also serves to reinstate gender binaries. The overstatement of masculinity reconstitutes the exclusion of femininity and the necessary avowal that boxing is for 'real men'. Masculinity is also constructed in relation to femininity through the inclusion of actual women in the narrative or of recognisably feminine traits and attributes and the status of women within the fight film genre. This raises questions about the fixity or fluidity of gender identities and the spaces occupied by women in these stories of heroic masculinity. How can women 'do' the versions of masculinity which are played out in films? What sort of figures of heroism might be made available for women? These questions are all located within the context of films as a particular aspect of representation marked out by fantasy. So where do boxing films fit into these debates?

Out of the ring and into the mainstream

The sport of boxing has a very special place in film history and boxing films represent a long tradition. There have been some 150 films made, starting with some very early recordings of fights, including eight minutes of Gentleman Jim Corbett against Peter Courtney in East Orange, New Jersey in 1894 (Mitchell, 2005c). Boxing was seen to have enormous potential as a spectator sport as early as the late nineteenth century, which transforming technologies could make more widely available and which could benefit the development of those very technologies. Performance and display are integral to boxing as was argued in Chapter 5. It was a 'Gentleman Jim' Corbett fight, the 1897 Fitzsimmons–Corbett fight in the US, which was the site of the first such representations. This was not just a technological experiment. 'Filming of the fight was always integral to its planning' (McKernan, 1998). This event in a wooden amphitheatre, with peepholes for cameras, in Nevada to which 17,000 were invited, although only 4,000 were able to attend, was crucial in shaping future links between film, spectacle and fighting. The National Film and Television Archive has 11,000 feet of film remaining. Sadly, the final stages of the fight are not included in this footage, because when Corbett assaulted Fitzsimmons the ring was filled with a crowd that was eager to join in (McKernan, 1998). Boxing can certainly excite a crowd, but there is a more general point about the appeal of spectacle, especially that which focuses upon violence, which is considered in this chapter in relation to the particular draw of motion pictures.

Over a century of cinematic history since these early films were made has seen a large range of productions that could loosely be called 'boxing films'. It is a loose affiliation and there is enormous diversity, ranging from those films which explicitly tell a boxing story, for example Robert Rosen's *Body and Soul* (1947), Robert Wise's *The Set-up* (1949) and Mark Robson's *Champion* (1949), to films like David Fincher's *Fight Club* (1999) which are more tangentially concerned with the sport of boxing. Other films like Quentin Tarantino's *Pulp Fiction* (1994) have a boxing/fight element and can be cited illustratively, but could not be said to be 'about boxing', although boxing films are never *just* about boxing. The internal conflicts of *Fight Club*, like the Palahniuk novel upon which it is based, is concerned with dislocation and alienation played out in scenes of violent pugilism. *Fight Club* explicitly engages with psychic conflict and brings together the discursive regimes of pugilism, especially as enacted outside the law and the workings of the internal, psychic drama of its main protagonist. The films that might be more narrowly categorized as 'boxing films' have often been bio-pics, some of the most notable being the Ali movies. Boxing biographies reconstruct heroes, largely through chronological life stories, like Michael Mann's *Ali* (2001) and Robert Wise's *Someone Up There Likes Me* (1956) about Rocky Graziano. They also focus on pivotal moments in boxing history, such as the *Rumble in the Jungle* (1974), classified as a documentary film and its reincarnation in 1996 in Leon Gast's, *When We Were Kings* and, in 2000, *One Nation Divisible*, on the Frazier–Ali rivalry, again arising from key boxing moments.

The late 1940s and 1950s could be seen as the golden era of boxing movies. Fight films of this period were somewhat pessimistic and brooding, demonstrating the relevance of the economic and social context of film-making and the ways in which cinema can engage with contemporary concerns. The post-war era with its 'rampant inflation, unemployment, labour strife, shifting social patterns' (Telotte, 1989: 4) and the politically anxious climate of the cold war provided a space in which the boxing film which adopted the passive hero characterized by a crisis of masculinity in the face of the criminals, aggressive state agencies and vampiric women of *film noir* could flourish. The boxing film provides a most appropriate vehicle for the exploration of existential angst, especially in relation to masculinity, at a time of change. The ring and all that goes with it becomes a moral arena for the interrogation of identity. Deborah Thomas goes further and suggests that: 'What was normal during the war – close male companionship, sanctioned killing . . . and more casual sexual behaviour – became deviant in the context of post-war calm' (1992: 60). A film like *The Set Up* (1949) can be seen as the apogee of the heroic boxer who secures authenticity through suffering and is able to overcome the forces of corruption ranged against him. Such a film could be seen as representing the moral high moment coded as both 'true' and authentic, but which it has been difficult to regain (Mellor, 1996). The one-on-one combat of boxing affords a representational site where elemental oppositions, involving good and evil, the inauthentic and the authentic and the 'real' and the 'not real' might be accessed. This is a complex issue in film. As Vivian Sobchack argues, the *not real* is: 'Clearly contrasted to our cultural and historical sense of what constitutes the real (as in a patently "impossible", "fantastic" or even "implausible" fiction)' (2004: 258).

The boxing film, especially in some of the exaggerations of the later *Rocky* series, appear to engage with the 'not real', as the impossible. However, in the drama of boxing the ring is itself exaggerated and carries the threat of excess. For those who engage in the sport and those who watch, there is always the threat of 'what if' things went too far. The one-on-one corporeality of boxing makes this engagement all the more authentic and, although the spectator in the cinema is not drawn into the reality of the fight which invokes responses from all the senses, for Sobchack, even when viewing films, there is no separation between vision and visibility and embodiment, or between the viewer and what is seen. The response is still embodied in all senses.

Films which engage with violence may reflect violence in the wider cultural terrain and are historically specific. However, confronting the excesses of violence and negotiating aggression and anger is not always on the public agenda. Films reflect and reproduce contingent gender identities. The growth of pacifism in the 1960s might have been inimical to the heroism of the pugilist (James, 1996). However, the 1970s saw the production of films engaging with the cultural construction of masculinity often framed in terms of what it meant to be a 'real man', for example in relation to the development of the *Rocky* series and *Raging Bull*. More recently there has been greater diversity with *Ali*, *Rumble in the Jungle*,

When We Were Kings and *The Boxer*, set in a UK context and focusing on the Troubles in Northern Ireland, as well as films which include women boxers, such as *Girlfight* (2000) and *Million Dollar Baby* (2005), retelling the narrative of exclusion and the transition from the trailer park or the ghetto to the ring.

Boxers become part of the popular imagination through their place in the movies, whether they are actual fighters or fictional ones like Rocky Balboa, a film character albeit reputedly based on the actual boxer, Chuck Wepner. Some boxers might have passed into cultural oblivion, apart from the memories of the boxing cognoscenti, if it had not been for cinematic representation. Were it not for Robert de Niro's Academy Award winning performance and Martin Scorsese's direction of *Raging Bull*, Jake La Motta might not be still remembered (Tosches, 1997). Cinema plays an important role in the reconfiguration of heroes and boxing heroes and villains are always implicated in the social and cultural processes through which they are constituted. Transforming identities and the processes of identification are historically specific, although there are emerging patterns in the fight film genre.

Representation, film and fantasy

Films demonstrate the discursive meanings attached to changing masculinities and the processes through which they are transformed or reproduced. These cinematic meanings articulate with some of the continuities of psychic investment in these identities. Film offers a particular field of representation which links language and meaning to culture. All representation has some relationship with what it represents. The term literally means presenting something again. The process of representation alters the reality of the original; in films representation involves making a claim on and about reality. Thus the process of representation when applied to film involves maximizing the experience so that the audience is drawn into the drama. For example, 'films use continuity editing to create the illusion, not that this *is* the real world, but that the world the film creates has a reality of its own, a reality that acts in much the same way as the reality of the world outside the text behaves' (Grossberg *et al.*, 1998: 179). Film makers deploy a range of technologies so that the audience 'forgets' that this is a text and is absorbed and taken up in the world of the film and can imagine the actualization of the world that is being represented. Representation in the cinema is not, of course, always realist, but it is always making a claim about reality. Realism, as a genre, focusing upon the sordid or horrific or the banal and the minutiae of the everyday, displayed in black and white and employing the devices of the documentary, is the most obvious way in which particular texts like boxing films with all their potential for low life depiction and bloody detail, can make claims about what is real. However, realism always operates ideologically in that the text, in this case the film, makes claims about the world in which the audience lives and about what is real and possible. However fantastical the *Rocky* series has become, for example in their deployment of virtual technologies and somewhat crude political oppositions, they are still making a stake in the real world of boxing. Films as representations have to be believable even if their links with the world outside the cinema are tenuous. Boxing films are also part of the culture which mediates and makes meanings, not only in the ring, but also in the wider cultural field and the social world in which the sport is performed and experienced. In discussing the significance of films I am taking what Hall calls a constructionist approach to representation in that representation can never be purely reflective or innocent in the processes that are implicated in making meanings (1997). Much is made of reality and authenticity in boxing films in relation to the socio-economic reality of the boxers' lives and the authenticity of boxing itself and of its practitioners. However, they are not only realist in the techniques deployed to support a mimetic reflection of the real world outside the screen. Films also constitute a discursive reality, for example in particular versions of heroic masculinity, and can be read discursively. Representations are produced through symbolic systems and sets of practices, language and image, but an analysis of the discursive alone may be insufficient to explain the draw of such representations and much of the work undertaken in film studies has necessarily engaged with psychoanalytical perspectives.

Do we need psychoanalytic film theories?

There are strong arguments for understanding the making of masculinity through narrative tropes, which can be read discursively. However, so violent an enterprise, whether in practice or in representation, also demands explanations which go beyond that which can be understood as manifestation of the practices of rational individuals or the outcome of particular mechanisms and apparatuses of regulation. Much of the critical analysis of the different elements in cinema, including text and spectatorship has been framed within psychoanalytic theories, which engage with unconscious meanings as well as those of the conscious mind. As Stuart Hall has argued, 'many of the images' "effects" operate, not just "discursively" but at the symbolic and psychic level of the unconscious' (1999: 311). Hall cites Jacqueline Rose's use of the links noted by Freud between sexuality and visual representation (1986). On the journey to adult sexuality the child takes as a model scenes or staged events, *mise-en-scène*,

> which demonstrate the complexity of an essentially visual space . . . The sexuality lies less in the content of what is seen than in the subjectivity of the viewer . . . The relationship between the viewer and scene is always one of fracture, partial identification, pleasure and distrust.
>
> (1986: 411)

It is through such scenes that meanings are constructed, however fragmented and ambivalent these meanings may be. A psychoanalytic framework offers the advantage of incorporating subjective experience into an analysis of visual, cinematic images and narratives and accords some importance to the significance of looking and the symbolic power of the visual image with its identificatory potential, for example in recruiting gendered subjects. Such images and scenes are crucial in the process of forming racialized and gendered subjects. Cinema both engages with the threat of excess and the trauma of instability. This is a space within which insecurity and ambivalence can be accommodated, if not resolved. Boxing heroes offer the fantasy of a stable masculinity.

One way of marking out bounded masculinity is by the exclusion of femininity and the establishment of the security of mythical, often embodied borders which cannot be breached. The 'othering' of femininity is effected through the dynamics of exclusion. Part of what masculine selves have to pre-empt is association with the perceived fragility of femininity. In the spaces created by the fight film genre these borders are secured, or rather there are attempts to secure them, through particular narratives through which masculinity is constructed and reconstructed.

The vulnerability and instability of masculinity, even in men's boxing where it might be at its most hegemonic and secure, makes the 'Object Relations' school understanding of the defended self attractive as an explanatory framework for making sense, not only of participation in boxing, but also of its cinematic pull. Kleinians argue that it is the projective processes which are linked to the preservation of the self and the irrational defence mechanisms which are operating. Many male boxers cite the experience of being bullied as a child as reason for their taking up boxing as a means of defending themselves from playground bullies (Woodward, 2004). Tony Jefferson's work on Mike Tyson supports this explanation by tracing the origins of Tyson's transformation from 'fairy boy' to 'destroyer' and world champion (1996). In a space hitherto securely marked out as masculine, there may be some awareness of the threat of invasion, for example by women boxers and by 'new' masculinities which challenge this version of hegemony. Deep-rooted identity structures are unsettled and projected outwards. The heroes of boxing films resolve both the material problems of economic disadvantage and social exclusion and the personal insecurities of vulnerability, many of which relate to bodily experience and fear of physical weakness.

However, the psychoanalytic approaches which have been most influential in exploring the field of cinematic representations are undoubtedly the Lacanian, with Laura Mulvey's now famous 1975 article, 'Visual pleasure and the narrative cinema' amounting to what could be called a seminal text; it has certainly provoked an enormous engagement with debate about the sexual subject and its relationship to the cinema, which has been most fruitful. It is worth revisiting here because of its impact in the field of film studies and, more especially, because of the resonance of its implications for analyses of fight films with their strong patriarchal trajectories. Mulvey used Jacques Lacan's reworking of Freud to explore the representation of subjectivity in cinema with the intention of using psychoanalytic theory to demonstrate how patriarchal society has structured film.

As she states at the start of her original article, she 'intends to use psychoanalysis to discover where and how the fascination of film is reinforced by pre-existing patterns of fascination already at work within the individual subject and the social formations that have moulded him [sic]' (1975: 6).

In her use of Freud's understanding of scopophilia, as the desire to look at another as an erotic object, it is 'the gaze' which is central to Mulvey's original critique. Her original claim that 'the male gaze', which is the main mechanism of filmic control and which thus constructs the male gaze as active and female spectatorship as passive, has been challenged in many different ways since she first propounded her theory. Mulvey claimed that the gaze was male. The camera is usually operated by a man, the look of male actors within the film is structured to objectify women and create male power and the gaze of the male spectator mediated through the camera and the male actors further conspires to a representation of women which is fetishistic. Even when women look at women on screen they do so through men's eyes. Mulvey's reconsideration of her original work in 'Afterthoughts on "Visual pleasure and narrative cinema"' (1989) reiterates much of her critique of mainstream, especially Hollywood cinema, with Hollywood genre films being seen as structured around masculine pleasure and offering only masculine identification for the female character and spectator.

Others have claimed that whilst Mulvey's insights are particularly productive in their combination of psychoanalytic theory and narrative and focus upon gender, they are also limited in their rejection of mainstream cinema and rejection of a more democratic gaze (King, 1992) for example, a female gaze and a gay gaze. Although Mulvey's work has been located within a politics that seeks to overcome inequalities and injustices, especially in relation to gender, the universal claims of psychoanalysis make it difficult to address the material specificities of 'race', 'ethnicity' and class. However, Mulvey's work does reveal the normative power of the male gaze in dominant systems of representation, such as Hollywood films, which can be applied to other forms of looking. For example, the female nude is not so much a representation of heterosexual male desire, but a form of objectification which endorses and reinstates male dominance over the apparatus of representation itself and thus, I would argue, hegemonic masculinity. Kobena Mercer, in his analysis of Black Males, the work of the photographer, Robert Mapplethorpe, has suggested that this can be applied to other forms of racialized representation, using black skin as a most visible marker of racial difference, rather as the female nude is presented as the most obvious marker of gender difference and the male gaze. Mercer analyses these photographs as cultural artefacts which can be used to explore how white people 'look' at black people, especially black men, for whom, in these representations, male sexuality is seen as excessive and 'other' (Mercer, 1990). Mercer suggests that Mapplethorpe appropriates elements of common racial stereotypes and aestheticizes them into works of art, playing with the ambivalence of the colonial discourse of black men as represented either as sexual threats to white male dominance or as subordinate and passive. In Mapplethorpe's photographs of black men they are both feminized as objects of the gaze and as models in an art work and represented as beautiful and sexually powerful. This example is cited here to illustrate the relevance of an approach which focuses upon the power that is implicit in ways of looking, which operate at the level of the psyche and the possibilities that are afforded by different cinematic representations through the desires with which they engage.

In her later work Mulvey has reflected on her own films and the role of the avant-garde and especially the transforming technologies of film-making (2005), but what is important for my purposes here is the 'putting into discourse' by Mulvey of theories of subjectivity which have allied the techniques of film-making to spectatorship. This approach sets out the idea that the spectator's pleasure in looking is shaped by the structure and language of the film. The subject is always constituted within a set of psychical relationships and fantasies which relate to the public arena of representations of which cinema is one.

Fantasy and reality?

The concept of fantasy is not only a prime concern of psychoanalysis, it is also used extensively in everyday language to encompass imagined scenarios and unattainable desires which may be contrasted with a more mundane and routinely realizable reality. Fantasy, with its etymological roots in 'making visible', has come to be understood to refer to that which is there, but not seen directly. Fantasy involves different levels, of material reality and of conscious thoughts and unconscious desires. Psychoanalysis provides a particularly useful application to films (Cowie, 1999). Freud claimed that fantasy hovers between three time modes, 'the present provides a context, the material elements of the fantasy; the past, the wish, deriving from earliest experiences; the dreamer then imagines a new situation, in the future which represents a fulfilment of the wish (Cowie, 1999 [1997]: 365). The relationship between material reality cannot be simply translated into a conventional binary of real life and fiction. Freud acknowledged that there is a necessary distinction between psychical reality and the material world (1953 [1900]), 'Fantasy [is] a privileged terrain on which social reality and the unconscious are engaged in a figuring which intertwines them both' (Freud, 1953 [1900]: 265).

Freud makes a distinction between unconscious fantasies, such as dreams and conscious fantasies, such as daydreams, although he sees both as doing the same psychic work so that the two cannot be separated (Laplanche and Pontalis, 1968). In film, fantasy occupies the public terrain, bringing together the desires of the unconscious into the expression of fantasy in a space which is publicly available. The psychoanalytic concept of fantasy offers a route into understanding the appeal of the heroic narratives of boxing films and their status in the constitution of masculinity. Fantasizing, whether unconsciously, for example as in dreams which may then be interpreted in the conscious waking hours, or consciously, constitutes the psychic reality through which subjectivity is created. Films offer a space in which subjects are recruited through the fantasies re-presented in the text, which is a public story. Similarly, for the individual, fantasy is not simply a matter of summoning up imaginary objects. It involves staging a scenario and putting that which is submerged into the picture as a *mise-en-scène*; that is, occupying 'the space between perception and consciousness' as Jacques Lacan later described it (1977: 56).

Psychoanalytic theories prioritize the original fantasy which is located within the family, notably in the experience of the resolution of the Oedipus conflict, suggesting that all fantasies revert to the original, which might imply that all fantasies follow the same path. As Roland Barthes has argued, 'Doesn't every narrative lead back to Oedipus? Isn't storytelling always a way of searching for one's origins, speaking one's conflicts with the law, entering into a dialectic of tenderness and hatred?' (1973: 47).

However, the search for belonging does not always take the journey of a search for the 'myth of origin' related to psychoanalytic understandings of entry into the Lacanian 'Law of the Father'. The desire to belong and to secure an identity position can also be seen as operating in very diverse ways through fantasies in public stories as well as private ones. The 'dialectic of tenderness and hatred' is not only played out repetitively in the public stories that are told in films, but also in fantasized scenarios which are infinitely various and 'shifting with the new impressions received every day, changing to fit the new situations and contexts of the subject' (Cowie, 1999: 365).

Boxing films offer specific and changing representations that bring together these different and multi-faceted levels of fantasy and material reality. This material reality is manifest in corporeal reality, for example in the representations of fight sequences. Materiality is also presented by highlighting the social, economic and political circumstances of the boxers. These aspects of materiality support the claim that these films are characterized by realism, which is evident in the cinematic techniques deployed to convey the poverty of the spatial locations of the boxer and the gym and the brutality of the ring. As the series has progressed, the *Rocky* films have become increasingly far removed from any classification as realist, or even, it can be argued, as boxing films; Oates argues that they are 'scarcely about boxing, as we know it . . . but [are] effective as pop-iconographic success stories starring Sylvester Stallone as Rocky . . . the sweet guy, the perpetual underdog who cannot lose even against overwhelming odds. Rocky is a comic book boxer' (1987: 58). The tone of the series is exploitative of the genre, but they are useful to the analysis of the links between fantasy and reality for a number of reasons, including, especially, the relationship between celebrity, actor and movie text as part of the mainstream cinema.

These elisions between fantasy and reality, between actor, actual boxer and the role in the movies are complicated. As Richard Dyer argues, there is an instability in the relationship between the star actor in the movies and the part being played. At times the fit is perfect and he cites Sylvester Stallone as Rocky Balboa as presenting the viewer with no problems in perceiving Sly as Rocky. He *is* Rocky. Dyer suggests this is because 'there is a set of cultural categories to which both

Figure 6.1 Stallone *is* Rocky (Photo: © Empics)

role and star image refer, beyond that of performer in movies' (1998: 509). Stallone presents the viewer with a convincing narrative of white working-class advancement which fits Rocky 'like a glove'. Stallone understands perfectly the symbiosis between boxing and its cinematic, on-screen representation. This may be due to his skill as an actor, but why does it have such resonance? Stallone is relatively short, but in the films he becomes a heavyweight; he realizes the aspirations to the status of being heavyweight champion of the world. It is almost so excessive and caricatured that it appears ironic. However, whatever the excesses of *Rocky IV* especially, it may not always be entirely playful. Throughout the series, Rocky's transition into a champion may be too good to be true but, the 'rags to riches' narrative still has too powerful a purchase in the history of boxing and of dispossessed masculinities to be read simply as parody. Even *Rocky IV*, located somewhat absurdly in the consumer rewards of Reaganite postmodernity deploying technological devices to enhance its virtuality, still uses the familiar boxing film trope of engaging with the dreams of stardom.

The inspiration for Rocky Balboa, purported to be Chuck Wepner (Mitchell, 2005c) had little chance of realizing this dream, although his difficult, if interesting, life led Stallone to make the *Rocky* films. Wepner was a sufficiently good boxer to share the ring with Muhammad Ali on one occasion and his biography has some dramatic elements including a spell in prison. In some senses Wepner was a 'proper tough guy rather than a merely fictional one' (Mitchell, 2005c: 39). The social reality of Wepner's life might accord more closely with the material circumstances of a boxing career which are, in *Rocky*, transformed into the fantasies of achieving a recognized and recognizable success. The cinematic version has 'resonance and impact', however much it might be dismissed as over-sentimental and 'merely' fictional and by implication less 'real'.

Another aspect of reality is the opposition between real, understood as according with the lived experience of boxers, for example the actual Chuck Wepner, and the unreal, as inaccurate or even false. In this instance what is not real deviates from the actualities of experience rather than being an exaggeration or metaphor. Sporting narratives are imbued with tensions between the authentic and the inauthentic sometimes articulated as between the 'real' and the fake. In the practice of sport this dichotomy with its appeal to what is real and authentic is often located within a discussion of fandom. For example, in football (soccer) in the UK, 'real' fans are those who attend every match and have been supporters of one team or throughout their lives (Robson, 2000). In boxing and especially in boxing films, the discursive real, by which I mean the ways in which people appeal to authenticity and what is real in the text, and talk about reality and authenticity, is largely invoked in relation to the social and economic world of the boxer and, in films in particular, to the raw brutality of the ring which follows the gruelling regime of training and preparation.

Sexuality: beautiful bodies?

The material reality of boxing is closely implicated in representations of the body and the attraction of these bodies lie not only in their athletic competences but also in their aesthetic appeal as beautiful bodies. Boxing films offer a great opportunity for the display of beautiful, fit, male and very occasionally, female, bodies. William Hazlitt in his famous nineteenth-century description of *The Fight* prefigures much later writing and representation of boxers in film, 'Hickman might be compared to Diomed, light vigorous, elastic and his back glistened in the sun as he moved about like a panther's hide' (1982: 91).

However, boxing bodies are broken and damaged as well as fit and beautiful, as was argued in Chapter 3. If boxing bodies are sexualized then their viewing is deeply troubled. The spectator is drawn into a problematic terrain and positioned as the voyeur. Nick James points out that the dilemma for film makers is to maintain audience empathy for the boxer who nonetheless has to be portrayed as brutal and savage in the ring, yet attractive to women, especially within the heterosexual frame of Hollywood movies, and sympathetic in his life outside the ring. There are tensions underpinning the translation of sexuality into the terrain of violence in the ring, which has been informed by the traditional practice of keeping men and women separate, for example before a fight. This is common a practice in many sports and is based upon the idea that sexual activity might weaken the sportsman (*sic*) and reduce his aggression towards his opponents. The practice has much wider currency in men's sports than in women's. Whilst women athletes might need to concentrate on the competition there is the biologically reductionist idea that male athletes need to divert their sexual energies into the competition rather than into sexual activity, which might be coded in terms of aggression and competitiveness, linking male sexuality to a testosterone-fired hostility in a particular, over-simplified version of masculinity. However the understanding that fighters are redirecting sexual energy in combat does seem to compound the troubled alliance between aggression and sexuality; sex and combat can become interchangeable (James, 1996: 114).

Another expression of sexuality, explicitly heterosexuality, in mainstream boxing films is the ubiquitous relationship between the male boxer and a woman. Not only is sexuality a key component of identity, but also some version of gender difference is universal in identificatory processes. Masculinity is constructed in relation to the othering of femininity at myriad points within knowledge systems and practices. Women can be boxers, as in *Girlfight*, and *Million Dollar Baby*, where relationships between women and men are more often coded in a familial, father–daughter relationship. In *Girlfight* it is significant that Diana challenges her father's authority in taking up boxing and in *Million Dollar Baby*, Maggie's relationship with Frankie, the older, white, male trainer, which is central to the drama puts her in the position of a surrogate daughter. In the traditions of malestream, mainstream films women are often more marginal to the drama. They may be wives or girlfriends, who are the object of the boxer's violence outside the ring; they may be call-girls decorating the periphery. In each case women serve to affirm heterosexuality and serve to settle the troublesome homoeroticism of boxing. Women may occupy the position of comforter, such as the maternal figure witnessing the suffering in the ring as in *The Set Up*. In the 1940s and 1950s women represented protection from and resistance to the temptations of the world. The two figures available to women were as Madonnas, saintly wives/ mothers or whores, for example call-girls. They were also marked by their absence, such as in instances where they could not bear to be spectators and to look. The empty seat of the woman who cannot bear to witness the brutality of the ring in *The Set Up* is a poignant illustration of this.

Women are also part of the crowd. Since the mid-1970s women have also become tormentors from their ringside seats, for example in *The Harder They Fall*, the woman shouts aggressively from the ringside, 'You yellow dog!' when the dying Dundee is carried out on the stretcher. In *Pulp Fiction*, Esmerelda Villa Lobos is a more glamorous femme fatale witnessing the death of a fighter. However, she is not cheering at the ringside. She is more remote: coolly listening to the fight on her radio.

Viewing aggression in the ring with its subtext of diverted sexual energy also involves the concomitant notion that the spectator is drawn into an eroticized pleasure in viewing. The problem of the representation of violence is compounded by the difficulties that beset reproducing violence. Scorsese resolves this through

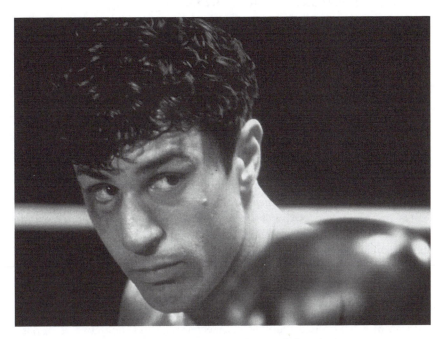

Figure 6.2 Robert de Niro in *Raging Bull* (Photo: © Empics)

his carefully constructed storyboards (French, 2004) which enable him to direct a stylized aesthetic of violence deploying choreographed, but convincing, flash-lit intensity in the ring that evokes the raw physical power of actual aggression. The beautiful, sexualized body is always mediated, however, by the ghosts of the broken body and the threat or promise of the unfit, aging body.

Raging Bull might be construed as re-presenting a nostalgic homage to the beautiful body which, in the narrative of the film, La Motta loses in his transition from lean, vicious destroyer to overweight, sad comic. This film, whatever its aesthetic risks and brilliant technical direction, remains within the boxing tradition of heroic narratives and, not only the story of the climb from rags to riches, but also that of the fall from grace, so often represented in the transformation of the beautiful body. Pam Cook argues, '*Raging Bull*, like its predecessors in the boxing genre, presents the powerful male body as an object of desire and identification, but moving towards the loss of male power. This loss activates the desire to call it up once more' (1982: 45).

The dilemmas of boxing films are those that belong to the contradictory field of the making and remaking of gender identities. The ambivalences of sexuality also constitute the narratives through which masculinities are constructed and reproduced. How do boxing films address some of their own particular conflicts in relation to sexuality, especially in the context of masculinity and heterosexuality?

The homosocial and the homoerotic

Sex sells at the movies, but this poses problems for the boxing film. Is that which is sexualized and eroticized the straight sex of the mainstream cinema or is there something else going on in the translation of sport, especially the corporeal contact of boxing, onto the screen? Is there the possibility of an accommodation of diverse sexualities in the masculinities enacted within this cultural terrain? There can be a love interest that accompanies the main thread of the drama but in men's sport, especially boxing, there remains the much-heralded celibacy before the match and, in boxing especially, the idea that the main protagonist, instead of concentrating his fantasies on a woman, must move the emphasis to his opponent. Joyce Carol Oates refers to the female–male gender binary in relation to heterosexuality as, 'Where woman has been. Opponent must be' (1987: 30).

Boxing masculinities are consistently constituted in relation to femininity. Oates' insistence that 'boxing is for men' (1987) resonates through the culture of boxing, especially men's boxing. The practice in gyms of excluding women, the massive financial input in the men's game which is still lacking in the women's and the media coverage of the sport all contribute to gender polarization. Boxing films take their context from the social world in which most gyms and most fights appear to be homosocial spaces where men not only set the agenda, but the cultural terrain is also coded masculine. These are homosocial spaces reconstructed through institutionalised routines and mechanisms and the networks through which relationships, alliances and friendships are forged in the gym and outside.

Boxing offers a field where one might expect the reinstatement of heterosexual hegemonic masculinity, with its emphasis on the separation of women and men and its strong traditions of male bonding and associated affiliations outside the sport itself, and retold in cinematic narratives. However, this is a more complicated terrain, as I have already suggested in Chapter 2. It may be a male space but the proximity of men to each other in states of undress may also be unsettling to what Judith Butler has called the heterosexual matrix, through which heterosexual imperatives close off other possibilities and permit only particular, heterosexual identifications (1993). Oates goes further in noting the potential of this space for alternatives to a heterosexual norm,

> No sport appears more powerfully homoerotic: the confrontation in the ring – the disrobing – the sweaty heated combat that is part chance, courtship, coupling – the frequent urgent pursuit by one boxer of the other . . . surely boxing derives much of its appeal from this mimicry of a species of erotic love?
>
> (1987: 30)

As Nick James points out, the movie business, too, is part of the establishment sexual norms and 'likes its male icons to have primarily a hetero-sexual appeal and a homosexual appeal only as a by-product. Yet the erotic content of boxing is exclusively homoerotic' (1996: 113). Whilst it may be quite acceptable to present men as the objects of a sexualized gaze, Steve Neal suggests that in a largely heterosexual and patriarchal society, 'the male body cannot be marked explicitly as the erotic object of another male look: that look must be motivated in some other way, its erotic component repressed' (1992: 281). It is the unsettling elision of violence and eroticization which is problematic in fight films. Boxing films can be unsettling in unexpected ways, but nonetheless they highlight contradictions and dilemmas that also occupy spaces outside the sport. The homoeroticism of boxing, especially as represented on screen offers a disruption of the heterosexual imperative, however insistently it may be imposed through gendered narrative structures in film.

Heroic narratives

In the rags-to-riches trope of the cinema, the central character is not always male, although boxing films often carry a central narrative of heroic masculinity. Even when these are films which have a woman who boxes as a central character, heroism is encoded within the genealogy of masculinity. For example, *Million Dollar Baby*, tells the story of a young, white woman's attempt to become successful as a boxer and to look after her family. In this instance it is her family of origin and not her own partner and children, a more familiar format when men are the boxers, who constitute the 'family'. Clint Eastwood, the film's director, producer (and star), himself claims that the film is 'not really a boxing story' (in Buscombe, 2005: 67). The film centres on a female boxer and its main narrative is constructed around the recurrent *American Dream* story of how boxing can provide a route out of poverty and into acceptance, wealth and celebrity. In the film the home town of Maggie, the boxer, is described as between 'nowhere and goodbye' in an image resonant of so many tales of honest escape from the ghetto and from poverty. However, her roots are not romanticized and her trailer-park family is shown as grasping and most ungrateful for her attempts to help them. Indeed, one of the best scenes in the film is the moment when Maggie goes with her trainer Frankie to show her mother and sister the house she has bought them. Far from expressing gratitude her mother is angry at the potential loss of her welfare benefits. Maggie, along with the more frequently featured male protagonists of such heroic narratives, is fired by ambition and determination and manifests great physical resilience. However, although at one level Maggie is the hero, struggling against not only the constraints of her 'trailer trash' roots but also her gender, the heroes of this film are male. First, Eastwood himself who plays the trainer Frankie and second, Scrap, played by Morgan Freeman, and who also provides the voiceover and the narrative continuity linking memories of boxing history, especially his own and Frankie's. The acting of all three characters is excellent, as was acknowledged by their Oscar victories in 2005, but Eastwood and Freeman are central because this is a story of masculinity, its routine networks and collusions.

Maggie is indeed a strong character; she is no cipher (Buscombe, 2005), but it is the two men who carry the film's iconic identities and identifications. Whilst Maggie may appear to be standing as a substitute for Frankie's estranged daughter, it is the relationship between the two men that weaves centrally through the film. The men are bound by ties that extend temporally and spatially, a long way beyond the specificities of their particular relationship. Frankie, as the trainer, carries the guilt of having allowed Scrap to continue in a fight which cost him an eye and this underpins their relationship: one that is characterized by bickering but also deep, if rarely stated, affection. The moral anguish of the film is Frankie's. He has been persuaded to allow Maggie to fight and he bears the guilt of her terrible fate in the ring. His relationship with the Catholic priest to whom he turns for guidance through the film and who refuses to support Frankie's final decision to support Maggie's plea for euthanasia informs the narrative and this version of honourable and heroic masculinity.

Although the film is at one level about a 'woman boxer' and she is the central character in the narrative, women's agency is often marginalized or subordinated to that of men. Maggie is the vehicle for exploring Frankie's life and his problem, which represent those of contemporary masculinity. Women are constructed negatively: there is Frankie's absent daughter and Maggie's 'bad mother'. The ultimate tragedy of the film is played out on Maggie's body; her attempts to be included in this male world being doomed to most terrible failure in spite of early apparent successes in the ring after she has persuaded Frankie to train her. For the male boxer it would be his tragedy because he is the hero of the narrative and its author; in this film the heroes of the story are the male ex-boxer and trainer.

Figure 6.3 Clint Eastwood at the Oscars (Photo: © Empics)

Figure 6.4 Hilary Swank at the Oscars (Photo: © Empics)

Cinematic narratives bring together celebrity and heroism, embodied in the actor who takes the part of the hero of the film. Films combine the fantasy and the reality in particular ways in sport, especially in boxing. The actor who plays Muhammad Ali takes just a little bit of the glory that is Ali's. However, for women this is slightly different. These narratives of heroism are constructed around other stories. Hilary Swank's portrayal of Maggie in *Million Dollar Baby* also received extensive media coverage. She, like every actor who has ever played the part of a boxer, had to follow a rigorous training programme: one which transformed her body from that of a healthy, attractive young woman into a super-fit athlete. Male actors enhance their masculinity and become 'fighters', often trained by professional boxers, such as Barry McGuighan, as Daniel Day Lewis was for his lead role in *The Boxer*. However, the media coverage of Hilary Swank, for example, focused more upon the transformation of an already beautiful body into an even more beautiful body.

Women's magazines celebrated Swank's achievements in becoming 'sexy, powerful and gorgeous . . . after putting on 19lb of muscle' (Gannon, 2005: 118). This embodied transformation is sexualized and Swank is quoted as saying, 'My husband watched me at the gym and said to my trainer, "I used to love Hilary's butt – I can't believe how amazing it is now." He was totally knocked out' (Gannon, 2005: 124). The whole project is situated in the context of strategies for cosmetic enhancement, which might even be adopted by other women, such as the readers of the magazines, on a more modest scale. Swank was trained by a boxing trainer who worked with her nutritionist. Although, the notion of empowerment through the body is acknowledged and given significant coverage in some accounts, the main emphasis is on the whole process as a beauty project. Swank is reported as wanting to retain some of her muscle power. 'I never felt as truly physically gorgeous as when I played Maggie. I loved the feel of my body . . . What I've learned is I like to be a bit bigger and I want some of that muscle and strength to stay' (Gannon, 2005: 124). However, the desire is not for too much muscle: just six pounds not the full nineteen. This is still a body project, framed with a sexualized, gendered discourse. There is no reference to pugilistic possibilities or to a femininity that might be enhanced by the strength that is associated with aggression. Assurances are given that it is possible to retain a more traditional, heterosexual femininity in spite of this, albeit temporary engagement in the noble art. Gender differences are interconnected with those of class, 'race' and 'ethnicity' and whilst there may be moments at which gender is fore-grounded it is impossible to unravel the interrelationship between these dimensions of diversity and inequality; an inequality which is frequently interpreted through the performance and voice of anger. The expression of rage which is so often worked through the narrative of boxing films is often most closely linked to inequalities of class and race.

Expressions of anger: 'race', 'ethnicity' and class

Boxing stories retold in the cinema are part of the mythology of the sport. They are also both reflective and constitutive of its material circumstances, for example of the economic, social and cultural factors which create the neighbourhoods from which so many boxers are drawn. Personal and psychic investments in boxing masculinities cannot be disentangled from the material, social circumstances in which they are made. Similarly, psychic investments are enmeshed with affectivity and emotion. Anger is a powerful emotion that provides some explanation for the engagement in what is often a violent and damaging sporting activity by people in particular economic circumstances marked by social exclusion. Films are able to provide a space for the representation of this anger which can be located within the specificities of class, racialization and ethnicization which give rise to the strength of the rage which can be expressed by boxers, real and fictional. Films also recreate and reinstate stereotypes of the body in relation to gender, class and 'race', especially as articulated in the figure of the working-class, dispossessed hero. The film, *Ali* structured within the framework of the boxer's biography, presents some explicit engagement with the political articulation of emotion and rationality expressed in anger and resistance to racism, which necessarily has to acknowledge the agency of its main protagonist.

However, racialization is often expressed through the locality, for example in the location of the gym around which the narrative is constructed. The cinematic gym, like its material counterpart is invariably located in a downtown, impoverished, ethnically diverse or predominantly black area. In boxing films, the gym often serves as an indicator of a culture which cannot express its own anger through more explicit articulations of political practice and rhetoric. For example, in the *Rocky* series the gym is initially the site of a language of realism and conforms to the visual landscape of post-industrial dereliction in Philadelphia in the mid-1970s. Social exclusion is represented visually more than verbally and through the actions of the protagonists more than through the expression of cognitive processes. The politics of resistance may be more or less explicit and dispossession and social and political exclusion may not be embodied in the agency of the boxer. It may be embedded in the locality as a more internal, ethnicized politics of exclusion is in *The Boxer* which is set in Northern Ireland incorporating a familiar strand of boxing's genealogy: the Irish are a longstanding part of boxing's ethnicized traditions.

'Race' is significantly marked by visible difference. As Frantz Fanon argued so powerfully in his psychoanalytic critique of the representational force of racism and its intersection with corporeality, skin becomes the focus of alienation because it is inescapable because of its striking visibility (1967). Stereotypes are constructed through the setting of clear boundaries and through the exaggeration of particular characteristics often set in binary oppositions, such as those between active and passive, seeing and being seen, masculine and feminine, black and white, aggressor and victim. Such stereotypes incorporate gender, ablebodiedness, 'ethnicity', 'race' and class. One of the most powerful stereotypical figures in sport and in boxing in particular is that of the black male athlete. As Keith Piper suggests, 'The genesis of the involvement of black men in the arena of prize-fighting embodies a complex set of markers which have fixed and influenced wider social readings of black boxers ever since' (1996: 71).

From its earliest days, prizefighting has been a practice situated within a relationship between a powerful elite and the dispossesed 'others'. It has been sponsored by that elite and contested by those at the bottom of the social spectrum, as was demonstrated in Chapter 2. The figure of the black athlete is deeply embedded in the discourse of colonialism and this legacy has manifest associations. A significant double burden has rested on the prizefighter. The former burden of standing both for his sponsor, the slave owner and for his people as the repository of their dreams, whereby the struggles of the ring could be seen as a metaphoric narrative for the daily struggle for survival, has been replaced by a new translation of this dual role. The slave owner has been replaced by the entrepreneur, the media mogul, the criminal syndicate or the promoter, and boxers today, as Mike Marqusee has pointed out, 'have less power over their bodies and careers than almost any other sports people' (1995: 3) tied as they are to sponsors, television companies and managers. However, they still carry the burden of speaking for the communities from which they come and, as the visibility of the boxer increases, so their symbolic role, including its representation in film and other such public fields, demands that boxing champions stand as symbols of national and racial superiority (Sammons, 1988). The working-class hero, anti-hero or victim in boxing films is inflected by the specificities of 'race' and 'ethnicity'. As Homi Bhabha has argued 'an important feature of colonial discourse is its dependency on the concept of fixity in the ideological construction of otherness' (1983). The fighter can be seen as one of a series of stereotypes of black men along with other athletes, entertainers, hoods and hoodlums in film (Denzin, 2002). Female characters in boxing films seem to foreground this version of black masculinity more visibly through its juxtaposition with white femininity. There is the presence of the spectral white woman who appears to haunt the boxer, like Vicki in *Raging Bull*. Stereotypes are also coded within a discourse of role models, which Norman Denzin suggests operates strongly within different film genres, many of which are coming-of-age all-male narratives conveying a uniform moral message which frequently includes negative representations of black men. In boxing, role models usually fit into the class-based, rags-to-riches narrative and form part of a journey to success across a tempestuous and troubled terrain often marked by crosses with the law, but the hero figure is often the white boxer, like Rocky.

Such stories may present a linear moral tale with very clear-cut notions of right and wrong expressed within a framework of authenticity. As David Mellor has argued, however: 'the racialized romantic-modernist representation of existential man in all his bleak grandeur attained definition in Hollywood post-World War 11 . . . the cinematic boxer was an involuntary cinematic saint . . . Generally the boxer gained that dimension of authenticity through passages of suffering and sacrificial violence' (1996: 81).

Mellor cites the figure of the 'Afro-American Manager as Despot', who confronts the boxer, as a key motif in boxing films. This is one figure that recurs in the genre. For example, in *Pulp Fiction* the white boxer and African-American manager (Marcellus) relationship, is confirmed yet inverted in terms of race and visible difference. In *Rocky V*, however, the relationship becomes an absurd caricature with Duke Washington, the Don King-style African-American manager attempting to persuade Rocky back into the fight game in spite of his brain trauma. Mellor suggests that an attempt such as this in *Rocky*, to recapture the modernist narratives of good versus evil is unsuccessful, for example in using Washington to represent evil incarnate as a bragging showman 'who has denuded boxing of its moral worth' (1996: 82). It is not only a failure of authenticity; it is complicit in a racialized articulation of the boxer–manager relationship.

Class and 'race' intersect in the central narratives of boxing films, articulated in different ways through the tropes that are deployed to explore the fight game and what it can deliver in terms of addressing issues of winning and losing, inclusion and exclusion. 'Outsider' status, whether in relation to class, 'ethnicity' or 'race' is central to boxing and especially to the stories that are told and the ways in which the boxer is represented. Boxing engages so well with hopes and with the fight against injustice and exclusion as well as winning and losing that it is also about what *might* have been.

I could have been a contender

A crucial figure which provides the central focus in Scorsese's *Raging Bull* and in Avildsen's *Rocky* is Marlon Brando's Terry Molloy in *On the Waterfront* (1954). The use of an earlier text and the techniques of self-reference and intertextuality have been much more fully developed and deployed in recent years, but in boxing films they have a special resonance. *On the Waterfront* is not really a boxing film at all, but the central character, Molloy, has been a boxer, although his career is over by the start of the film. He has taken up work as a stevedore in the docks and as an errand boy. Scorsese saw *On the Waterfront* as a pivotal moment carrying iconic significance (1989). Molloy's relationship with his girlfriend is fragile and sentimental and positioned in a gendered dichotomous opposition between the inarticulate, masochistic man and the sensitive, emotional woman; rather like Beauty and the Beast in traditional fairy stories. The notion of a central character who has to 'be someone' permeates the first *Rocky* film through Rocky's journey to success through boxing and his inarticulate relationship with his wife Adrian and is developed more in *Rocky II* (1979), in an articulation of the rags-to-riches narrative which elides masculinity with the job a man does. As Rocky says to his girlfriend when she presses him to retire from boxing: 'I never asked you to stop being a woman. Please don't ask me to stop being a man.' This representation of the boxer as embodying masculinity demonstrates the power of Oates' claim that 'boxing is about men' (1987). It pervades the fight film genre and articulates with familial genealogies and male networks in boxing. In Robert Wise's *Someone Up There Likes Me*, Rocky Graziano's father tells him 'Be a champ like I never was' (1954). These masculinities represent the attempt to establish boundaries around an identity position which seems to be fragmenting and constantly under threat (Whitehead, 2002). Brando's method acting and performance in *On the Waterfront* both spoke to fantasies of securing identity and establishing the boundaries of masculinity and reinstated these as part of a recognised identity of masculinity. Gerald Early (1994) argues that this was further compounded, not only by the style of acting, but by the off-screen relationship between Brando, the boxer Rocky Graziano, and actors Paul Newman and James Dean. Hegemonic masculinity is worked and reworked through the interweaving of different levels, times, practices and relationships all of which feed into and reconstruct fantasies through which subjectivities are reconstituted. This version of masculinity with its halting inarticulacy is, as Early suggests, somehow more true, more authentic and more poetic as an expression of 'the misunderstood, anti-social youth' (1994: 90).The anger felt as a result of both social exclusion located within the context not only of losing, which boxing can deal with, but of not actually being an agent in control of his own destiny, even knowing who he is and an inability to articulate those feelings is perfectly condensed in Brando's words which echo through these boxing films. The monosyllabic rage of Robert de Niro as Jake La Motta in *Raging Bull* carries a threat of authenticity. This is most dramatically brought home through its association with the dispossessed working-class hero drawing on Terry Molloy's words in *On the Waterfront*,

> I could have been somebody
> I could have been a contender

The trope clearly depends upon de Niro's skill as an actor and upon Marlon Brando's in the original film, of course, but there is a synchrony with a particular version of masculinity. The actual Jake La Motta traded upon this masculinity himself after *Raging Bull*, which makes this a very powerful identity position which is embodied in Marlon Brando's Terry Molloy, but which has resonance throughout the genre and reverberates at myriad sites at which masculinities are forged. It clearly expresses both smouldering rage and the fantasies that drive the aspirations of this masculinity and indeed in the wider arena of marginalized and excluded subjectivities. The force of the regretful claim that 'I could have been a contender' has a particular place in the genealogies of masculinity with its associations of heroism through combat, whether in the military or sporting fields. What is so powerful about this statement is also its incorporation of the agency, for example as represented in Sartre's existential figure of the boxer, discussed in Chapter 3, who can or could shape his own identity, illustrated by dealing with his anger and the acknowledgement of structural constraints, especially those of class, racialization and ethnicization.

Watching the films: can you take it?

Not only is there a view, often strongly expressed that boxing is for men, but there is also some element of bravado in the viewing of cinematic violence. As a woman, I have been asked more frequently by my male peers in the academy about my unexpected interest in boxing films and whether I could stand the violence, for example in a film like *Fight Club*, than any inquiries by practising boxers about whether I can manage to watch an actual fight. This may hint at some of the collusions of hegemonic masculinity which, as Bob Connell argues, is constituted through its associations as well as those who perform hegemonic masculinity overtly (1995). Valerie Walkerdine expresses her responses to such films in the context of her research using a family viewing of a video of *Rocky* (1986). Her own first response is to see the fight scenes as distressingly violent, but when she views the film again on her own she finds that she is drawn into the narrative of the working-class boxer whose only route out of poverty is to fight. In attempting to find some explanation for the two phenomena; the first being her identification with Rocky when she viewed the video alone, but not at the first viewing with family and the second being why she, having no previous interest in boxing, should identify with Rocky at all. In what is albeit a very small-scale project, for example, criticized by Elspeth Probyn as a 'small industry' and as evidence that the 'me generation lives on' (1993: 10), Walkerdine makes some useful points. She suggests that, in answer to the first point, when viewing the film with the family, the father, Mr Cole, as a working-class man who would understand very well the links between class struggle, masculinity and 'fighting the system' (1997: 55) occupies a particular psychic space in the small audience in the home, which she, as an 'outsider', is not therefore able to take up. In response to the second point Walkerdine uses the idea of intertextuality, to explain how she too, given her own working-class background, is able to get caught up in the narrative of Rocky's struggle and, far from being sickened by the macho violence, at her second viewing she is rooting for Rocky and completely committed to the fight and to his victory, whatever it takes. She argues that for identification to take place there have to be associations; 'meanings in the film meant something to the viewer because of other places in which those meanings were constituted in their lives' (1997: 54). Her claims perhaps underestimate the structure of the film and the boxing story that is framed in the ring. Boxing is inherently about a winner and a loser, however much a spectator may watch the fight to assess the skills and techniques of the boxers. The stark binary between winning and losing make it almost impossible not to be on one side or the other. Walkerdine suggests that the theories of identification in this context have to on board the fantasies of the spectator and what is brought to the viewing, as well as what is represented on screen. Whilst she engages with this using her own experience, it is also possible to argue from collective consciousness of spectatorship which shares the fantasies so represented in the construction of gendered identities. Just as Judith Butler argues that Foucault needs psychoanalysis, Walkerdine suggests that psychoanalysis needs a Foucauldian discursive approach (1997). She suggests that Foucault's work offers a means of escaping an essentialist understanding of the working-class subject, whether in economic or psychological terms. She is critical of the Lacanian approach of Laura Mulvey which contributed to what has been called the *Screen* approach discussed above (pages 128–30). Although this theoretical perspective was very influential in the 1970s and 1980s, Walkerdine argues that its emphasis is too much upon the universal and it does not engage with the particular and contingent relationship between the subject and the popular culture. This view supports the importance of discourse theory to demonstrate how subjects are produced and addresses questions about the operation of power in the construction of subjectivities including the subjectivity of the researcher in the process. 'My own feelings and fantasies must, I felt, have some bearing on my, and therefore anybody's, interpretation and explanation' (1997: 54). The strength of Walkerdine's argument is her psychosocial placing of an analysis of fantasy in the ideological terrain of social reality in which fantasies circulate.

In examining the impact of popular culture, she is using ideology in the Marxist sense of not simply a false consciousness, but as the social effect of knowledge so represented that people 'do not know it but they are doing it'; a not knowing on the part of the subject. As Slavoj Žižek says, 'The main point is to see how the reality itself cannot reproduce itself without this so-called mystification. The mask is not simply hiding the real state of things; the ideological distortion is written into its very essence' (1989: 28).

Notions of false consciousness and deception are crucial to the identification processes that take place in boxing cultures, whether in the practice of the sport or in spectatorship, either at the ring or in the cinema. Bourdieu's concept of *illusio*, discussed in Chapter 3, can be used to explain how boxing and this version of masculinity, can be 'in the blood' without the boxer being seen as duped or deceived. Walkerdine addresses the problem of the tension between deception and the idea that, for example, the working class is deceived by the images of popular culture which distort social reality and resistance, that is, the notion that there can be opposition and people are not simply duped by the mass media and popular culture. In attempting to explain the responses of the family with whom she views *Rocky* and her own later responses, her question relates to how far the working-class psyche can be explained outside a model that sees the class either as duped and deceived or as exercising agency and resisting deception and even expressing agency, for example through the rags-to-riches trope of the boxing story.

A similar question could be posed in relation to masculinity at this site. Is the working-class masculinity which pervades boxing and its cinematic expressions a resistant heroism and a route for the agentic subject to escape oppression? Or, on the other hand, is this masculinity wrought by fantasies which induce deception and reinforce dependence and the persistence of inequality? It is both. Walkerdine suggests that it is through incorporating an analysis of the psyche and subjective experiences with a discursive critique, that the accusation of false consciousness can be avoided.

Working-class masculinities are implicated in the economic, social and cultural world that is constitutive of class difference and the inner spaces of psychic investment in heroic working-class masculinity. Gender, 'race', 'ethnicity' and class belonging interrelate, but also occupy different spaces, and allegiances both coincide and collide. Walkerdine's negative reaction to the violence in the film *Rocky* when watching with the family, her notion of the psychic space occupied by the father of the family preventing her from taking up that subject position resonates with the arguments presented in Chapter 5 about the colluding masculinity which makes it difficult for women to take up subject positions within that space. This is not to suggest that women cannot perform that masculinity, but their inclusion is impeded by the difficulties of occupying the psychic space, which can constitute even more powerful a threat to hegemonic masculinity than the space of social reality, for example as practitioners in the gym and in the ring. Questions about being able to 'take the violence' as projected into on-screen fantasies, are part of the process of 'othering' women and creating an outsider status in relation to a protected mainstream of gendered identity.

In addressing the issue about the possibility of being drawn into the narrative of the film if one has no interest in boxing, it can be argued that the associations of different relationships between fantasies and social reality, for example in relation to class, make sense of the viewer's understanding of the narrative and create psychic investment in the fantasies expressed and embodied in the central character's struggles. Whilst Walkerdine does not offer her work as an alternative to more familiar forms of audience research, her 'autobiographical turn' (Moores, 1993: 68) does present useful insights into the relationship between the fantasies on screen and how these are linked to the social world in which they circulate as well as demonstrating that class can transcend gender in the process of identification and that this could be one aspect of women 'doing masculinity'.

Conclusion

Films are about fantasy and provide one of the links between the technologies and practices of identity formation and the fantasies which inform them. Films offer one cultural vehicle through which such fantasies are shared through the psychic space between the text and the spectator. There has to be a wider community of understanding of these dreams and aspirations in order for them to be operative, or for them to have any purchase. These films are historically specific and this chapter has traced some of the transformations that have taken place, notably since the 1940s and 1950s into the new cinematic age of the twenty-first century. However, there is some continuity in the narrative structures of boxing, especially in their gendered discourses of heroism located within social exclusion, racial and ethnic inequality and the enormous contrast between the poverty that motivates boxers and the affluence to which they aspire in a sport that has offered great financial rewards to individual fighters, especially to heavyweights. Boxing films are all haunted by the rags-to-riches trope as well as the threat of failure. The films, like the sport, are as much about losing as about winning and provide a means of making sense both of aspirations to heroism and the difficulties of dealing with failure as well as success. Such masculinities present both aspirational identifications and pre-empt the fear of failure through an accommodation of the tension between winning and losing.

In looking at transformation in gender identities over a period of economic, social and cultural change, which has been marked by the emergence of new identities, which ascribe more caring affective attributes to men and more agency to women, especially in the labour market and in relationships with men, it appears that the boxing film genre like the sport has made few concessions to change. Hegemonic masculinity has been challenged by the articulation of more ambiguous versions of masculinity framed within a more complex matrix of gendered identities, but boxing in the cinema, and largely in the sport itself, has made only limited modifications. Boxing films do provide some cognisance of change, but more importantly they engage with major continuing concerns that are relevant to the making and remaking of identities. What persists is the psychic space of spectatorship, which can still be occupied by traditional masculinities, although the performance of masculinity at this site has undergone some transformation in relation to the social, economic and cultural contexts in which films are made.

Masculinity is still constituted in relation to femininity, although relationships between women and men are represented in different ways. There is some continuity in the marginalization of women, even in those films where they are the main protagonist, like *Million Dollar Baby*, as I have argued in this chapter. Particular female figures persist, for example those of the Madonna and the whore, the self-effacing Marian wifely figures, white women and call-girls, although they are reconstituted, if not completely changed, especially in films like *Pulp Fiction*, which is not strictly a boxing movie. 'Doing masculinity' can include identification with heroic figures and is not confined to a directly gendered recognition, as I have suggested.

The psychoanalytic theories which have frequently been deployed in film criticism offer one route into understanding the ways in which identities are formed and in particular why interpellation works; why some versions of masculinity recruit subjects and others do not and what are the anxieties and fears as well as the aspirations to which films as cultural products speak. Psychoanalytic theories address the formation of subjectivity and the identification processes that are implicated in the representation of gender identities and present a means of understanding spectatorship as well as focusing upon the meanings that are produced within the texts of the films. One of the most powerful processes of identification in fight films is not only with heroes but also with the possibility of failing and the genre could be said to be most relevant in this respect.

The violence of cinematic representations, as well as of spectatorship of boxing in the ring occupies spaces outside what can be symbolized as well as being legitimized within symbolic systems. One of the ways in which legitimacy is achieved is through the narratives of heroism and the notions of 'making good' for the kid from the wrong side of the tracks. The dilemma explored in boxing is the tension and contradiction between the honour of heroism and the pull of celebrity and between the fantasy and its realization. 'I could have been a contender' resonates through this film genre, largely, but not always coded masculine. However, this statement retains its ambiguities and differently inflected meanings in relation to the contender as fighter and the contender who 'is someone'. The aspiration and regret condensed in the desire to have 'been someone', who is recognised and heard has particular force in addressing contemporary constructions of masculinity at a moment when young men are resorting to political acts of violence because they claim they are not heard even by those who are said to represent them.

Chapter 7

Conclusion
I Could Have Been A Contender

Introduction

Boxing, far from being an anomaly the persistence of which is hard to explain in contemporary societies, has a great deal to offer in explaining the processes of identification. The uncertainties and instabilities which characterize the processes of making sense of the self in the wider social field are deeply embedded in boxing where there is a strong sense of engaging with insecurity and anxiety and with attempting to establish a sense of belonging. The re-production of boxing masculinities resonates with the dynamics of identification through personal and public stories in diverse areas of social and cultural life in uncertain times. These are the routine masculinities reconfigured through every day, embodied regimens and cultural practices and the pre-emptive masculinities which seek to accommodate the fears and uncertainties of making up the self. Identification involves finding some settlement of tensions and contradictions, and boxing culture offers an excellent example of dealing with ambivalence, disruptions and polarities. These tensions are experienced and enacted at a personal level and are represented in the discursive field of the sport in which psychic and social elements are imbricated. Not only does boxing illustrate how the social field recruits subjects through its appeal to unconscious desires for a unity of the self, but the social terrain is itself structured by such desires. The social operates within the psyche and the psychic is in the social.

Boxing and its associated cultural practices are marked by the persistence of collusive masculinities, frequently reproduced in opposition to femininity. There are significant continuities in the discourses of boxing in the reconstitution of masculinities and there is limited evidence of the transformations of masculinity which incorporate more inclusive, less polarized versions of identity. This collusion compares to the complicity of hegemonic masculinity (Connell, 1995) and is one of the distinctive features of the masculinities reconstructed in the field of boxing. However, those who actually engage in the body practices of boxing largely receive limited benefit from the patriarchal dividend and their benefits may be outweighed by their class-based, ethnicized and racialized disadvantages. Men in sport clearly do gain overall from the more general subordination of women, but the gains may be greater in the wider networks of masculinity than for most boxers.

One of the most powerfully expressed polarities in boxing is that based on gender, which is why this book has focused upon masculinity as a gendered identity. The language of sport remains largely unaffected by gender neutral discourses of diversity that permeate social and political life in the west. In the actual sport of boxing women and men are clearly classified and differentiated, although, as in most major sports, it is women who are marked as such, as in 'women's boxing' or 'women's football', whereas the men's sport is not marked; it is 'boxing' or 'football' where gender is unstated, but it is the men's sport that is meant. The universality of gender difference is explicit in boxing, whereas it is frequently obscured in other fields and the identity work in boxing persists in forging and securing particular masculinities. To aver the persistence and continuities of gender differentiation is not to suggest that they are either fixed or biological. However, they are embodied and gendered, material bodies are central to identity work. A view of selfhood which emerges from an analysis of bodily reflexive practices in boxing is one that can accommodate agency and structural constraints and the lived, experienced and represented body. This is an agentic self which is empowered through the practices of the sport. Critiques of embodiment, such as Wacquant's, drawing upon the work of Merleau-Ponty and Bourdieu especially, have offered convincing analyses of embodied selfhood. However, whilst the mind/body dualism has been most effectively challenged there are others that remain within the theoretical framework, notably that of gender and the female/male binary. Bodily practices and the *illusio* of engagement are gendered too.

There is, of course a strong traditional association of the sport with men and masculinity, but this is what also makes it so interesting for the exploration of gendered identities, especially in changing times. Gendered identities are transformed and transforming and stereotypes are there to be challenged and deconstructed, but their resilience in boxing might also pay tribute to a sport which often invites the performance and iteration of collusive masculinity, because the sport is so implicated with this particular version of masculinity. Its heroes are mostly men. Its stories are often about a risk-taking, self-denying, stoical, aggressive and, especially, honourable masculinity. This is changing, even within as traditional a sport as boxing women are emerging as heroes too and are beginning to tell their own stories, notably on the internet, which has provided a liberating space in some senses, encouraging both publicity for fights and training opportunities as well as a forum for debate about the contentious issues, including mixed fights. There are points of visibility for women boxers, although this is a complex and contested terrain in which sexualized ethical challenges have also to be negotiated. There are fewer public narratives, especially of any longevity, most notably of honour and heroism, which inform heroic boxing stories and it is through the stories that are told that identity positions become established, if only temporarily or even momentarily and reconstituted and reproduced. I have not suggested that women cannot 'do' masculinity or that masculinity is the prerogative of those who are classified or who would categorize themselves as men, but the stories of masculinity that are told and which take up so much of the public and personal space of boxing are those which feature people who are men, often excluding or marginalizing those people who are women or at least impeding the identificatory processes, especially in appropriating roles involving honour or heroism. It is difficult for women to imagine themselves into these identities because of the operation of a collusive masculinity and, even more so because of the narrative structures of boxing honour and heroism. This may present even more powerful exclusionary mechanisms than the engagement in boxing's body practices and the biologistic discourses that enforce them, for example in the history and current practices of regulating women's fighting.

Identities are forged in particular spatial and temporal contexts and in relation to both embodied selves and specific economic and social situations. Boxing has a long history of association with political activism and of resistance to social and economic exclusion and disadvantage. Although political struggles in the public arena have often been fought by men and it is largely black men whose struggles with white supremacy and racism that have been accorded status in boxing stories, even the Tyson myth incorporates an honourable narrative of heroism in the politics of 'race' in spite of the muddied waters of exploitation and gender politics which taint this story.

The public stories of rags to riches and of challenging racism resonate with more local, personal experiences and, especially, aspirations of many boxers. The meanings given to masculinities in boxing are strongly influenced by the dynamics of social and cultural change, even if there are consistencies in some of the sport's routines, practices and representations. In explaining how identities are reproduced in boxing culture I have brought together routine, habitual practices and more public, spectacular displays and manifestations of excess. The masculinities reconfigured in boxing incorporate routines, dreams and fears and identificatory processes embrace the habits of routine engagement, including body practices and the discursive terrain in which meanings are recreated and in which investments are made in these identities.

There are different measures of success in this sport which is so deeply marked by the distinction between success and failure, which can mean winning or losing in the ring or in the rigorous standards of personal achievement set in the gym. These tensions draw in those who do not practise the sport but whose measure of success in being included belongs in their complicity in an endeavour that carries such dangers and threats of violence, where success means not admitting fear and being part of the game. Terry Molloy's powerful statement in *On the Waterfront*, 'I could have been a contender' underpins the trajectories of so many boxing films from *Raging Bull* through the *Rocky* series to *Cinderella Man*. This claim does not only express regret for not having 'been someone' in the public eye, it also signifies the fear of failure of identification and of being able to belong and secure the self in this version of masculinity. Fear of losing can be applied to failure to secure an identity position. Belonging is often configured as 'being someone' and fitting into a bounded, seemingly secure identity position, however ephemeral. The over-simplification which boxing appears to invite, especially as stated in its oppositions, notably that between success and failure, is expressive of the desires and dreams of the sport and the aspiration to belong as well as to the concomitant fear of failure: the fear of not being up to it and of not being able to cope, which represents the dynamic between success and failure.

Pre-emptive masculinities

The masculinities forged in boxing in training regimes, which are organized around attempts to pre-empt failure, are also the means of accommodating the fear of not succeeding. The pre-emptive strike in the sport is a metaphor for this identification with a masculinity characterized by courage in the face of perceived danger, embodied bravery, agency and honour. The public history of boxing focuses on those who are or who have been contenders; those who have clearly 'been someone', whilst the sport itself is largely taken up by those who, whatever their dreams, engage its bodily practices for less dramatically aspirational purposes. Boxing has a very particular attraction. In its elemental, primitive combat between two people in the ring, it offers the promise, or threat of resolution. There is no real escape from the binary of winning or losing, but this is also what is so attractive about boxing; it provides a space in which this anxiety can be confronted. This stark dualism, which haunts boxing frames its relationship to an understanding of identity and highlights the dilemmas of identification. The metaphor of the contender pre-empts accusations of failure and demonstrates the desire to set some boundaries around the self and to experience a sense of belonging and even some temporary and ephemeral point at which one recognises oneself. It also brings together the temporal frame in which identities are forged as a space for present reflection upon the roots and origins that have constituted the drama and which inform and reconstruct aspirations projected into the future

Some of the key organising questions that boxing most strongly evokes relate to explanations, not only of why boxers box, but why spectators watch. These questions inform the whole process of identity formation. Boxing provides its spectators with the experience and the non-experience of violence. There is always the promise of going too far, which the spectator wants and does not want. The violence of the spectacle is a representation of excess and of the transgression of the boundaries of civilization and restraint. However, the violence is contained, disciplined and made regular by the institutionalization of boxing as a legitimate sport. The possibility of total breakdown is pre-empted by the disciplines of regulation. In this sense the spectator is not offered the experience of anarchic excess, although sometimes, just very occasionally the tragedy is real. We are given the promise of 'what if' in the ring and for ourselves as spectators complicit in the engagement. What if there were no rules? What if I let go? What if I, a 'civilized', non-violent person let rip and started hitting someone? What if it went too far and someone died? These are terrible and terrifying possibilities and, of course, people *do*, if rarely, die in the ring as the amateur boxer Becky Zerlentes did in 2005.

Boxing is a space in which there is the possibility of dealing with these unstated fears and anxieties. It goes beyond the 'attraction of repulsion' (Stallybrass and White, 1986) to a manifestation of what cannot be said, but can be represented by boxing. This is also part of the distinction between amateur and professional boxing and the particular lure of the professional heavyweight contest. The amateur professional sport gives different interpretations to honour and heroism across the globe, but the heavyweight contest, with all its histories of 'race', class and politics, occupies a special place in the representation and experience of honourable conflict. The greater status of the professional sport, manifest in the enormous rewards at the top levels, is linked to perceived risk. There are more fatal casualties in other sports, but the point about boxing is that, in competition, the aim of one boxer is to knock the other unconscious; to direct punches at the head. The focus of the whole project is to hit the opponent, but at all costs to escape injury oneself. This is premised on the possibility and the concomitant fear of being hit or injured. All defensive action is mirrored by attack and the need to pre-empt injury, just as the emotions of spectators are expressed within a framework of sport. However, the unstated underside of this is fear and the promise of extreme violence and even the possibility of the breakdown of social order. Boxing re-presents that fear. In so highly regulated a sport, part of the rationale of which is to train young men to fight in a disciplined arena and to keep them from fighting in the streets, the threat or promise of violence is always present. There is some awareness of this in the sport. Boxing aficionados and practitioners who defend the sport against those who would like it banned, suggest that it would 'go underground' in this event and there would be no rules, no health-care for boxers and a return to bare-knuckle fighting. In practice there is still strong demand for the unregulated pugilistic activities, as if recreating the Ancient Greek pankration, which suggests that the desire for the dangers of transgression, albeit one step removed through spectatorship remains very strong.

Rather than drawing upon primordial, elemental human spirit these contests remain socially constituted whilst appealing to contradictory desires which may indeed be more universal. They are written in a history and language of political conflict and power struggles. The combat incites the anxiety and the negotiation of pre-empting disaster as well as feeding any existing need to watch the spectacle. The repetition of such phenomena at different points in human history is more indicative of the power of the spectacle than of some fundamental need to view violent conflict. The ring, which constitutes a kind of theatre in the round, with its bounded frame from which there is no escape, is reminiscent of the site of Roman gladiatorial conflict, performed in the amphitheatre, which literally constituted a watching space that provided a view all the way round, and reconstructs the power of the gaze of the spectator. This is a contradictory power.

Whilst those brave and strong enough to fight in the ring have the physical strength to overpower any of the individual spectators, the spectators are positioned as controlling the subordinated performer and, similarly, are offered the possibility of controlling their fears. Muhammad Ali has expressed this most powerfully in the context of the racialized memory of the slaves as boxers and the white men as spectators (Ali and Durham, 1975). They have paid to watch and the performers are paid to perform. There must remain not only an element of pre-empting death or severe injury, but also the rebellion of those in the subordinated position. Another act of transgression might be the overthrow of existing social inequalities and an exploitative order, which can be and has been, of course, translated into political action at key points in boxing history.

Routine masculinities

The collusive networks of masculinity in boxing are also reproduced through routine and iterative practices as well as in dramatic moments. The routine of boxing includes embodied practice in the gym and the routines of following the sport and knowing its histories and culture. Technologies of self that permit individuals to operate on and through their own bodies and conduct in order to transform them also include the practices that are associated with being part of collusive networks. Boxing more than any other sport exerts a contradictory draw, not only through engagement in the sport, but through spectatorship and through the networks of association that are part of its imperative. 'The Fancy' of the nineteenth century has some resonance in the twenty-first century and there are collusions and closures around these associations that even draw in the researcher who seeks to investigate the site. This is a collusive, routine masculinity which can also operate to create boundaries between insider and outsider status in the research process, if it remains unsituated and unacknowledged.

It is not only body practices that are shared and re-iterated; it is also stories and identificatory moments, combining to create co-travellers in journeys to particular, routine masculinities. The whole process of recall of personal achievements and the local fights as well as the big moments in Manila, Kinshasa or Madison Square Garden create these affinities and complicities in this version of masculinity. Boxing, like so much of sport culture, is characterised by memory, both of successes and failures and of the failure of memory, in the desire to establish networks through what is half-remembered and what might have been half-invented. It is through these stories that the collective memories, however partial and disputed they are in their re-creation of past triumphs and failures, as well as the quantifiable, measurable details of each fight, that these routine masculinities are also reconstructed.

The mechanisms through which masculinities are reconstituted in local and public spaces often marginalize women's place in the sport. The intimacy of routine masculinities either renders women invisible, or excludes them more explicitly. However, the increased visibility of women in the sport, although often contradictory, offers some scope for re-negotiation, maybe through affiliations, including those of kinship. For example, in the case of Laila Ali, there are mechanisms for the reconfiguration of women's identifications through the sport. Women might engage in the shared practices of routine masculinities, which constitute regimes of truth that are contingent and could be transformed through different configurations and practices.

Conclusion

I have argued for a synthetic approach insofar as identification cannot be seen as operating outside the histories of the identities that are so formed. Gendered, embodied, ethnicized and racialized identities are produced through routine processes and the elision of public and private stories. The public stories have to be included in order to understand the racialized genealogies of gender. Gendered identities are made and remade through identification processes through points of recognition and of interpellation. These are not purely discursive positions into which people are fitted. The process demands personal, psychic investment. Boxing masculinities offer seductively secure, bounded identities and an intimacy of routine masculinity that is at times untroubled by having to engage with femininity.

Identities are constituted through social, cultural and economic processes and boxing illustrates these well, offering the possibility of the investment of physical capital within the *habitus* that encompasses a gendered, racialized domain of life and a set of dispositions. The sport has long been associated with narratives of escape, whether from class, 'race' or 'ethnic' oppression and the heroic figure of the boxer who succeeds has a strong identificatory position in the creation of boxing masculinities especially in terms of the honour and self respect so achieved. As has been demonstrated through the history of the sport this operates in different ways, but there is a strong thread of materiality in relation to socio-economic class in the sport, which articulates with 'race' in particular ways. However, what is also important to note, is the dominance of gender at moments in the sport which can override other affiliations, especially in the networks through which gender identities are also forged. Boxing, more than any other sport, offers a complicity that implicates those who do not engage in actual combat or demonstrate physical prowess. This collusive masculinity combines the routine and the pre-emptive in its synthesis of personal and public arenas. Its dangers offer a special pull, for example, through public representations such as cinema. This masculinity is not only concerned with *being* physically fit and being able to face such corporeal dangers and to inflict them, it is also about being able to watch them; about being able to 'take it'. This is a masculinity that women may also perform, although pre-emptive masculinity has more powerful associations for men. This is because of personal investments as well as the genealogies of corporeal masculinity with its links to physical power, competition and an honour imbricated with the dangers of transgression. This transgression is illustrated by the example in the activities associated with boxing that are not within the parameters of the law, in a culture which enables the exclusion of women to operate so pervasively.

It is through the elision of public and private stories that gendered identities are secured, especially through the mechanisms of collusion and exclusion. However powerful these mechanisms may be, boxing masculinities are not passive subjectivizations. They demonstrate both agency and resistance and thus the possibility of transformation. The masculinities discussed in this book are fluid and contingent but also beset by uncertainty and insecurity, especially through its body practices. Work on the routine body practices, especially in so challenging a physical activity as boxing, demonstrates well the agentic body and the incorporation of a self-regulating embodied identity, but I have suggested that ground-breaking as this work has been in overcoming the agency–structure binary it has often failed to acknowledge the gendered dimensions of embodiment. The embodied identifications that take place within the sport are both local and specific to the bodies involved and contextualized by a framework of histories and cultural constraints which can be negotiated in different ways and which offer both the possibility of conformity and resistance.

Not only are masculinities constructed and experienced within sport through routine body practices, they are situated within a transforming and yet sometimes unchanging cultural terrain. Identificatory processes have to embrace both the psychic investment made by individuals, which frequently admits ambivalence and contradiction, which counters any notion of the fixity of bounded hegemonic masculinity. Boxing masculinities encompass the search for belonging and the accommodation of anxiety both through routine and pre-emptive collusions. Boxing is a sport which takes courage; you have to be very brave to take part.

Bibliography

Akrich, M. and Pasveer, B. (2004) 'Embodiment and disembodiment in childbirth narratives', *Body and Society*, 10 (2–3): 63–84.

Ali, M. and Durham, R. (1975) *The Greatest: My Own Story*, New York: Random House.

Althusser, L. (1971) *Lenin and Philosophy and Other Essays*, London: New Left Books.

Armstrong, G. and Giulianotti, R. (eds) (1999) *Football Cultures and Identities*, Basingstoke: Macmillan.

Atherton, M. (2005) 'Batting for Hemingway', Radio 4, 11.30 a.m., 19 May, London: BBC.

Bakhtin, M. (1984) *Rabelais and his World*, Bloomington, IN: Indiana University Press.

Barrett, M. (1991) *The Politics of Truth*, Cambridge: Polity.

Barthes, R. (1972) *Mythologies*, London: Cape.

Barthes, R. (1973) *The Pleasure of the Text*, trans. R. Miller, New York: Hill and Wang.

Bauman, Z. (2004) *Identity Conversations with Benedetto Vecchi*, Cambridge: Polity.

Beattie, G. (1997) *On the Ropes: Boxing as a Way of Life*, London: Indigo, Cassell.

Beattie, G. (2003) *The Shadow of Boxing: Prince Naseem and Those he Left Behind*, London: Orion.

Benjamin, W. (1999) [1936] 'The work of art in the age of mechanical reproduction', in J. Evans and S. Hall (eds) *Visual Culture: The Reader*, London: Sage pp. 71–9.

Berbick, T. (2004) *Independent*, 31 July, 2004.

Bhaba, Homi K. (1983) 'The other question: the stereotype and colonial discourse', *Screen*, 24 (4): 18–36.

Birrell, S. and Donnelly, P. (2004) 'Reclaiming Goffman: Erving Goffman's influence on the sociology of sport', in R. Giulianotti (ed.) *Sport and Modern Social Theorists*, Basingstoke: Palgrave Macmillan, pp. 49–64.

Bordo, S. (1993) *Unbearable Weight: Feminism, Western Culture and the Body*, Berkeley, CA: University of California Press.

Bourdieu, P. (1977) *Outline of a Theory of Practice*, Cambridge: Cambridge University Press.

Bourdieu, P. (1978) 'Sport and social class', *Social Sciences Information*, 17(6): 819–40.

Bourdieu, P. (1986) *Distinction: A Social Critique of the Judgement of Taste*, trans. R. Nice, London: Routledge.

Bourdieu, P. (1990a) [1987] *In Other Words*, Cambridge: Polity.

Bourdieu, P. (1990b) *The Logic of Practice*, trans. R. Nice, Stanford, CA: Stanford University Press.

Bourdieu, P. (2000) *Pascalian Meditations*, Cambridge: Polity.

Bourdieu, P. (2001) *Masculine Domination*, trans. R. Nice, Cambridge: Polity.

Bourdieu, P. and Wacquant, L. (1992) *An Invitation to Reflexive Sociology*, Cambridge: Polity.

Braidotti, R. (1994) *Nomadic Subjects: Embodiment and Sexual Difference in Contemporary Feminist Theory*, New York: Columbia University Press.

Brailsford, D. (1988) *Bareknuckles*, Cambridge: Lutterworth Press.

Burkitt, I. (1999) *Bodies of Thought: Embodiment, Identity and Modernity*, London: Sage.

Burkitt, I. (2002) 'Technologies of the self: habitus and capacities', *Journal of Social Behaviour*, 32:2

Buscombe, E. (2005) *Million Dollar Baby*, London: British Film Institute (BFI), pp. 67–8.

Butler, J. (1990) *Gender Trouble: Feminism and the Subversion of Identity*, New York: Routledge.

Butler, J. (1993) *Bodies that Matter*, New York: Routledge.

Butler, J. (1999) 'Performativity's social magic', in R. Shusterman (ed.) *Bourdieu: A Critical Reader*, Oxford: Blackwell.

Carrington, B. (2002) 'Masculinity and Black cultural resistance', in J. Sugden and A. Tomlinson (eds) *Power Games: A Critical Sociology of Sport*, London: Routledge, pp. 267–91.

Cashmore, E. (2004a) *Beckham*, Cambridge: Polity.

Cashmore, E. (2004b) *Tyson: Nurture of the Beast*, Cambridge: Polity.

Cashmore, E. (2005) *Making Sense of Sports*, 4th edn, London: Routledge.

Chandler, D. (ed.) (1996) *Boxer: An Anthology of Writing on Boxing and Visual Culture*, London: Institute of International Visual Arts.

Collings, M. (ed.) (2001) *Muhammad Ali: Through the Eyes of the World*, London: Sanctuary.

Connell, R.W. (1983) *Which Way is Up? Essays on Sex, Class and Culture*, London: Allen and Unwin.

Connell, R.W. (1995) *Masculinities*, Cambridge: Polity.

Connell, R.W. (2000) *The Men and the Boys*, Berkeley, CA: University of California.

Connell, R.W. (2002) *Gender*, Cambridge: Polity.

Connell, R.W. (2005) 'Change among the gatekeepers: men, masculinities and gender equality in the global arena', *Signs: Journal of Women in Culture and Society*, 30 (31), University of Chicago.

Cook, P. (1982) 'Masculinity in crisis: tragedy and identification in *Raging Bull*', *Screen*, Oct/Nov.

Cowie, E. (1999) [1997] 'Fantasia', in J. Evans and S. Hall (eds) *Visual Culture: The Reader*, London: Sage, pp. 356–69.

Crossley, N. (1995a) 'Body techniques, agency and intercorporeality: on Goffman's relations', *Public Sociology*, 29: 133–50.

Crossley, N. (1995b) 'Merleau Ponty, the elusive body and carnal sociology', *Body and Society*, 1: 43–63.

Crossley, N. (1996) 'Body-subject/body-power: agency, inscription and control in Foucault', *Body and Society*, 2: 99–116.

Crossley, N. (2001) *The Social Body: Habit, Identity and Desire*, London: Sage.

Crossley, N. (2004) 'The circuit trainer's habitus: reflexive body techniques and the sociality of the workout', *Body and Society*, 10: 37–69.

Crossley, N. (2005) 'Mapping body reflexive techniques: on body modification and maintenance', *Body and Society*, 11: 1–35.

Culbertson, L. (2002) 'Leading with the left: boxing, incarnation and Sartre's progressive regressive method', in J. Sugden and A. Tomlinson (eds) *Power Games: A Critical Sociology of Sport*, London: Routledge.

Curry, T.J. (1991) 'Fraternal bonding in the locker room: a pro-feminist analysis of talk about competition and women', *Sociology of Sport Journal*, 8: 119–35.

Daily Telegraph (2005) *Daily Telegraph*, 12 August, http://www.telegraph.co.uk,p.1.

Department of Media, Culture and Sport/Social Unit (DCMS/SU) (2002) *Game Plan: A Strategy for Delivering Government's Sport and Physical Activity Objectives*, London: Cabinet Office.

de Garis, L. (2000) 'Be a buddy to your buddy', in J. McKay, M. Messner and D. Sabo (eds) *Masculinities, Gender Relations and Sport*, London: Sage.

Denzin, N. (2002) *Reading Race: Hollywood and the Cinema of Racial Violence*, London: Sage.

Descartes, R. (1988) *Selected Philosophical Writings*, Cambridge: Cambridge University Press.

Donzelot, J. (1980) *The Policing of Families*, London: Hutchinson.

Dunn, K. (2002) 'Defending Tyson', in D. O'Connor (ed.) *Iron Mike: A Mike Tyson Reader*, New York: Thunder's Mouth Press, pp. 247–56.

Dunning, E. (1999) *Sport Matters: Sociological Studies of Sport, Violence and Civilization*, London: Routledge.

Dunning, E. and Rojeck, C. (eds) (1992) *Sport and Leisure in the Civilizing Process: Critique and Counter-critique*, London: Routledge.

Dunning, E., Murphy, P., Newburn, W. and Williams, J. (1988) *The Roots of Football Hooliganism*, London: Routledge.

Dyer, R. (1998) 'Idol thoughts: orgasm and self reflexivity in gay pornography', in N. Mirzoeff (ed.) *The Visual Culture Reader*, Oxford: Blackwell, pp. 504–15.

Early, G. (1994) *The Culture of Bruising: Essays on Prizefighting, Literature and Modern American Culture*, Hopewell, NJ: ECCO.

Early, G. (ed.) (1999) *I'm a Little Special: A Muhammad Ali Reader*, London: Yellow Jersey Press, Random House.

Early, G. (2002) 'Mike's brilliant career Transition 71: Fall, 1996', in D. O'Connor (ed.) *Iron Mike: A Mike Tyson Reader*, pp. 197–208.

Egan, P. (1812) *Boxiana; or sketches of ancient and modern pugilism; from the days of the renowned Broughton and slack to the heroes of the present milling era*, London: Sherwood.

Elias, N. (1978) *The Civilizing Process, Volume 1: The History of Manners*, New York: Pantheon Books.

Elias, N. (1983) *The Court Society*, Oxford: Basil Blackwell.

Elias, N. (1994) *The Civilizing Process: The History of Manners and State – Formation and Civilization*, Oxford: Basil Blackwell.

Elias, N. and Dunning, E.G. (1986) *The Quest for Excitement*, Oxford: Basil Blackwell.

Ellison, R. (2001) [1947] *Invisible Man*, Harmondsworth: Penguin.

Engel, M. (2002) 'Nowhere to run, nowhere to hide for Mike Tyson', *Guardian Sport*, 10 June.

Eskin, L. (1974) 'Complete history of women's boxing', *Boxing Illustrated*, August/September, pp. 25–32.

Evans, J. and Hall, S. (eds) (1999) *Visual Culture: The Reader*, London: Sage.

Fanon, F. (1967) *Black Skin, White Masks*, trans. C.L. Markman, New York: Grove Press.

Foucault, M. (1972) *The Archaeology of Knowledge and the Discourse on Language*, London: Pantheon.

Foucault, M. (1973) *The Birth of the Clinic*, London: Routledge.

Foucault, M. (1977a) [1975] *Discipline and Punish: The Birth of the Prison*, trans. A.M. Sheridan Smith, Harmondsworth: Penguin.

Foucault, M. (1977b) 'Nietzche, genealogy, history', in D. Bouchard (ed.) *Language, Counter-Memory, Practice*, Ithaca, NY: Cornell University Press, pp. 139–64.

Foucault, M. (1978) *The History of Sexuality: An Introduction*, trans. R. Hurley, Harmondsworth: Penguin.

Foucault, M. (1986) *The Care of the Self, History of Sexuality*, vol. 3, trans. R. Hurley, Harmondsworth: Penguin.

Foucault, M. (1988) 'Technologies of the self', in L.H. Martin, H. Gutman and P.H. Hutton (eds) *Technologies of the Self: A Seminar with Michel Foucault*, Cambridge, MA: Massachusets Institute of Technology (MIT).

Fraser, M. and Greco, M. (eds) (2005) *The Body: A Reader*, London: Routledge.

French, K. (2004) 'Art by Directors', *Granta*, 86, Summer, 2004 pp. 95–128.

Freud, S. (1953) [1900] *The Interpretation of Dreams: The Standard Editions of the Complete Psychological Work, Vol. V*, trans. J. Strachey, London: Hogarth Press.

Frosh, S. (2002) *Afterwords*, Basingstoke: Palgrave.

Gannon, L. (2005) 'Sexy Lady', *Elle*, April, UK Edition, pp. 118–24.

Gatens, M. (1991) *Feminism and Philosophy: Perspectives on Difference and Equality*, Cambridge: Polity.

Giddens, A. (1991) *Modernity and Self Identity*, Cambridge: Polity.

Gilroy, P. (1998) 'Race ends here', *Ethnic and Racial Studies*, 21(5): 838–47.

Gilroy, P. (2004) *Postcolonial Melancholia*, New York: Columbia University Press.

Giulianotti, R. (ed.) (2004) *Sport and Modern Social Theorists*, Basingstoke: Palgrave Macmillan.

Giulianotti, R. (2005) *Sport: A Critical Sociology*, Cambridge: Polity.

Goffman, E. (1959) *The Presentation of Self in Everyday Life*, New York: Doubleday.

Goffman, E. (1963) *Behaviour in Public Places*, London: Allen Lane.

Goffman, E. (1967) *Interaction Ritual*, New York: Anchor Books.

Gorman, B. and Walsh, P. (2002) *King of the Gypsies*, Lytham: Milo Books.

Gorn, E.J. (1986) *The Manly Art: Bare Knuckle Prize-Fighting in America*, London: Robson Books.

Gramsci, A. (1971) *Selections from the Prison Notebooks*, London: Lawrence and Wishart.

Grindon, L. (1996) 'Body and soul: the structure of meaning in the boxing film genre', *Cinema Journal*, 35(4) June, Society for Cinema Studies, University of Texas Press, www.guardian.co.uk accessed 12 August 2005.

Grossberg, L., Wartella, E. and Whitney, C. (1998) *Media Making*, Thousand Oaks, CA: Sage.

Guardian (2005) *Guardian*, 12 August, http://www.guardian.co.uk, p. 1.

Guardian Sport (2002) Headline, p. 1, 10 June.

Hall, G.S. (1920) *Morale, the Supreme Standard of Life and Conduct*, New York: Appleton.

Hall, S. (1985) 'The rediscovery of ideology', in V. Beechey and J. Donald (eds) *Subjectivity and Social Relations*, Milton Keynes: Open University Press, pp. 23–55.

Hall, S. (1990) 'Cultural identity and diaspora', in J. Rutherford (ed.) *Identity, Community, Culture, Difference*, London: Lawrence and Wishart.

Hall, S. (1996) 'Introduction: who needs identity?', in S. Hall and P. DuGay (eds) *Questions of Cultural Identity*, London: Sage.

Hall, S. (1997) *Representation: Cultural Representations and Signifying Practices*, London: Sage.

Hall, S. (1999) 'Looking and subjectivity: introduction', in J. Evans and S. Hall (eds) *Visual Culture: The Reader*, London: Sage, pp. 309–14.

Halpert, C. (1997) 'Tough enough and woman enough: stereotypes, discrimination and impression management among women professional boxers', *Journal of Sport and Social Issues*, 21: 7–36.

Hammersley, M. and Atkinson, P. (1995) *What's Wrong with Ehnography: Methodological Explorations*, London: Routledge.

Hammersley, M. and Atkinson, P. (2003) *Ethnography: Principles in practice*, 2nd edn, London: Routledge.

Haraway, D. (1991) *Simians, Cyborgs and Women: the Reinvention of Nature*, London: Routledge.

Haraway, D. (1992) 'The promises of monsters: a regenerative politics for Inappropriate/d others', in L. Grossberg, C. Nelson, and P. Treichler (eds) *Cultural Studies*, London: Routledge.

Haraway, D. (2000) [1985] 'A manifesto for cyborgs', in G. Kirkup, L. Janes, F. Hovendon and K. Woodward (eds) *The Gendered Cyborg*, London: Routledge.

Hargreaves, J. (1994) *Sporting Females: Critical Issues in the History and Sociology of Women's Sports*, London: Routledge.

Hargreaves, J. (1996) 'Bruising peg to boxerobics: gendered boxing – images and meanings', in D. Chandler (ed.) *Boxer: An Anthology of Writing on Boxing and Visual Culture*, pp. 121–31.

Hargreaves, J. (1997) 'Introducing images and meanings', *Body and Society*, 3(4): 33–49.

Harris, O. (1998) 'The role of sport in the Black community', in G. Sailes (ed.) *African Americans in Sport*, New Brunswick, NJ: Transaction Publishers.

Hauser, T. (1991) *Muhammad Ali: His Life and Times*, New York: Simon and Schuster.

Hauser, T. (2004) 'When they were kings', *Observer Sport Monthly*, pp. 22–8.

Hauser, T. (2005a) 'The unforgiven', *Observer Sport Monthly*, September, no. 67, pp. 46–50.

Hauser, T. (2005b) 'The ten greatest moments in US sport', *Observer Sport Monthly*, July, no. 65, pp. 6–7.

Hawkes, T. (1988) *Structuralism and Semiotics*, London: Routledge.

Hayward, P. (2005) 'Local hero Hatton hits the big-time', Sport Monday, *Daily Telegraph*, London.

Hazlitt, W. (1982) 'The fight', *William Hazlitt, Selected Writings*, Harmondsworth: Penguin.

Heath, S. (1981) *Questions of Cinema*, Basingstoke: Macmillan.

Hemingway, E. (1936) 'Fifty Grand', *The Short Stories of Ernest Hemingway*, New York: Scribner, pp. 243–65.

Hennessy, J. (1990) *Mike Tyson*, Mumbai: Magna Books.

Hirst, P. (1979) *On Law and Ideology*, Basingstoke: Macmillan.

Horowitz, A. (2005) 'The power and the glory', *Sunday Telegraph*, 4 September, Review, p. 3.

Howson, A. (2005) *Embodying Gender*, London: Sage.

Humm, M. (1997) *Feminism and Film*, Edinburgh: Edinburgh University Press.

Irigaray, L. (1991) 'This sex which is not one', in M. Whitford (ed.) *The Irigaray Reader*, Oxford: Basil Blackwell.

James, N. (1996) 'Raging bulls: sexuality and the boxing movie', in D. Chandler (ed.) *Boxer: An Anthology of Writing on Boxing and Visual Culture*, London: Institute of International Visual Arts, pp. 113–19.

Jamieson, L. (1998) *Intimacy: Personal Relationships in Modern Societies*, Cambridge: Polity.

Jefferson, T. (1996) 'From "little fairy boy" to "compleat destroyer": subjectivity and transformation in the biography of Mike Tyson', in M. Mac an Ghaill (ed.) (2002) pp. 153–67.

Jefferson, T. (1997) 'The Tyson rape trial: the law, feminism and emotional "truth"', *Social and Legal Studies*, 6: 281–301.

Jefferson, T. (1998) 'On muscle, "hard men", and "Iron" Mike Tyson: reflections on desire, anxiety and the embodiment of masculinity', *Body and Society*, 4: 77–98.

Jordan, J. (2002) 'Requiem for the Champ', in D. O'Connor (ed.) *Iron Mike: A Mike Tyson Reader*, New York: Thunder's Mouth Press, pp. 158–164.

Jones, K. (2004) Boxing: life at court when they are kings, *Independent*, London, 28 July.

Kay, S. (2003) *Žižek: A Critical Introduction*, Cambridge: Polity.

King, C. (1992) 'The politics of representation: a democracy of the gaze', *Imagining Women*, Cambridge: Polity, pp. 131–39.

Kristeva, J. (1987) 'A new type of intellectual: the dissident', in T. Moi (ed.) *The Kristeva Reader*, New York: Columbia University Press.

Lacan, J. (1977) *The Four Fundamental Concepts of Psychoanalysis*, ed. J.A. Miller, trans. A. Sheridan, London: Hogarth Press.

Lafferty, Y. and McKay, J. (2005) '"Suffragettes in satin shorts?" Gender and competitive boxing', *Qualitative Sociology*, 27(3): 249–76.

La Motta, J. with Carter, C. and Savage, P. (1997) [1970] *Raging Bull: My Story*, 1st edn, New York: De Capo Press.

Laplanche, J. and Pontalis, J.B. (1968) 'Fantasy and the origins of sexuality', *The International Journal of Psychoanalysis*, 49: 1.

Lemert, C. (2003) *Muhammad Ali: Trickster in the Culture of Irony*, Cambridge: Polity.

Lewis, L. (2001) 'Foreword', in M. Collings (ed.) *Muhammad Ali: Through the Eyes of the World*, London: Sanctuary, pp. 9–10.

Mac an Ghaill, M. (ed.) (1996) *Understanding Social Relations and Cultural Arenas*, Buckingham: Open University Press.

McKay, J. (1997) *Managing Gender*, Albany, NY: Suny Press.

McKay, J., Messner, M. and Sabo, D. (2000) *Masculinities, Gender Relations and Sport*, London: Sage.

McKernan, L. (1998) 'Sport and the silent screen', *Griffithiana*, no. 64, October, pp. 80–141.

McRae, D. (1996) *Dark Trade: Lost in Boxing*, Edinburgh: Mainstream.

Mailer, N. (1991) [1975] *The Fight*, Harmondsworth: Penguin.

Marqusee, M. (1995) 'Sport and stereotype: from role model to Muhammad Ali', *Race and Class*, April–June, vol. 36, London: Institute of Race Relations.

Marqusee, M. (2005) [2000] *Redemption Song*, London: Verso.

Marshall, P.D. (1997) *Celebrity and Power*, Minneapolis, MN: University of Minnesota Press.

Mauss, M. (1973) [1935] 'Techniques of the Body', *Economy and Society*, 2(1): 71–88.

Mead, G.H. (1934) *Mind, Self and Society*, Chicago, IL: University of Chicago Press.

Mellor, D. (1996) 'The ring of impossibility, or, the failure to recover authenticity in the recent cinema of boxing', in D. Chandler (ed.) *Boxer: An Anthology of Writing on Boxing and Visual Culture*, London: Institute of International Visual Arts.

Mennesson, C. (2000) '"Hard" women and "soft" women', *International Review for the Sociology of Sport*, 35(1): 21–33.

Mercer, K. (1990) *Welcome to the Jungle: New Positions in Black Cultural Studies*, London: Routledge.

Merleau-Ponty, M. (1962) *Phenomenology of Perception*, New York: Routledge.

Merleau-Ponty, M. (1968a) *The Visible and the Invisible*, Evanston, IL: North Western University Press.

Messner, M. (2002) *Taking the Field: Women, Men and Sports*, Minneapolis, MN: University of Minnesota Press.

Messner, M.A. and Sabo, D.F. (eds) (1994) *Sex, Violence and Power in Sports*, Freedom, CA: Crossing Press.

Michner, J. (1976) *On Sport*, London: Secker and Warburg.

Mitchell, K. (2003) *War, Baby: The Glamour of Violence*, London: Yellow Jersey Press.

Mitchell, K. (2005a) 'Were these fights even better?' in T. Hauser, 'The unforgiven', *Observer Sport Monthly*, September, no. 67, p. 49.

Mitchell, K. (2005b) 'You can right McClellan's plight, *Observer*, 20 February, p. 13.

Mitchell, K. (2005c) 'Fights, camera, action', *Observer Sport Monthly*, July, no. 65, London, pp. 36–41.

Moi, T. (1985) *Textual/Sexual Politics: Feminist Literary Theory*, London: Methuen.

Moi, T. (1999) *What is a Woman?*, Oxford: Oxford University Press.

Moore, H. (1994) *A Passion for Difference: Essays in Anthropology and Gender*, Cambridge: Polity.

Moores, S. (1993) *Interpreting Audiences: The Ethnography of Media Consumption*, London: Sage.

Morgan, D. (1992) *Discovering Men*, London: Routledge.

Mossop, J. (1997) 'Lewis looks forward to a bout of unification after McCall fiasco', *Sunday Telegraph*, 9 February, S7.

Mulvey, L. (1975) 'Visual pleasure and narrative cinema', *Screen*, Autumn, 16(3): 6–18.

Mulvey, L. (1989) 'Afterthoughts on "Visual pleasure and narrative cinema" inspired by *Duel in the Sun*', in *Visual and Other Pleasures*, London: Macmillan, pp. 29–39.

Mulvey, L. (2005) *Death Twenty-four Times a Second: Reflections on Stillness in the Moving Image*, London: Raktion Books.

Neal, S. (1992) 'Masculinity as spectacle', *The Sexual Subject: A Screen Reader in Sexuality*, London: Routledge.

Nye, R.A. (2005) 'Locating masculinity: some recent work on men', *Signs: Journal of Women in Culture and Society*, 30(31), University of Chicago.

Oakley, A. (1982) *Sex, Gender and Society*, London: Temple Smith.

Oates, J.C. (1997) [1987] *On Boxing*, London: Bloomsbury.

Oates, J.C. (2002) 'Rape and the boxing ring', in D. O'Connor (ed.), *Iron Mike: A Mike Tyson Reader*, New York: Thunder's Mouth Press, pp. 153–8.

O'Connor, D. (ed.) (2002) *Iron Mike: A Mike Tyson Reader*, New York: Thunder's Mouth Press.

Oliver, A. and Simpson, P. (eds) (2004) *The Rough Guide to Muhammad Ali*, Harmondsworth: Penguin.

Pindar (1997) *The Odes and Selected Fragments*, trans. G.S. Conway, revised R. Stoneman, London: Everyman, J.M. Dent.

Pink, S. (1997) *Women and bullfighting: Gender, Sex and the Consumption of Tradition*, Oxford: Berg.

Piper, K. (1996) 'Four corners: a contest of opposites', in D. Chandler (ed.) *Boxer: An Anthology of Writing on Boxing and Visual Culture*, London: Institute of International Visual Arts, pp. 71–9.

Plimpton, G. (2002) Foreword, in D. O'Connor (ed.) *Iron Mike: A Mike Tyson Reader*, New York: Thunder's Mouth Press, pp. xiii–xvii.

Polkinghorne, D. (1988) *Narrative Knowing and the Human Sciences*, Albany, NY: State University of New York.

Price, J. and Shildrick, M. (1999) *Feminist Theory and the Body: A Reader*, Edinburgh: Edinburgh University Press.

Probyn, E. (1993) *Sexing the Self: Gendered Positions in Cultural Studies*, London: Routledge.

Ramazanoghu, C. and Holland, J. (2005) *Feminist Methodology: Challenges and Choices*, London: Sage.

Randall, C. (2004) 'Students mix brawn with brains', *Sport Telegraph*, London, 10 December, p. S4.

Rawling, J. (2005) 'Glovy night for gutsy Hatton', *Guardian*, 6 June, pp. 16–17.

Rawling, J. (2006) 'Masterful Calzaghe stakes his claim to greatness', *Guardian*, 6 March, p. 15.

Reid, J. (1971) *Bucks and Bruisers*, London: Routledge and Kegan Paul.

Remnick, D. (1998) *King of the World: Muhammad Ali and the Rise of the American Hero*, New York: Random House.

Ricoeur, P. (1991) 'Narrative identity', trans. D. Wood, in D. Wood (ed.) *On Paul Ricoeur: Narrative and Interpretation*, London: Routledge.

Robson, G. (2000) *'No One Likes Us, We Don't Care': The Myth and Reality of Fandom*, Oxford: Berg.

Rose, J. (1986) *Sexuality in the Field of Vision*, London: Verso.

Rose, N. (1996) *Inventing Our Selves*, Cambridge: Cambridge University Press.

Rose, N. (1998) *Lifelines: Biology, Freedom, Determinism*, London: Penguin.

Rose, N. (1999) [1989] *Governing the Soul: The Shaping of the Private Self*, London: Free Association Books.

Rutherford, J. (1990) (ed.) *Identity, Community, Culture, Difference*, London: Lawrence and Wishart.

Ryle, G. (1949) *The Concept of Mind*, Harmondsworth: Penguin.

Sammons, J. (1988) *Beyond the Ring: The Role of Boxing in American Society*, Chicago, IL: University of Illinois Press.

Sartre, J.P. (1963) *The Problem of Method*, trans. H.E. Barnes, London: Methuen.

Sartre, J.P. (1991) *Critique of Dialectical Reason, Vol II: The Intelligibility of History*, trans. Q. Hoare, London: Verso.

Scambler, G. (2005) *Sport and Society: History, Power and Culture*, Milton Keynes: Open University Press.

Scorsese, M. (1989) *Scorsese on Scorsese*, London: Faber.

Scraton, S. and Flintoff, A. (2002) (eds) *Gender and Sport: A Reader*, London: Routledge.

Segal, L. (1987) *Is the Future Female? Troubled Thoughts on Contemporary Feminism*, London: Virago.

Segal, L. (1997a) *Slow Motion: Changing Masculinities, Changing Men*, 2nd edn, London: Virago.

Segal, L. (1997b) *New Sexual Agendas*, London: Macmillan.

Smith, D. (1997) 'Comment on Hekman's "Truth and method: feminist standpoint theory revisited"', *Signs*, 22(21): 392–7.

Smith, R.R.R. (1991) *Hellenistic Sculpture*, London: Thames and Hudson.

Sobchack, V. (2004) *Carnal Thoughts: Embodiment and Moving Image Culture*, Berkeley, CA: University of California Press.

Stallybrass, P. and White, A. (1986) *The Politics and Poetics of Transgression*, London: Methuen.

Stanley, L. and Wise, S. (1993) *Breaking Out Again: Feminist Ontology and Epistemology*, London: Routledge.

Sugden, J. (1996) *Boxing and Society: An International Analysis*, Manchester: Manchester University Press.

Sugden, J. and Tomlinson, A. (eds) (2002) *Power Games: A Critical Sociology of Sport*, London: Routledge.

Telotte, J.P. (1989) *Voices in the Dark: The Narrative Patterns of Film Noir*, Champaign, IL: University of Illinois Press.

Thomas, D. (1992) 'How Hollywood deals with the deviant male', *The Movie Book of Film Noir*, London: Studio Vista.

Tosches, N. (1997) 'Introduction', in J. La Motta with C. Carter and P. Savage (eds) *Raging Bull: My Story*, 1st edn, New York: De Capo Press, pp. vii–xii.

Turner, B.S. (1984) *The Body and Society*, Oxford: Blackwell.

Turner, B. (1992) *Regulating Bodies: Essays in Medical Sociology*, London: Routledge.

Virgil (1956) *The Aeneid*, Book V, trans W.F. Jackson Knight, Harmondsworth: Penguin.

Wacquant, L. (1993) 'Positivism', in W. Outhwaite and T. Bottomore (eds) *The Blackwell Dictionary of Twentieth Century Social Thought*, Oxford: Blackwell.

Wacquant, L. (1995a) 'Pugs at work: bodily capital and bodily labour among professional boxers', *Body and Society*, 1 (1): 65–93.

Wacquant, L. (1995b) 'The pugilistic point of view: how boxers think about their trade', *Theory and Society*, 24 (4): 489–535.

Wacquant, L. (1995c) Review article, 'Why Men Desire Muscles', *Body and Society*, 1: 163–79.

Wacquant, L. (2001) 'Whores, slaves and stallions: languages of exploitation and accommodation among professional fighters', *Body and Society*, 7: 181–94.

Wacquant, L. (2004) *Body and Soul: Notebooks of an Apprentice Boxer*, Oxford: Oxford University Press.

Wagg, S. (2004) *British Football and Social Exclusion*, Oxford: Blackwell.

Walkerdine, V. (1986) 'Video replay: families, films and fantasies', in *Formations of Fantasy*, London: Methuen.

Walkerdine, V. (1997) *Daddy's Girl*, Basingstoke: Macmillan.

Walters, J. (2005a) 'I'll take on men, says woman boxer', *Observer*, 29 May, p. 22.

Walters, J. (2005b) 'Meet the real Million Dollar Baby', *Observer Sport Monthly*, July, 65: 42–3.

Wheaton, B. (2002) 'Babes on the beach, women in the surf', in A. Tomlinson, and J. Sugden (eds) *Power Games: A Critical Sociology of Sport*, London: Routledge.

Whitehead, S.M. (2002) *Men and Masculinities*, Cambridge: Polity.

Whyte, W. (1954) *Street Corner Society*, New York: McGraw Hill.

Williams, Z. (2004) 'The gloves are on', *Guardian*, 30 September, p. 10.

Witz, A. (2000) 'Whose body matters? Feminist sociology and the corporeal turn on feminism and sociology', *Body and Society*, 6: 1–24.

Witz, A. and Marshall, B.L. (2003) 'The quality of manhood, masculinity and embodiment in the sociological tradition', *Sociological Review*, 51(3): 339–56.

Women's Boxing Archive Network (WBAN) (2005a) http://www.womenboxing.com (accessed 10 June 2005).

Women's Boxing Archive Network (WBAN) (2005b) http://www.womenboxing.com. whats.htm (accessed 8 June 2005).

Woodward, K. (1997a) 'Concepts of identity and difference', in K. Woodward (ed.) *Identity and Difference*, London: Sage.

Woodward, K. (1997b) *Whose Body?* BBC television programme, Open University/BBC.

Woodward, K. (2002) *Understanding Identity*, London: Arnold.

Woodward, K. (2004) 'Rumbles in the jungle. Boxing: racialization and the performance of masculinity', *Leisure Studies*, 23(1): 1–13.

Woodward, K. (2005) 'On and off the pitch: diversity policies and transforming identities', Working Paper no. 8, Centre for Research on Socio-Cultural Change (CRESC): Manchester.

www.telgraph.co.uk accessed 12th August, 2005.

Young, I.M. (1990) *Throwing Like a Girl and Other Essays on Feminist Philosophy and Social Theory*, Bloomington and Indiapolis, IN: Indiana University Press.

Žižek, S. (1989) *The Sublime Object of Ideology*, London: Verso.

Žižek, S. (1999) *The Ticklish Subject: The Absent Centre of Political Ontology*, London: Verso.

Žižek, S. (1992) *Enjoy Your Symptom: Jacques Lacan In Hollywood and Out*, London: Routledge.

Žižek, S. (1993) *Tarrying with the Negative: Kant, Hegel and the Critique of Ideology*, Durham, NC: Duke University Press.

Žižek, S. and Dolar, M. (2002) *Opera's Second Death*, London: Routledge.

Index

Related titles from Routledge

Sport, Culture and Society

Grant Jarvie

An exciting new textbook exploring all of the key themes covered in undergraduate sport studies and introducing students to critical thinking about the complex and symbiotic relationship between sport and its wider social context.

Hbk: 978–0–415–30646–1
Pbk: 978–0–415–30647–8

Available at all good bookshops
For ordering and further information please visit:
www.routledge.com